ENCYCLOPAEDIA OF INDIAN GOVERNMENT: PROGRAMMES AND POLICIES

ENCYCLOPAEDIA
OF
INDIAN GOVERNMENT:
PROGRAMMES AND POLICIES

Vol. 28

Finance

Edited by

Satish Tiwari

ANMOL PUBLICATIONS PVT. LTD.

NEW DELHI - 110 002 (INDIA)

ANMOL PUBLICATIONS PVT. LTD.
4374/4B, Ansari Road, Daryaganj
New Delhi - 110 002

Encyclopaedia of Indian Government: Programmes and Policies

First Edition, 2000
ISBN 81-261-0515-1 (Set)

[Responsibility for the facts stated, opinions expressed, conclusions reached and plagiarism, if any, in these volumes is entirely that of the Editor. The Publisher bears no responsibility for them whatsoever.]

PRINTED IN INDIA

Published by J.L. Kumar for Anmol Publications Pvt. Ltd., New Delhi - 110 002 and Printed at Mehra Offset Press, Delhi.

Contents

Preface

Encyclopaedia of Indian Government: Programmes and Policies contains authoritative information on about fifty departmental policies and their future developmental programmes.

Organised to be completed in 40 volumes, this gigantic work covers Agriculture; Atomic Energy; Chemicals and Fertilizers; Coal; Commerce; Communication; Culture; Defence; Education; Environment and Forests; External Affairs; Finance; Food & Consumer Affairs; Food Processing Industries; Health and Family Welfare; Home Affairs and Internal Security; Human Resources; Industry; Information and Broadcasting; Labour; Law, Justice and Company Affairs; Non-conventional Energy Sources; Ocean Development; Parliamentary Affairs; Personnel, Public Grievances and Pensions; Petroleum and Natural Gas; Planning and Programme Implementation; Planning and Statistics; Posts and Telegraphs; Power; Rural Development; Science and Technology; Social Justice and Empowerment; Space; States Affairs; Steel; Steel and Mines; Sugar and Edible Oils; Surface Transport; Textiles; Tourism; Urban Development; Water Resources; Women and Child development etc.

Based on the information derived from authoritative sources, this work contains authentic facts and figures. I am deeply beholden to all the scholars whose writings are cited or substantially made use of in the present work. I am also thankful to Anmol Publications Pvt. Ltd. for undertaking publication of this encyclopaedia. I am solely responsible for shortcomings in presentation of matter.

Encyclopaedic in nature, this will prove a dependable reference work for scholars and academics besides those appearing for different competitive examinations.

—Satish Tiwari

1

Department of Economic Affairs

Economic division

The Economic Division tenders expert advice to the Government on important issues of economic policy The Division monitors economic policies and advises on policy measures relating to macro-management of the economy and on reforms.

As part of its regular activities, the Economic Division brings out the annual Economic Survey which is placed in Parliament prior to the presentation of the Central Government Budget. The Economic Survey provides a comprehensive overview of important developments in the economy. It also analyses recent economic trends and gives an appraisal of policies in a perspective frame. Over the years the Economic Survey has acquired the status of an authoritative source and a useful compendium of the annual performance of the Indian economy.

The Division also brings out the Economic and the Functional Classification of the Central Government's Budget which is also presented to the Members of both Houses of parliament. The publication presents an estimate of the savings of the Central Government and its departmental undertakings, gross capital formation and the magnitude of the development and consumption expenditure broken up under broad functional heads.

The Division's Monthly Economic Report provides a synoptic view of the current economic situation and helps in monitoring the performance of the economy. This is submitted to the Cabinet and senior officers of the Government and Indian Missions abroad. The division also brings out every month an abstract entitled "Selected Economic Indicators" which gives the latest available data on the key sectors of the economy. The Division prepares, from time to time, briefs on the performance of the infrastructure sector, agriculture and industrial production, the price situation, trends in tax collection, the balance of payments and the monetary situation. The Division also undertakes short-term forecasting of key economic variables.

As part of its advisory functions, the Economic Division prepares analytical notes and background papers on important policy issues and also provides briefs for meetings of the consultative committees and working groups set up by the Government. The officers of the Economic Division participate in the consultations with various missions from international institutions, such as, International Monetary Fund (IMF), the World Bank & WTO etc. The Division works in close cooperation with the Reserve bank of India, The Planning Commission, The Central Statistical Organisation, the Ministry of Commerce and the Economic and Statistical Wings of other Ministries.

The work of the Economic Division is organised under the following units:

1. External Sector
2. Public Finance & Fiscal Policy
3. Industry & Infrastructure
4. Prices and Agriculture
5. Coordination and Administration Unit

6. Social Sector and Data bank
7. Money & Capital Markets.

During 1997-98 the officers of the Economic Division served on a number of official Committees and Working/ Monitoring Groups which included the Permanent Review Committee on Export and Import Policy; Technical group of Ministry of Petroleum & Natural Gas; Board of Directors of United Bank of India; Empowered Committee on Oilseeds and Diary Development; FCI's Higher Level pricing committee for open market sale of food grains; Committee for appraisal of Project Reports for the setting up of Allahabad Bank and Executive Council of Regional Computer Centre, Calcutta; Sub-Group on Unorganised/Unregistered Industrial Sector; Technical Advisory Committee on Economic Census 1996, Working Group relating to industrial sector for the IX Plan including Sub-Group on data Base and information System for the Small Scale Industries. Empowered Steering Committee on the Montreal Protocol as well as its Technology and Finance Committee; Expert Group on Commercialisation of Infrastructure; Expert group on Pricing Policy of Department of Telecommunication; Special Action Committee on Secretaries on Monitoring Prices; Tripartite Advisory Group on Equality, Employment and Status of Woman; Advisory Committee on National Accounts; Expert Committee on Social Burden on Railway; Specialised Group to prepare State level IIPs, High Powered Committee on MDHs of PSEs etc.

The External Sector Unit monitors and reviews the emerging trends in India's foreign trade and balance of payments position. It was associated with the Ministry of Commerce in various consultations and discussions relating to Import & Export Policy of the Government, multilateral trade negotiations, trade liberalisation and economic cooperation. It was also associated with meetings of the IMF, IBRD, WTO and other international conferences. It is also responsible for monitoring and effective management of external debt and planning sustainable future borrowing levels. It is the nodal agency for implementing Special Data Dissemination Standards, established by the IMF, to which India subscribed w.e.f. 1.1.1997. External Sector Unit also assisted in the preparation of the Working Group Report on balance of Payments for the ninth plan.

On the recommendations of the Task Force/Policy Group on External Debt Statistics, an External Debt Management Unit (earlier DUES, Debt Unit for External Sector) was set up in the Ministry of Finance, Department of Economic Affairs as the apex Unit for external debt monitoring and management exercises. The broad functions of this Unit are as under:

1. periodically update external debt statistics for India;
2. supervise and co-ordinate computerization of external debt data on CS:DRMS (Commonwealth Secretariat: Debt Recording and Management System) at various data sites at Ministry of Finance and the Reserve Bank of India;
3. prepare Status Report on External debt; provide external debt related information for Economic Survey, RBI Annual etc.;
4. co-ordinate reporting of external debt data to the World Bank for publishing in World Bank's Global Development Finance report; carry out continuous reconciliation of external debt data with World Bank and other agencies to ensure correct reporting in international publications;
5. providing MIS inputs for debt management through scenario building, etc.;

6. be a forum for discussing conceptual and definitional issues relating to external debt;
7. carry out research on important debt related subjects;
8. answering Parliament Questions on total external debt.

The Public Finance and Fiscal Policy Unit deals with matters relating to public finance and the budgetary operations of the Central Government. Statistics relating to the budgetary operation of the Central and State Governments are compiled in this Unit. These are also used by the International Organisations such as, the International Monetary Fund in its annual publications with the International Monetary Fund. The unit prepares an Economic and Functional Classification of the Union Budget every year. Indian Public Finance Statistics present the revenue and expenditure of the Central and State Government classified by economic categories. Notes on various aspects of public finance prepared in the Unit for the Meetings of the Parliamentary Consultative Committee and the estimates Committee. It is also associated with the estimation of resources for the Central Sector Plan. The unit is intimately involved in the process of formulation of tax policies of the Government. In particular, it examines the various representations received from trade associations/institutions regarding tax matters. These representations are examined from a broader economic perspective keeping in view the issues of the equity and efficiency in the formulation of tax policies. Besides, this unit also maintains a close liaison and collaborates with institutions engaged in economic research outside the Government in the sphere of macro-economic modeling, policy and analysis on economic issues which are of interest of the Government. The Unit also monitors the performance of macro-economic aggregates and deals with necessary policy matters arising there from.

The Industry and Infrastructure Unit advises the Government on policy issues relating to industry and infrastructure at both macro and sectorial levels. The unit also monitors and reviews on a continuous basis the trends in industrial production, performance of basic, infrastructure, small scale industries and the public sector. It also analyses the investment climate both domestic and international, industrial sickness and industrial relations.

The Prices and Agriculture Unit monitors and reports on price situation and advises on general price policy matters relating to supply management, especially in respect of essential commodities and advises on policy matters relating agriculture sector. This unit also examines proposals from other ministries regarding price policy issues such as, fixation of minimum support price for crops and selected commodities and, the impact of price charges on general price level and other policy matter relating to Agriculture Sector, including Animal Husbandry, Commodity budgets, particularly, for wheat, rice, sugar, edible oils are kept under constant focus so as to anticipate measures needed for augmenting supply in case of market price rise due to shortages. The unit assists Committee of Secretaries on Monitoring of Prices and also Cabinet Committee on Prices. The unit produces weekly report on price situation followed up by a monthly summary that includes movement in consumer price indices to serve as a feed back for policy. The Unit also advises the Government on pricing policies relating to food and agriculture commodities.

The Coordination unit is entrusted with macro-economic policies, coordination management information system, computerization and administration.

It coordinates the pre-budget meetings of the Finance Minister with Economists, Agriculturists, Industrialists, Trade Union Leaders, representatives of small scale industries, Experts in Financial Markets, representatives from Consumer Organisations and Experts in the field of Science and Technology. It also coordinates the work relating to the Annual Economic Survey. The Unit prepares a comprehensive paper on the State of the Indian Economy for the meeting of the Aid-India Forum. It prepares analytical material and notes for use by the Finance Minister, Cabinet Secretariat and office of the President and Prime Minister. The Unit also Annual Action Plan of the Division.

The Social Sector Unit prepares the analytical notes on poverty, employment and other topics concerning social sectors. The unit also advises the Government on specific policy issues in social sectors, examines reports, draft policy papers/Cabinet Notes etc. prepared by other Ministries concerning issues on social sectors. The unit also brings out weekly Report "Statistical Highlights", "Monthly Economic Report" and Selected Economic Indicators" (monthly) on important macro-economic indicators

The Money and Capital Market Unit advises the Ministry on Money and Credit Policy and deals with issues relating to Capital & Financial Market developments. The Unit periodically reviews and monitors money supply (M3), bank credit to the Government, bank credit to the commercial sectors deposit and credit growth of the scheduled commercial banks that influences the liquidity level in the economy.

Banking division

Organisation and role

Banking Division is concerned with Government policies which have a bearing on the working of commercial banks and the term lending institutions excluding Life Insurance Corporation of India, General Insurance Corporation of India and Unit Trust of India. The Division is headed by a Special Secretary and operates through three sub-divisions each headed by a Joint Secretary dealing with (i) Industrial Finance (ii) Banking Operations and (iii) Priority Sector.

Implementation of official language policy in the banking division, banks and financial institutions

Banking Division ensures implementation of provisions of Official Language Act, 1963 and Official Language Rules, 1976 as well as instructions received from the Department of Official Language, Ministry of Home Affairs, from time to time, in the Division as also in 27 Public Sector Banks and Seven All India Financial Institutions (i.e. IDBI, IFCI, NABARD, EXIM Bank, SIDBI, IIBI, and NHB), besides the Reserve Bank of India (RBI).

An Official Language Implementation Committee is functioning in Banking Division. This Committee periodically reviews the progress made in the use of Hindi in RBI, Public Sector Banks and Financial Institutions and issues necessary instructions for effective implementation of Official Language Policy and the Annual Programme issued by the Department of Official Language. These Banks and Financial Institutions send their quarterly progress reports regarding use of Hindi in their Head Offices to the Banking Division. These progress reports are also reviewed in the meetings of Banking Division's Official Language Implementation Committee. RBI, Public Sector Banks and Financial Institutions also have their own Official Language Implementation Committees which also meet regularly to review the progress made in the use of Hindi. In addition, 24 Town Official Language Implementation Committees also monitor the progress of implementation of Official Language policy in Banks in different towns.

Workmen employee directors and officer directors

During the year 1998, Government appointed Workman Employee Directors on the Boards of State Bank of Travancore, State Bank of Mysore, State Bank of Saurashtra, State Bank of India, United Bank of India, Central Bank of India. Action for appointment of Workmen Employee Directors on the Boards of these banks. As on 14.12.1998 there were vacancies of Workman Employee Directors in (i) Bank of Maharashtra (ii) Canara Bank (iii) Punjab & Sind Bank. (iv) State Bank of Bikaner & Jaipur and (v) State Bank of India has also been initiated.

Introduction of a scheme for payment of ex-gratia to pre-1986 retirees in Reserve Bank of India and other public sector banks

In the year 1995 a pension scheme was introduced in the public sector banks (except State Bank of India) in lieu c contributory provident fund w.e.f. 1.11.93. This scheme was also, extended to those employees, who retired from the bank's service on or after 1.1.86 and opted for pension scheme. Subsequently, Government received several representations from various quarters to extend the benefit of pension to pre-1986 retirees c at least to provide them some relief by way of ex-gratia payment The matter was examined and Government have decided that banks may provide ex-gratia relief to all such ex-employee who retired before 1.1.86, provided they had rendered at least twenty years of continuous service prior to their superannuation and a not getting any pensionary benefits from the bank. Subject fulfillment of these conditions, the ex-gratia at the rate Rs.300/- per month may be paid w.e.f. 1.11.97. On this amount of ex-gratia beneficiaries are also entitled to dearness relief the rate of 0.67% for every rise of four points in the All India working Consumer Price Index (base 1960=100) over 600 points. The amount of ex-gratia including dearness relief payable as on 1.11.97 work out Rs.873/- per month.

The ex-gratia is, however, not admissible to (a) those who were dismissed/removed from service and (b) those who resigned from service

Representation of scheduled castes/scheduled Tribes in public sector banks/financial institutions

The representation of SCs and STs, ex-serviceman, Physically handicapped persons and other backward classes in 19 Nationalised Banks, State Bank of India and its Associate Banks, Reserve Bank of India, Industrial Development Bank of India, Industrial Investment Bank of India, National Bank for Agriculture and Rural Development, Export Import Bank of India, National Housing Bank and Small Industries Development Bank of India as on 31.12.1997 was as under:-

Scheduled caste/scheduled tribes

Category	*Total No. of employees*	*Number of employees belonging to*	
		Scheduled Castes	*Scheduled Tribes*
Officers	252072	2995	10098
Clerks	465780	69902	22416
Sub-staff	183061	42567	11275
Sub-staff (Sweepers)	43509	22864	2449

Ex-Servicemen

Category	*Total No. of Ex-servicemen employed*
Officers	1980
Clerks	13601
Sub-staff	41011
Sub-staff (Sweepers)	55

Physically Handicapped

Category	*Blind*	*Deaf & Dumb*	*Orthopaedically Handicapped*
Officers	17	46	996
Clerks	463	540	4576
Sub-staff	119	215	1829

Other Backward Classes

Category	*Total No. of OBCs*
Officers	626
Clerks	2718
Sub-staff	2439

Vigilance

Central Vigilance Commission have in exercise of powers conferred under Section 8(l)(h) of the Central Vigilance Commission Ordinance 1998 notified the Special chapter on banking which has been finalised in consultation with RBI, IBA, CBI and Banking Division of Ministry of Finance. The Special Chapter was prepared taking into account the special needs of bank managers-who have to take risky decisions as an integral part of the business of banking. It addresses the problems faced by them in their day to day functioning and has been made with the objective that the vigilance activity in the banks does not stifle the ability of bank managers in taking business decision or obstruct the achievement of organisational goals and objectives set for them by their managements.

Public sector banks

An analysis of financial results of Public Sector Banks as on March 31,1997 and 1998 reveals that the number of Public Sector Banks (PSBs) recording net profit has gone up from 24 to 25.

The Operating and net profit of Public Sector Banks a on March *31, 1997* and March, *31, 1998* is as under:

(Rs. crore)

Banks	*March 31, 1997*		*March 31, 1998*	
	Operating Profits	*Net Profits*	*Operating Profits*	*Net Profits*
State Bank Group	4457.81	1649.94	4780.61	2459.77
Nationalised Banks	4440.82	1445.48	5531.19	2567.28
Total for PSBs	8898.63	3095.42	10311.80	5027.05

(Bank)

Banks	March 31, 1997 Operating Profits	Net Profits	March 31, 1998 Operating Profits	Net Profits
State Bank Group	8	8	8	8
Nationalised Banks	16	16	18	17
Total for PSBs	24	24	26	25

Out of 27 Public Sector Banks only two banks viz. Indian Bank and UCO Bank have incurred net loss as on March 31, 1997 and March 3.1,1998.

United Bank of India reported net profit of Rs.9.62 crore as on March 31, 1998 as against net loss of Rs.113.64 crore for the year 1996-97.

The number of banks which reported operating loss reduced from three (Indian Bank, UCO Bank and United Bank of India) in 1996-97 to one (Indian Bank) in 1997-98.

Public Sector Banks as a group have shown remarkable improvement in the performance during the fiscal year 1998 as compared to the previous fiscal year. Total operating profit of PSBs during the relevant periods were Rs.10311.80 crore and Rs.8898.63 crores respectively. The net profits registered an increase of Rs.1931.63 crores from Rs.3095.42 crores in 1997 to Rs.5027.05 crores in 1998.

Private sector banks

The private Sector Banks earned net profit aggregating Rs.839.65 crore as on March 31, 1998 as against Rs.683.91 crore during the previous year. The net profit of new private sector banks amounted to Rs.397.79 crore as on March 31, 1998.

Working of Indian Banks' branched abroad:

The policy with regard to the overseas operations of Indian Public sector banks continued to be one of consolidation and selective expansion. Presently there are

8 public sector banks and one private sector bank operating in 25 countries with a network of 97 branches. Besides the network of the branches, there are 25 representative offices, 8 joint ventures and 13 subsidiaries. Some of these banks have been rendering management services under contracts to bank affiliates and Exchange Houses at overseas centres.

Aggregate balance sheet size of the overseas branches of the 9 banks for the year ended 31st Match, 1997 and 1998 is given in the table below:

(US $ Million)

1997	1998
15,675	16,578

The asset expansion of the overseas branched has been in compliance with the prudential norms. The growth recorded has been steady and the banks are cautious in improving their portfolios. The bank-wise profitability ending March, 1997 and 1998 is given below:

(Rs. crores)

	31.3.1997	31.11.1998
State Bank of India	+40.21	+40.03
Bank of India	+31.08	+21.61
Bank of Baroda	+12.87	+19.53
Indian Bank	+0.48	+0.09
Indian Overseas Bank	+ 4.77	+3.68
UCO Bank	+11.46	+2.37
Syndicate Bank	+5.27	+0.76
Canara Bank	-6.86	+6.23
Bharat Overseas Bank	+0.57	+0.98

All the Indian banks with overseas operations (except Indian Bank and UCO Bank) had achieved the CRAR as per their global balance sheet and also met the respective norms prescribed by the host country regulatory authorities.

Restructuring of capital of nationalised banks

The equity by Corporation Bank in 1997-98 was Rs.304.00 crore including premium of Rs.266.00 crore.

The return of capital by Punjab National Bank to the Government was Rs.138.33 crore during the fiscal under review.

During the year 1996-97 and 1997-98, the Government contribution to the capital in the form of Recapitalisation Bonds to nationalised Banks was of the order of Rs.1509 crore and Rs.2700 crore, respectively. The details are given in the table below:

(Rs. crore)

Name of the Bank	*1996-97*	*1997-98*
Andhra Bank	165.00	Nil
Canara Bank	Nil	600.00(*)
Central Bank of India	500.00	Nil
Indian Bank	Nil	1750.00
Punjab and Sind Bank	150.00	Nil
UCO Bank	54.00	350.00
United Bank of India	338.00	Nil
Vijaya Bank	302.00	Nil
TOTAL	1509.00	2700.00

Raising of bonds by nationalised banks

Punjab National Bank, Indian Overseas Bank, Vijaya Bank, Central Bank of India, Syndicate Bank, Canara Bank have been given permission to raise Tier 11 Capital in the form of non-secured redeemable bonds to strengthen their capital base.

Performance obligations and commitments 1998-99

RBI held discussions with the following nationalised banks to review their performance during 1997-98.

1. UCO Bank
2. United Bank of India

3. Vijaya Bank
4. Allahabad Bank
5. Punjab and Sind Bank
6. Central Bank of India
7. Indian Bank

The discussions focused on the strategies for the coming years in the emerging scenario in banking in India. The priority for banks now is to contain the Non-Performing Assets which is an area of serious concern. Details road maps are required to be prepared by the banks to tackle the problem not only in respect of the yearly accretions to NPAs but also to effect recoveries even from old and hard-core NPA accounts. The meetings noted the need for reducing operational costs by improving the deposit mix, dependence on high cost of deposits and funds and noted the need for increasing the levels of staff productivity. The tightening of prudential norms and the concomitant provisioning requirements are likely to exert pressure on the bank's bottomlines. Therefore, Interest spread was the key to increased profitability. The banks have to fine tune their systems to return the cutting edge in the face of competition.

Packages for revival of weak public sector banks

Following the consultants' reports on UCO Bank and United Bank of India (UBI), turnaround packages were framed. At the instance of the Government, UCO Bank prepared a three year Strategic Revival Plan covering the period 1997-98 to 1999-2000. UBI also chalked out an Action Plan for its turnaround. During 1997-98 the Government contributed Rs.350 crore towards recapitalisation of UCO Banks.

At the instance of the Government, Indian Bank prepared a three year Strategic Revival Plan covering the period 1997-98 to 1999-2000. During 1997-98 Government contributed Rs. 1750 crore towards recapitalisation of the Bank.

In the fiscal 1996-97, Central Bank of India improved its working by earning a net profit of Rs.150.83 crore and moved into the 'A'category.

The performance of these banks continue to be monitored.

Scheme for collection of information on defaulters and suit filed accounts

Based on the information collected, RBI has circulated to banks and financial institutions, information on the defaulting borrowers with outstanding of Rs.1 crore and above classified as 'Doubtful' or 'Loss' or where suits have been filed for the half year ended March 31, 1997, September 30.1997 and March 31, 1998.

The list of borrower accounts against which banks and Financial Institutions have filed suits for recovery of funds as on 31st March, 1997 and 31st March, 1998 have been published by RBI.

The position regarding defaulting borrowers of banks and Financial Institutions as on 31st March.

Entry of new banks in the private sector

After the issue of guidelines in January, 1993 for the entry of new private sector banks following 10 banks have started operations:

1. UTI Bank Ltd.
2. Indus Ind Bank Ltd.
3. ICICI Bank Ltd.
4. Global Trust Bank Ltd.
5. HDFC Bank Ltd.
6. Centurion Bank Ltd.
7. Bank of Punjab Ltd.

8. Time Bank Ltd.
9. IDBI Bank Ltd.
10. Development Credit Bank Ltd.(*)

Debts recovery tribunals

Under the provisions of the Recovery of Debts Due to Banks and Financial Institutions Act, 1993 which provides for establishment of Recovery Tribunals and Appellate Tribunals for expeditious adjudication and recovery of debts due to Banks and Financial Institutions and matters connected therewith or incidental thereto, the Central Govt. have established the following Tribunals:-

	Location	*Date of establishment*	*Jurisdiction*
1.	Debts Recovery Appellate Tribunal, Mumbai	July 12, 1994	Over all the Debts Recovery Tribunals.
2.	Debts Recovery Tribunals		
	(i) Calcutta	April 27, 1994	West Bengal, Andaman & Nicobar Islands
	(ii) Delhi	July 5, 1994	National Capital Territory of Delhi
	(iii) Jaipur	August 30, 1994	Himachal Pradesh, Punjab, Haryana, Rajasthan & Chandigarh.
	(iv) Bangalore	November 30,1994	Karnataka and Andhra Pradesh.
	(v) Ahmedabad	December 21,1994	Gujarat, UT of Dadra and Nagar Haveli, Daman & Diu.
	(vi) Chennai	November 4,1996	Tamil Nadu, Kerala & U.T. of Pondicherry

(vii) Guwahati	January 7, 1997	Assam and Other North Eastern States and Sikkim
(viii) Patna	January 24, 1997	Bihar & Orissa
(ix) Jabalpur	April 7, 1998	Madhya Predesh and Uttar Pradesh

In addition to the above it has been decided to establish five more DRTs one each at Chandigarh, Allahabad, Cuttak, Hyderabad & Ernakulam and four more DRATs one each at Delhi, Calcutta, Chennai and Allahabad. Consequently jurisdiction of DRTs/DRATs would be suitably changed. Each Tribunal is manned by a Presiding Officer with necessary supporting staff.

On a Writ Petition filed by Delhi High Court Bar Association challenging the validity of the Recovery of Debts Due to Banks and Financial Institutions Act, 1993 the Delhi High Court quashed the Notification regarding establishment of Debts Recovery Tribunal for Delhi Region and declared the Act as unconstitutional and void on March 10, 1995. The Union of India filed a Special Leave Petition and the Hon'ble Supreme Court stayed the judgement of Delhi High Court. Subsequently the Supreme Court has on 18.3.96 directed that notwithstanding any stay order passed in any of the Writ Petitions sought to be transferred the Debts Recovery Tribunals established under the Recovery of Debts Due to Banks and Financial Institutions Act, 1993 shall resume their functions. The hearing of the SLP in the Supreme Court is in progress.

Shipping finance

In pursuance of the Shipping Development Fund Committee (Abolition) Act, 1986, the functions of the Shipping Development Fund Committee (SDFC) were taken over by the Ministry of Finance (Banking Division) with effect from 3rd April, 1987. Sanction/release of loan's to shipping companies in the private sector against past commitments of SDFC and recovery of dues from shipping and fishing companies is accordingly being done by the Banking Division through Industrial Credit and Investment Corporation of India Limited (ICICI) with effect from 15th April, 1997 (previously through SCICI Ltd.), the designated person.

Government disbursed an amount aggregating Rs.90.45 crores till March, 1998 and no amount has been disbursed during 1998-99 (Till December 1998) for meeting the commitments of the erstwhile SDFC relating to shipping companies in the private sector. This is apart from Rs.113.35 crores unspent balance of SDFC transferred to erstwhile SCICI Ltd. (now ICICI) for disbursement and Rs.0.22 crores disbursed by erstwhile SCICI out of sale proceeds for this purpose. Two shipping companies viz. India Steamship Company Limited (ISS) (including Ratnakar Shipping Company Ltd. which merged with ISS with effect from 1st April, 1989) and Surendra Overseas Ltd. are under rehabilitation.

The funds in respect of erstwhile SDFC assisted fishing companies are provided by Ministry of Food Processing Industries (MFPI) from their budget provisions. Erstwhile SDFC had sanctioned loans to 85 fishing companies to acquire trawlers. Since the fishing companies, except three companies, were not repaying their loans, MFPI constituted a Technical Committee on the Deep Sea Fishing Industry in India, to suggest corrective measures for the rehabilitation of the sick units. The recommendations made by the Committee were considered and accepted by the Government with certain modifications. Accordingly, rehabilitation scheme for SDFC assisted fishing companies was announced by

ICICI, the designated person on 5th May, 1997. 33 fishing companies have finally availed of the scheme.

Industrial credit and investment corporation of india (ICICI)

Sanctions by ICICI during 1997-98 aggregated Rs.25532 crore recording an increase of 81 % over those in the previous year. Disbursements (including guarantees issued) went up by 47% to Rs.1 8230 crore. ICICI's total assets as on March 31, 1998 stood at Rs.45920 crore of which the major portion was made up of loans and advances (Rs.28721 crore) and investments (Rs.7330 crore). The Corporation declared a dividend of 55% for the year 1997-98 as compared to 45% for 1996-97.

Sanctions by ICICI during April-November 1998 aggregated to Rs.24671 crore showing an increase of 54.0% over those in the previous year. Disbursements went up by 34.3 per cent to Rs.11727 crore. ICICI's total disbursements as on march 31, 1998 stood at Rs.68400 crore.

SCICI Ltd. was merged with ICICI with restrospective effect from April 1, 1998, after the merger was sanctioned by the Bombay High Court on April 3, 1997.

Industrial development bank of india (IDBI)

Aggregate assistance sanctioned during 1997-98 recorded an increase of 41.9% (Rs.24199 crore compared to Rs.17050 crore in the previous year) whereas disbursements at Rs. 15165 crore registered a growth of 32.6% over disbursements of Rs.11439 crore in the previous year. Total assistance outstanding at the end of March 1998 stood at Rs.51570 crore higher by 17.8% as compared to the outstanding at the end of the previous year (Rs.43769 crore).

Industry-wise distribution of the IDBI's assistance indicates that core/infrastructure sectors and other manufacturing sectors received a major proportion of assistance sanctioned during 1997-98. The infrastructure sector, comprising power telecom roads and ports shared 33.9% during the year. Core sector industries, such as iron and steel, oil exploration refining cement and fertiliser accounted for 18.7% of the assistance sanctioned. Other major industries which accounted for a sizeable share of sanctions included chemicals and chemical products (10.8%) electronic & electrical products (3.9%), textiles (6.2%), food manufacturing (2.7%) and artificial fibres (2.4%).

During the year 1997-98 IDBI earned a pre-tax profit of Rs.1 800.3 crore as against Rs. 1482.3 crore during the previous year. A sum of Rs.219 crore was transferred to the Government of India, representing a return of 45% on the equity capital of IDBI.

Industrial finance corporation of india (IFCI)

IFCI was restructured from a statutory corporation to a company from 1st July, 1993. During the year 1997-98 overall sanctions of IFCI under its various schemes of assistance aggregated to Rs. 10983 crores for 303 projects as compared to sanction of Rs.7212 crores for 304 projects during 1996-97. Total disbursements during the year aggregated Rs.5650 crores as against Rs.5157 crores disbursed during 1995-96 registering 10% growth.

Cumulatively, sanctions accorded by IFCI under its various schemes upto the end of March, 1998 amounted to Rs.49226 crore for 5067 projects. The overall disbursements upto 31st March, 1998 were of the order of Rs.30757 crores.

During the year, IFCI's assistance to projects in notified less developed districts/areas amounted to Rs.4836 crore in respect of 133 projects, which constituted 44% of the total assistance sanctioned. Cumulatively, upto the March 31, 1998, IFCI had sanctioned financial assistance aggregating Rs.22869 crores to 2239 projects located in notified less developed districts/ areas which constituted 47% of IFCI's overall net cumulative sanctions.

During the nine month period of the current year 199899 i.e. April 1998 to December 1998, IFCI sanctioned assistance of Rs.6822 crores and disbursed Rs.3159 crores as against the sanction and disbursements of Rs.6799 crores and Rs.3843 crores respectively, made during the corresponding period of the previous year i.e. April 1998 to December 1998.

Industrial investment bank of India limited

IIBI, as a development financial institution provides finance for the establishment of the new industrial projects as well as for expansion, diversification and modernisation of existing industrial enterprises. Financial assistance is generally provided in the form of term loans, asset credit, equipment finance, short/ medium term loans for capital expenditure/working capital gap, margin money for working capital, subscription to debentures/equity shares and deferred payment guarantees. IIBI is a SEBI registered category-I Merchant Banker and its services include inter alia structuring of suitable instruments for raising resources by the client companies from the market through public/rights issues, preparation of prospectus/offer documents and working as lead manager in these issues. IIBI is also active in debt syndication and specialised services for merger and acquisitions.

The total assistance sanctioned and disbursed by the IRBI during the year 1997-98 was Rs.2061.04 crores and Rs. 1153.18 crores respectively as compared to Rs.816.01 crores and Rs.549.60 crores respectively during 1996-97. Cumulative sanctions and disbursements as on March 31,

1998 were Rs.6311.67 crores and Rs.4311.95 crores respectively. The sanctions and disbursements of IIBI during the period was Rs.1529.40 crore and Rs.1090.53 crores respectively.

Export import bank of india

Export Import Bank of India has a menu of 37 major programmes covering all the stages of export cycle. During the year ended March, 1998 Export Import Bank of India sanctioned loans of Rs.1840 crores under various lending programmes as compared to sanctions of Rs.1242 crores in the previous year. Disbursements during 1997-98 were at Rs.1 370 crores, as against Rs. 1257 crores in the previous year. Loan outstanding increased by 13.5% moving upwards to Rs.3917 crores on March 31, 1998 from Rs.3451 crores as on March 31,1997.

During 1997-98, the bank made commitments in principle amounting to Rs.718 crore for loans and Rs.1219 crores for guarantees to support export bids of Indian companies. Sanction of guarantees aggregated to Rs.403 crores and guarantees amounting to Rs.191 crores were issued during the year. Net profit of the bank in the period April 1997 to March 1998 on account of General Fund was Rs.201.6 crores registering a 33% increase over the previous year's profit of Rs.1 51.6 crores. Net worth of the bank increased to Rs.1206 crores comprising Rs.500 crores as equity and reserves of Rs.706 crores. Rs.41 crores was paid to the Government of India towards dividend as compared to Rs.31 crores in 1996-97.

Cumulative sanctions and disbursements of funded assistance as at March 31, 1998 were Rs.17425 crores and Rs.1 4427 crores respectively. Cumulative guarantees sanctioned as on that date amounted to Rs. 1769 crores and guarantees issued were Rs.1388 crores. As at March 31, 1998 the outstanding guarantees were Rs. 1209 crores.

During April to November 1998 Exim Bank's aggregate sanction under its various lending programmes amounted to Rs.1 369 crores as against Rs.1137 crores during the corresponding period last year. Disbursements during April-November 1998 amounted to Rs.597 crores as compared to Rs.591 crores during the corresponding period last year. Loan outstanding as on November 30 1998 amounted to Rs.4002 crores as against Rs.3472 crores during the corresponding period last year.

Sanctions for guarantees during April-November 1998 amounted to Rs.230 crores as compared to Rs.239 crores during the corresponding period last year. Guarantees amounting to Rs.63 crores were received during the same period as against Rs.38 crores during the pervious year. Guarantees outstandings as on November 30, 1998 amounted to Rs.1029 crores as against Rs.1072 crores as on November 1997.

Exim Bank's authorised capital has been raised from Rs.500 crore to Rs.1000 crore with a provision that Central Government may, by notification, increase the said capital to Rs.2000 crores. The Export-Import Bank of India Act 1981 has been amended to increase the authorised capital.

Small industries development bank of india (SIDBI)

SIDBI completed eight years of its operations on March 31, 1998. During the year ending March 31, 1998 total sanctions and disbursements by SIDBI were Rs.7485 crores and Rs.5239 crores respectively. The sanctions recorded growth of 15.4% over the previous year whereas the disbursements recorded a growth of 14.3% over the same period.

The aggregate assistance sanctioned by SIDBI over the period of eight years amounted to Rs.36262 crores and disbursements Rs.26700 crores. The compound annual growth rate for the eight year period upto March, 1998 has been 17.6% for sanctions and 16.1 % for disbursements.

SIDBI caters to the credit requirements of small scale units directly through tailor-made schemes of assistance and indirectly through the vast network of primary lending organisations mainly in the form of refinance. Availment of refinance by the credit institutions has been on the decline since 1991-92. On the other hand, SIDBI's operations under its schemes of direct assistance have been recording significant growth.

While the year 1998-99 continued to witness sluggish industrial growth rate SIDBI undertook various policy measures to enhance the flow of credit to the small scale sector. These measures helped in achieving an overall growth in sanctions and disbursements of 61 % and 37% respectively during the first half of 1998-99 over the corresponding period of the previous year. The initiative taken by SIDBI include an overhaul of refinance scheme in tandem with the changing requirements of the Primary Lending Institutions and greater emphasis on direct assistance schemes The Banks declared the year 1998-99 as "Techno Mission Year" and paid special emphasis for enhancing flow of assistance under Technology Development and Modernisation Fund (TDMF) Scheme. Consequent to certain relaxations and liberalised approach, the Scheme has shown a health growth at 121 % during the period April-September 1998 over the corresponding period of previous I year. Besides, measures have been taken to enhance the scope of development and support service with special emphasis on micro credit. SIDBI, during 1998-99 has launched a Rs.1 00 crores SIDBI foundation for Macro Credit (SFMC) to assist Non Governmental Organisations (NGOs) and Voluntary Organisations on soft terms which in turn would extend micro credit to poor people. The Foundation will promote an entirely new channel conducive to the needs of the poor borrowers in the years to come.

Total income from operations during the year was Rs.1408.54 crores with a net profit of Rs.405.23 crores. Out of the net profit a sum of Rs.271.83 crores has been transferred to Reserves; Rs.5.75 crores to Investment Reserve, Rs.1 0 crores to the Marketing Development Assistance Fund; Rs. 15 crores to National equity Fund, Rs.20 crore to Venture Capital Fund, Rs.1 crore to Mahila Vikas Nidhi, Rs.1crore to Mahila Udhyam Nidhi, Rs.1 crore to Staff Welfare Fund. After providing for Rs.1 2.5 crores toward dividend tax for the years 1996-97 and 1997-98, the balance amount of Rs.67.50 crores has been transferred to IDBI in terms of Section 29(2) of the SIDBI Act, 1989 as return on capital.

State financial corporations (SFCs)

State Financial Corporations (SFCs) operating at the State level form an integral part of the development financing system in the country. They function with the objective of financing and promoting small and medium enterprises for achieving balanced region socio-economic growth, catalysing higher investment, generating greater employment opportunities and widening the ownership base of industry.

At present, there are 18 SFCs in the country, 17 of which were set up under State Financial Corporations Act, 1951. Tamil Nadu Industrial Investment Corporation Ltd., set up in 1949 under the Companies Act also functions as a full fledged State Financial Corporation. SFCs extend financial assistance to industrial units by way of term loans, direct subscription to equity/ debentures, guarantees and discounting of bills of exchange. SFCs operate a number of schemes of refinance and equity type of assistance formulated by IDBI/SIDBI which include schemes for artisans, special target groups such as Scheduled Caste/Scheduled Tribe women, ex-servicemen, physically handicapped etc. and for transport operators, setting up hotels, tourism related activities, hospitals and nursing homes etc.

Based on the report of a Committee set up by the Government to review the State Financial Corporation Act, 1951 certain amendments in the Act are under consideration of the Government.

Board for industrial and financial reconstruction (BIFR)

The Board for Industrial and Financial Reconstruction (BIFR), set up under the Sick Industrial Companies (Special Provisions) Act, 1985 (SICA) became operational w.e.f. May 15 , 1987. The Board looks into cases of sick industrial companies in the large and medium sector with a view to achieving, inter alia, the objectives of timely detection of sickness and determination of preventive, ameliorative, remedial and other measures in respect of such companies and expeditious enforcement of the measures so determined.

The sick Industrial Companies (Special Provisions) Bill, 1997 to replace the Sick Industrial Companies (Special Provisions) Act, 1985 was introduced in the Lok Sabha on 16th May, 1997. However, due to dissolution of the Lok Sabha in December, 1997 the Bill has lapsed.

The progress of work of the BIFR as on 31.12.1998 as follows:-

1 .	References received	3483
2.	Registration declined	1018
3.	Under Scrutiny	11
4.	References registered	2454
5.	Dismissed as non-maintainable	453
6.	Rehabilitation Schemes approved/sanctioned	617

7.	Winding up recommended to the concerned High Courts	610
8.	Draft Schemes Circulated	33
9.	Winding up Notices issued	30
10.	Under Inquiry	561
11.	Schemes failed and reopened	23
12.	Pending cases remanded by AAIFR	22
13.	Stay ordered by Courts	44
14.	Schemes by AAIFR/Courts	28
15.	Net worth became positive during enquiry and hence dropped	27
16.	Declared no longer sick	217

Appellate authority for industrial and financial reconstruction

The Appellate Authority for Industrial and Financial Reconstruction has been set up under the provision of Sick Industrial Companies (Special Provisions) Act, 1985 to provide for a mechanism to hear appeals of sick industrial companies against the orders of the Board for Industrial and Financial Reconstruction (BIFR). The AAIFR started functioning w.e.f. 15th April, 1987.

During the year 1998 (upto March), the AAIFR disposed of as many as 56 cases. The other relevant statistics in this regard are shown below: New Office Building, Chandigarh

		1996	1997	1998	1999
1.	No. of appeals pending at the beginning of the year	144	103	84	105
2.	No. of appeals received during the year	233	253	160	-
3.	No. of appeals disposed of during the year	274	272	139	-

Customer services

Reserve Bank of India (RBI) has issued instructions to public sector banks from time to time for improving customer service in banks. RBI has formulated and implemented an Ombudsman Scheme for expeditious and inexpensive resolution of customer complaints against banks. At present 15 Banking Ombudsman are functioning within their area of jurisdiction. The details of names & addresses etc. alongwith area of jurisdiction is at Annexure. The scheme of Banking Ombudsman has been given wide publicity to have awareness amongst the masses in the leading newspapers so that the scheme could be availed of for quick and inexpensive redressal of grievances of customers.

Besides the above, each public sector bank was asked to appoint a Nodal Officer, who would handle the customer grievances and their prompt disposal. Indian Banks' Association (IBA) has given publicity through newspapers for awareness of the general people in the country about the Grievance Officers appointed by each public sector bank, who would be looking after customer complaints/grievances.

In addition, all the public sector banks have also adopted 'Citizens Charter' and have published booklets indicating various services/facilities provided by them to its customers. Some of the areas included in the Charter are provision of prompt and time bound services relating to preparation of Demand Drafts, issue of cheque books and encashment of cheque.

Banking Ombudsman Scheme

Name and address of Banking Ombudsman	*Area of jurisdiction*
Shri. B.N. Shetye C/o Reserve Bank of India, Garment House, Ground Floor, Dr. Annie Besant Road, Worli, Mumbai-400 018 Tel: 492 4607/496 0893 Fax: 022-4960912	Maharashtra and Goa

Address	Jurisdiction
Shri. S.K. Soni Jeevan Bharti Building, Tower No.1, 7th Floor, 124, Connaught circus, New Delhi-110 001 Tel:372 5445/372 5219 Fax: 011-3725218	Delhi, Haryana, Jammu & Kashmir and Ghaziabad district of Uttar Pradesh
Shri A.K. Pandya, C/o Reserve Bank of India, Hoshangabad Road, Post Box No. 32, Bhopal-462011 Tel: 573 772/573 776 Fax: 0755-573779	Madhya Pradesh
Shri J.C. Lynn C/o Reserve Bank of India 10/3/8, Nrupatunga Road, P. B. No. 6768, Bangalore- 560 022 Tel: 227 5629/ 227 5020 Fax: 080- 2244047	Karnataka
Shri R.C. Kapoor, C/o Reserve Bank of India, New Office Building, Sector-17, Central Vista, Opp. Telephone Bhavan, Chandigarh- 160017 Tel: 709 589/773 011 Fax: 0172-771880	Himachal Pradesh, C/o Punjab, Union Territory of Chandigarh
Shri S.A. Hussain, C/o Reserve Bank of India, 6-1-56, Secretariat Road, Saifabad, Post Bag No. 31, Hyderabad- 500 004 Tel: 210 013/210 248 Fax: 040-210014	Andhra Pradesh
Shri J.P. Sharma, C/o Reserve Bank of India, South of Gandhi Maidan, Post Box No. 182, Patna-800 001 Tel: 654 160/655 767 Fax: 0612-655 407	Bihar

Shri O.P Sodhani, C/o Reserve Bank of India, Ram Bagh Circle, Tonk Road, Post Box No. 12, Jaipur-302 004 Tel: 570 357/570 392/564 661 Fax: 0141-562 220	Rajasthan
Shri G.C. Agarwal C/o Reserve Bank of India, M.G. Road, Post Box No. 82, Kanpur-208 001 Tel: 361 191/310 593 Fax: 0512-362 553	Uttar Pradesh excluding District Ghaziabad
Shri H.N. Das C/o Reserve Bank of India, Station Road, Pan Bazar, Post Box No. 120, Guwahati-781 001 Tel: 540 445/510 054 Fax: 0361-540 033	Assam, Arunanchal Pradesh, Manipur, Meghalaya, Mizoram, Nagaland and Tripura
Dr. Sitakanta Mahapatra, C/o Reserve Bank of India, Pandit Jawaharlal Nehru Marg, Post Box No. 16, Bhubaneshwar-751 001 Tel: 418 007/418 008 Fax: 0674-418006	Orissa
Shri R. Ramalingam, C/o Reserve Bank of India, Fort Glasis, South Beach Road, Chennai-600001 Tel: 561 923/563 443 Fax: 044-432 1801	Tamil Nadu, Union Territories of Pondicherry and Andaman Nicobar
Shri S.L. Bose C/o Reserve Bank of India, 15, Netaji Subhash Road, Calcutta-700 001 Tel: 220 6222 Fax: 033-2205899	West Bengal and Sikkim

Shri S.A. Kamath C/o Reserve Bank of India, La Gajjar Chambers, Ashram Road, Ahmedabad-380 009 Tel: 658 2357 Fax: 079-658 3325105	Gujarat, Union Territories of Dadra and Nagar Haveli, Daman and Diu
Shri S.A. Rahman, C/o Reserve Bank of India, Bakery Junction, Post Box No. 6507, Thiruvananthapuram-695 033 Kerala.	Kerala, Union Territory of Lakshadeep

Regional rural banks (RRBs)

The Regional Rural Banks (RRBs) have achieved substantial growth over the years and have been able to take banking to the door-steps of the rural poor and providing them with institutional credit support. 196 RRBs are functioning in 23 States covering 427 districts in the country with a network of 14,475 branches (including satellite branches). The rural branch network of RRBs at 12344 constitutes 37.5% of the total rural credit outlets of the Scheduled Commercial Banks in the country. 94 out of 115 (82%) districts identified by the Planning Commission under Tribal Sub-Plan Area are covered by the RRBs.

The credit support provided by these banks amounted to Rs.9876.12 crores (outstanding in 12.03 million borrowal accounts). RRBs have disbursed credit aggregating Rs. 4584-03 crores the average amount of loan per account disbursed by them being Rs.12800. The aggregate deposits of RRBs increased from Rs.18032.01 crores in 1996-97 to Rs. 22197.80 crores in 199798 registering a growth of 23 per cent as compared to 26.9 per cent growth in 1996-97 and covered over 42.0 million accounts, The deposits as of March 1998 comprised of term deposits (53%), savings deposits (42%) and the current deposits (5%).

In order to supplement the limited resources of the RRBs, both NABARD and sponsor banks extended financial assistance to these institutions by way of refinance. The short-term credit limits sanctioned by NABARD for Seasonal Agricultural Operations (SAO) including Oilseeds Production Programme (OPP), National Pulses Development Programme (NPDP) and Development of Tribal Population (DTP) during the year 1997-98 stood at Rs. 881.47 crores registering an increase of 11.5 per cent over the limits sanctioned at Rs. 790.42 crores during the previous year. The limits sanctioned for 1997-98 included Rs. 92.96 crores for Oilseeds Production programme (OPP) (24 banks) and Rs.47.42 crores for the newly introduced Development of Tribal Population (DTP) (44 banks). As in the past, the RRBs in Andhra Pradesh with the sanctioned limits of Rs. 242.93 crores accounted for the largest share, followed by the RRBs in Karnataka with Rs. 192.33 crores. The overall utilisation under Short Term Seasonal Agricultural Operations (ST-SAO) amounted to Rs.823.58 crores and formed 93.4 per cent of the limits sanctioned. The outstanding was inclusive of the drawls under the previous year's limits and included Rs.37 crores in default (as on 31 October 1998) to NABARD. The Sanction of credit limits for Short-Term Other than Seasonal Agricultural Operations (ST-OSAO) purposes from NABARD during the year 1997-98 at Rs.1 91.53 crores was higher by about 8.3 per cent over the limit sanctioned during the previous year at Rs. 176.90 crores. NABARD's Medium Term (Non-schematic) (MT-NS) limit intended for financing the sporadic investments in agricultural allied activities and artisans was sanctioned to RRBs stood at Rs.1 4.20 crores and the drawls their against at Rs.8.5 crores formed 59.8 per cent of the limit sanctioned.

The outstanding borrowings by RRBs from NABARD (Rs.2750.68 crores) and sponsor banks (Rs.

480.33 crores) constituted 84.9% and 14.8% respectively of the total outstanding borrowing at Rs.3241 crores.

The annual losses of RRBs decreased substantially from Rs. 879.36 crores in 1996-97 to Rs. 230.75 crores in 199798. The net accumulated losses of the RRBs also decreased from Rs. 3040.57 crores as on 31 March 1997 to Rs.2805.30 crores as on 31 st March 1998. As many as 126 RRBs made a profit of Rs. 302.01 crores (Rs. 2.4 crores per RRB) as against a profit of Rs. 64.68 crores made by 44 RRBs (Rs. 1.58 crore per RRB) during 1996-97. The number of loss incurring RRBs decreased from 152 to 70 and the loss per loss incurring RRB decreased from Rs. 5.58 crores to Rs. 3.30 crores.

In pursuance of the recommendations of the Working Group on RRBs (Kelkar Committee) the issued capital of all the RRBs has been raised to Rs. 100 lakhs from Rs. 25 lakhs in a phased manner.

Other measures to improve the viability of RRBs include relieving of 69 RRBs of their service area obligations and allowing to finance throughout the area within their jurisdiction. Remaining RRBs are also allowed to extend loans in their entire command districts subject to fulfillment of their service area obligations. RRBs are allowed to issue guarantees on behalf of their customers and have been allowed to install lockers, issue drafts and effect mail transfers for increasing their range of services. In order to broadbase their investments and to provide them further scope for profitable investment avenues. RRBs have been accorded parity with commercial banks and permitted to invest in shares and debentures of corporates and units of mutual funds, subject to certain ceiling. The RRBs are also allowed to invest in the bonds of certain specified public sector undertakings and All India Financial Institutions, subject to exposure norms. The priority sector discipline as applicable to commercial banks has been made applicable to the RRBs as well with effect from 1.4.1997. The RRBs have been permitted to open new branches at potential centres on the condition that no additional staff is recruited by them. Further, with a view to bring uniformity in reporting of information in the Annual Reports of the RRBs, detailed guidelines have been issued by NABARD. As envisaged in the Union Budget for the year 199798, the sponsor banks have been entrusted with a greater role and responsibility in the management of the RRBs since November 1997.

Restructuring of RRBs: Various alternatives including merger were considered for revamping the RRBs and a decision was taken to revitalise them on "Stand Alone" basis. Towards this end, budgetary support of Rs.200.00 crores from Government in 1997-98 was provided for cleansing the balance sheets of afresh set of 15 RRBs through infusion of fresh capital and administering second dose of assistance to 75 RRBs selected under earlier phases. Further, an amount of Rs. 264.65 crores provided in the budget (Revised Estimates) for 1998-99 for this purpose is expected to be utilised to cover some more RRBs in addition to further recapitalisation of partially recapitalised RRBs (22).

Development Action Plans and signing of Memoranda of Understandings (MOUs): In order to achieve greater operational flexibility and providing avenues of profitability, a package of measures has been continued, which, inter-alia comprises of nontarget group lending, relocation of branches. Development Action Plans (DAPs) have been initiated for business improvement and viability attainment coupled with Memorandum of Understanding (MOU) between RRBs and Sponsor Banks to guide, control and facilitate DAP implementation. A system of execution of Annual MOU between the RRBs and the Sponsor Bank for the year 199899 has also been operationalised. Of the 196 RRBs 162, are reported to have already executed MOU for the year 1998-99 with their sponsor banks.

Priority sector lending

The Government have been giving considerable importance to the priority sector lending particularly in view of the need for quicker upliftment of the weaker and the down-trodden sections of the society. With a view to achieve this objective, the credit policy aims at channelising increasing flow of credit to priority sector and in particular to the weaker sections of society. Banks have been urged to step up priority sector lending so that they may respond effectively to the challenges before the nation for meeting the social concerns.

The priority sector lending of public sector banks was Rs. 79,131 crore as on the last Friday of March 1997 constituting 41.72 per cent of net bank credit (NBC) as against the target of 40 per cent. The performance of public sector banks has further improved with priority sector lending amounting to Rs. 91.319 crores (41.85 per cent of NBC) as on the last Friday of March 1998. Within the priority sector, lending to agriculture and weaker sections constituted 15.72 per cent and 8.31 per cent of NBC respectively as against the target of 18 per cent and 10 per cent respectively as on the last Friday of March, 1998.

Deposits and credit

The aggregate deposit of scheduled commercial banks as on March 27,1998 stood at Rs.6,05,410 crores recording an increase of Rs.99,811 crores (19.7 per cent) during the year 1997-98 as against an increase of Rs.71,780 crores (16.5 per cent) during the corresponding period of the previous year. Bank credit increased by Rs.45,677 crores (16.4 per cent) in 1997-98 as compared with an increase of

Rs.24,387 crores (9.6 per cent) in 1996-97. Non food credit increased by Rs.40,789 crores (15.1,per cent) during 1997-98 as compared with Rs.26,581 crores (10.9 per cent) in 1996-97. During the current financial year (1998-99), the aggregate deposits of scheduled commercial banks stood at 6,83,081 crores as on January 1, 1999, recording an increase of 12.8 per cent as against on increase of 11.6 per cent during the corresponding period of the previous year. Total bank credit stood at Rs.3.44,024 crores as on January 1, 1998 recording an increase of 6.2 per cent as against an increase of 7.9 percent during the corresponding period of the previous year. The Non-food bank credit stood at 3,27,922 crores recording an increase of 5.2 per cent as against an increase of 6.6 per cent during the corresponding period of the previous year.

Regional dispersal of credit

The Credit-Deposit (CD) Ratio is often considered to be an important indicator, among others, of the extent of contribution made by the banks to developmental activities in the concerned State. The C D ratio depends not only on the efforts made by the banks but also on various other factors such as credit-absorptive capacity of the region, infrastructural support, and the overall policy framework in the region. Banks are expected to have a CID ratio of 60 per cent in respect of their rural and semi-urban branches separately on an all-India basis.

Branch expansion

Under the extant branch licensing policy of the Reserve Bank of India (RBI), it is left to the judgement of commercial banks to open branches in metropolitan, urban and semi urban centres after assessing the need therefore and obtaining the approval of RBI. The proposal for opening of rural branches identified by the banks which are recommended by State Governments/ Union Territories are also considered by the RBI on merits. However RBI have given freedom to banks which fulfil the under mentioned criteria to open new branches:

(i) compliance with capital adequacy norm of 8 per cent;

(ii) minimum owned funds of Rs. 100 crores;

(iii) the banks showing net profits for three consecutive years;

(iv) non performing assets not exceeding 15 per cent of total outstanding loans.

RBI have advised the banks satisfying the above criteria to submit to them a yearly plan duty approved by their Board of Directors for opening branches to enable RBI to advise their concerned regional offices for issue of licences.

As at the end of March, 1998 a total of 66,137 branch offices of scheduled commercial banks were functioning in the country of which 32,918, 14,178, 10,436 and 8,605 offices were located in rural, semi-urban, urban and metropolitan centres, respectively. State/Union territory-wise number of branch offices of these banks as at the end of March 1998 are given in the Annexure-II.

Local area banks

With a view to providing institutional mechanism for promotion of rural savings as well as for the provision of credit for viable economic activities in the local areas, it has been decided to allow the establishment of new local area banks in the private sector. The area of operations of these banks shall be a maximum of three geographically contiguous districts. This is expected to bridge the gaps in credit availability and enhance the institutional credit framework in the rural and semi-urban areas., As per guidelines issued by RBI in this regard such a bank shall be registered as a public limited company under the Companies Act, 1956 and would be licensed under the

Banking Regulation Act, 1949. Further, it would be governed by the provisions of the Reserve Bank of India Act, 1934 and other relevant statutes. The minimum paid up capital for such a bank shall be Rs. 5 crores and the promoters contribution at least be Rs. 2 crores. Proposals having diversified share holdings will be preferred. The promoters of the bank may comprise individuals, corporate entities, trusts, and societies. The banks shall be subject to prudential norms and other policies laid down by RBI from time to time.

Reserve bank of India have approved eight proposals for setting up of Local Area Banks in the private sector.

State/Union Territory wise Credit Deposit (CID) ratios of all Scheduled Commercial Banks as on the last Friday of March 1996,1997 and 1998

State/Union	*Territory*	*C/D Ratio (per cent)*		
		March 1996	*March 1997*	*March 1998*
1.	Andhra Pradesh	80.8	77.6	72.1
2.	Arunachal Pradesh	10.4	10.7	13.1
3.	Assam	39.3	35.2	32.9
4.	Bihar	32.0	30.5	27.5
5.	Goa	26.9	25.0	24.6
6.	Gujarat	53.0	49.7	48.2
7.	Haryana	46.0	42.7	42.9
8.	Himachal Pradesh	25.8	23.4	21.6
9.	Jammu & Kashmir	38.2	38.8	37.4
10.	Karnataka	69.7	71.5	68.2
11.	Kerala	45.4	46.9	44.3
12.	Madhya Pradesh	57.1	52.3	51.4
13.	Maharashtra	75.7	68.7	72.3
14.	Manipur	53.7	57.6	58.8
15.	Meghalaya	14.4	14.3	15.2
16.	Mizoram	16.2	14.0	23.2
17.	Nagaland	27.4	24.0	18.3
18.	National Capital Territory of Delhi	74.7	66.9	61.9

19.	Orissa	54.8	49.0	45.2
20.	Punjab	41.9	39.1	38.6
21.	Rajasthan	46.6	44.2	47.4
22.	Sikkim	19.3	17.7	20.7
23.	Tamil Nadu	101.2	100.3	96.1
24.	Tripura	42.1	37.8	34.0
25.	Uttar Pradesh	34.2	31.6	28.6
26.	West Bengal	55.7	50.0	46.1
27.	Andaman & Nicobar Island	16.5	16.0	15.1
28.	Chandigarh	138.8	88.0	58.0
29.	Dadra & Nagar	20.7	18.6	21.4
30.	Daman & Diu	23.3	21.8	20.6
31.	Lakshadweep	9.6	8.8	10.0
32.	Pondicherry	41.9	39.0	35.9
	All-India	61.9	57.3	55.5

Monetary and credit policy

The overall objective of monetary policy for 1998-99 continued to aim at reasonable price stability and availability of adequate bank credit to support the grcwth of the real sector. The monetary policy for 1998-99 was formulated against the backdrop of developments that have taken place during the previous year and the broad economic objectives for the current year. The policy formulation during the current year was predicated by the developments like, higer than the projected growth of money supply in relation to growth in GDP in 1997-98, substantial increase in financial flows from banks to the corporate sector despite a slowdown in industrial growth, higher market borrowing requirements of the Government; and continued uncertainty in external currency and product markets. The short term economic objectives of the monetary policy were: the need to accelerate industrial investment and output in the economy; maintenance of low rates of inflation; continued pursuit of financial sector reform; moderation in interest rates; and improvement in credit delivery mechanisms, particularly for agriculture, medium and small sectors. With a view to achieving a balance among different objectives and the need or constant vigilance on the monetary front, short-term adjustments in monetary measures would be made on the basis of emerging developments.

It was further indicated that in view of the several important changes that have taken place in the regulatory framework for financial markets, much greater importance would be given to structural measures in the monetary and credit policy statement at the beginning of the year. As a matter of policy such structural measures would remain unchanged during the course of the year and also continue over the medium-term to enable banks to plan their operations and introduce organisational changes with the medium term monetary perspective in view. Short-term measures such as, changes in the Bank Rate, cash reserve ratio (CRR), Repo rate, access to refinance, etc. may also be included if it coincides with the timing of the announcement of Monetary and Credit Policy statements. Further, changes in short-term adjustments in monetary measures would be made at short notice in the light of actual developments and emerging external market conditions. The credit policy for the second half of the year would continue as before, but the October Statement would be in the nature of a mid-term review of monetary developments during the year and will not necessarily involve changes in credit policy measures.

Accordingly, the Statement on Mid-term Review of Monetary and Credit Policy for 1998-99 was made on October 30, 1998 setting out the stance of monetary policy for the second half of 1998-99 and measures to carry forward the monetary and financial sector reforms. No changes in short-term measures such as, the Bank Rate, Cash Reserve Ratio (CRR), Statutory Liquidity Ratio (SLR) Repo rate were announced.

The following are some of the important monetary and credit policy measures which were implemented during 1998-99 (upto December 1998):

Reserve requirements and refinance

Cash reserve ratio (CRR):

(i) On a review of the current foreign exchange and monetary conditions, it was decided to effect an increase in cash reserve ratio (CRR) as a temporary measure. Accordingly, effective from the fortnight beginning August 29, 1998, the CRR to be maintained by scheduled commercial banks [excluding Regional Rural Banks (RRBs)] was increased by one percentage point from 10.0 per cent to 11.0 per cent of net demand and time liabilities (NDTL).

(ii) It was decided on May 18, 1998, the remaining two-third balances impounded during the period May 4,1991 and April 17,1992 would be released in twelve equal monthly instalments from the fortnight beginning May 23, 1998 and extending upto March 13, 1999. One-third of the amount impounded during the period May 4,1991 and April 17, 1992 was released in three instalments in October 1992.

Statutory Liquidity Ratio (SLR)

SLR was announced during 1998-99 upto December 1998.

Refinance from RBI:

(i) With effect from the fortnight beginning May 9, 1988, export credit refinance was restored to the level prevailing as on January 16, 1998 i.e., 100 per cent (instead of 50 per cent effective from January 17, 1998) of the increase in outstanding export credit eligible for refinance over the level of such credit as on February 16, 1996.

(ii) In line with the reduction in the interest rate on export credit, with effect from August 6, 1998, scheduled commercial banks would be provided export credit refinance at 2.0 percentage point below the Bank Rate (i.e., 7.0 per cent per annum) upto March 31, 1999.

Interest rates

Bank rate: With effect from the close of business on April 2, 1998 the Bank Rate was reduced by one half of one percentage point from '10.5 per cent per annum' to 10.0 per cent per annum' which was further reduced by one percentage point from 10.0 per cent to 9.0 per cent effective from April 29, 1998.

Repo rate. The Reserve Bank reduced the Repo rate from 8.0 per cent to 7.0 per cent on April 3, 1998 and further to 6 and 5 per cent on April 30, 1998 and June 15, 1998 . On a review of the foreign exchange and monetary conditions, the Repo rate was raised to 8.0 per cent on August 20.1998.

Deposit rate With a view to providing greater freedom to banks in respect of several aspects of their deposit mobilisation, the following measures were announced:

(i) The minimum period of maturity of term deposits was reduced from 30 to 15 days.

(ii) Banks were permitted to determine their own penal interest rates for premature withdrawal of domestic/NRE term deposits and banks were advised to ensure that the depositors are made aware of the applicable penal rate along with the deposit rate.

(iii) Restriction on banks that they must offer the same rate on deposits of the same maturity irrespective of the size of such deposits was removed in respect of deposits of Rs. 15 lakh and over and bank boards to lay down the policy in this regard.

(iv) Taking into account the international development which reiterated the problems related to short-term external liabilities and large unhedged positions of corporates in some of the East Asian countries, to encourage the banks to mobilise long-term deposits, while simultaneously discouraging them to mobilise short term deposits, the interest rate ceiling on FCNR(B) deposits of one year and above was increased by 50 basis points and that on such deposits below one year and floating rate deposits were reduced by 25 basis points.

(v) Banks were permitted to fix their own overdue interest rates in respect of FCNR(B) and NRE deposits, subject to these deposits being renewed.

Lending rates

(i) With a view to providing greater freedom to banks in respect of their lending operations and with a view to removing the disincentive to the flow of credit to small borrowers, the, interest rates on loans upto Rs. 2 lakh was prescribed at not exceeding the Prime Lending Rate (PLR) which is available to the best borrowers of the concerned bank.

(ii) All advances against term deposits would be at an interest rate equal to PLR or less.

(iii) The existing regulations were reviewed and the ceiling amount on advances against shares to individuals was increased from Rs. 10 lakh to 20 lakh against dematerialised securities. The minimum margin subscriptions against dematerialised shares was also reduced from 50 to 25 per cent.

(iv) Interest rate on pre-shipment export credit upto 180 days was reduced from 12 per cent to 11 per cent with effect from April 30, 1998. Interest rate against incentives receivable from Government covered by ECGC guarantee in respect of pre-shipment credit upto 90 days was reduced from the existing 12 per cent to 11 per cent with effect from April 30, 1998.

(v) As a measure to effect a temporary revision in the interest rates on export credit upto March 31, 1999, with effect from August 6, 1998, the interest rates charged by scheduled commercial banks on pre-shipment rupee export credit and post-shipment rupee export credit were reduced by 2 percentage points. Further in respect of post shipment rupee export credit the ceiling rate of 'not exceeding 11.0 per cent per annum' applicable in respect of demand bills and usance bill upto 90 days and loans against incentives receivable from Government covered by ECGC guarantee upto 90 days was replaced by a fixed rate of 9.0 per cent.

Pre-shipment rupee export credit

Effective April 30, 1998 interest rate on pre-shipment rupee export credit upto 180 days was reduced from 12.00 per cent to 11.00 per cent per annum which was further reduced to 9.00 per cent with effect from August 6, 1998 valid upto March 31, 1999. As from 1 st April 1999, the interest rate applicable prior to August 6, 1998 i.e. 11.00 per cent per annum will come into force automatically unless notified otherwise.

Effective August 6, 1998, interest rate on pre-shipment rupee export credit beyond 180 days and upto 270 days was reduced from 14.00 per cent to 12.00 per cent per annum valid upto March 31, 1999. As from 1st April 1999 the interest rate applicable prior to August 6, 1998 i.e. 14.00 per cent per annum will come into force automatically unless notified otherwise.

Post-shipment rupee export credit

Effective August 6, 1998, interest rate on post-shipment rupee export credit upto 90 days was reduced from not exceeding 11.00 per cent to 9.00 per cent per annum' valid upto March 31, 1999. As from 1st April 1999, the interest rate applicable prior to August 6, 1998 i.e. not exceeding 11.00 per cent per annum will come into force automatically unless notified otherwise.

Effective August 6,1998, interest rate on post-shipment rupee export credit beyond 90 days and upto six months from the date of shipment was reduced from 13.00 per cent to 11.00 per cent per annum valid upto March 31, 1999. As from 1 st April 1999, the interest rate applicable prior to August 6, 1998 i.e. 13.00 per cent per annum will come into force automatically unless notified otherwise.

Issue of CP by SDs

In order to enable Satellite Dealers to have access to short-term borrowings by issuance of Commercial Paper, 'requisite guidelines were issued through notification dated June 7, 1998.

Payment of dues of units of SSI sector

In July 1998, banks were advised to ascertain from their medium/large industrial borrowers, the extent of their dyes to the SSI suppliers and the action proposed to be taken by them to clear off the overdues, if any. In case, overdues towards SSI 'suppliers still persist, banks should not hesitate to take it as a negative factor while fixing the rate of interest on the borrowings of corporate bodies.

Guidelines for sanction of working capital to IT industries

RBI recognised the problem/difficulties faced by: banks in assessing the credit requirement of the software industry, which is relatively new area, a set of guidelines on various aspects of lending to IT and SI were framed and issued to banks in August 1998 to bring about uniformity in their approach in lending to this sector. The guidelines broadly covered areas like eligibility, methodology for assessment of working capital, documents to be submitted for credit appraisal, nature of credit facilities that could be provided to the industry, margin, security, rate of interest, periodical reporting system, follow-up etc.

Money market developments

With effect from May 9, 1998, the minimum size of operation per transaction by entities routing their lending through Primary Dealers (PDs) in the call money market was reduced from Rs. 5 crore to Rs. 3 crore.

With effect from May 9, 1998, the minimum lock-in period for units of Money Market Mutual Funds (MMMFs) and the period of transferability for Certificates of Deposits (CDs) were reduced from 30 days to 15 days.

The following were announced as a part of the Midterm Review of the Monetary and Credit Policy for 1998-99

It was decided to withdraw the restriction of the minimum period of 3 days for inter-bank ready-forward (repo) transactions effective from October 31, 1998.

RBI decided in principle to create an environment that would facilitate introduction of interest rate swaps. RBI would examine, in consultation with market participants, relevant aspects such as standard documentation, the back-up by underlying transactions between parties, the bench-mark rate and maturity, and prudential prescriptions before allowing the interest rate swaps in the market.

The RBI took a view on some specific suggestions by the Narasimham Committee II relating to money market which are as follows:

The Reserve Bank concurs, in principle, with the Committee that the call/notice money market and term money market should be strictly restricted to banks and primary dealers and aims to ultimately move towards a pure inter-bank market including primary dealers. This will be implemented in a manner that the existing lenders in the market will have operational flexibility to adjust their asset-liability structure. Simultaneously, measures will be taken to widen the repo market and improve non-bank participation in a variety of their instruments.

The RBI also agrees with the Committee's suggestion that there must be clearly defined prudent limits for bank's reliance on the money market.

The RBI broadly agrees with the Committee's suggestion that the RBI support to the market should be through a Liquidity Adjustment Facility (LAF). It has been decided to initiate actions that will enable, in due course, to replace the present general refinance facility with LAF Collateralised intra-day/overnight facility with adequate margin is also being considered to facilitate smooth operation of payment and settlement system to be placed eventually on Real Time Gross Settlement (RTGS) basis.

Government securities market

With a view to deepen the market further, the practice of reverse repos with Primary Dealers in specified securities was dispensed with and instead, liquidity support against the security of holdings in Subsidiary General Ledger (SGL) accounts would be provided.

With a view to deepen the market further, 182-Day Treasury Bill auctions on a fortnightly basis would be reintroduced.

With a view to deepen the market further, the

periodicity of holdings 364-Day Treasury Bills auctions would be on a monthly basis as against the earlier arrangement of fortnightly auctions.

In the light of monetary policy of October 1997 wherein the RBI commenced pre-announcement of notified amounts in respect of Treasury Bill auctions and exclusion of non-competitive bids from the notified amounts, FIIs were permitted to purchase/ sell Treasury Bills within the overall approved debt ceilings.

In addition to the earlier three-day and four-day repos, one-day repos (including reverse repos) to absorb (or infuse) liquidity into the system would be introduced by the RBI. Further, fixed interest and auction based repos, as appropriate would be used.

The following were announced as a part of the Mid term Review of the Monetary and Credit Policy for 1998-99

It is proposed to introduce a uniform price auction method in respect of 91 day Treasury Bill auctions.

Besides, the following recent initiatives for developing the Government securities market are required to be implemented.

The move towards repeal of the Public Debt Act, 194 and its replacement by the Government Securities Act.

The proposed changes in the Securities Contracts (Regulation) Act, 1956 which will pave way for a more active repos market and introduction of new market features like when issued trading.

Credit delivery system

Agricultural Credit: In respect of agricultural credit, several procedural modifications were made in the light of recommendations of the Shri R.V. Gupta Committee or Agriculture. These include greater flexibility and discretion to the lending banks in matters of collateral, margin, security, dispensation of " no dues certificates", introduction of a composite cash credit limit to cover the farmers production, post-harvest and household requirements, etc. The Indian Banks' Association was also requested to work out simplified application forms of agricultural loans, and banks were advised to delegate sufficient powers to their branch managers. These procedural improvements would lead to a substantial reduction in paper work and simplify the delivery mechanism for flow of credit to farmers. Those recommendations of the Committee which fall within the purview of State Governments or which require consideration by Central Government would be forwarded to them for necessary action.

Credit to Small Scale Industries: With a view to accelerating the flow of credit to small scale industries, RBI had set up under the Chairmanship of Shri S.L. Kapur to review the working of credit delivery system for small scale industries with a view to making the system more effective, simple and efficient to administer, to make suggestions for simplification and improvements in strengthening the existing internal mechanism in banks for redressal of customer grievances. The recommendation of the Committee was submitted to the RBI in June 1998.

Interest rates

Prior to April 1998 policy statement, lending rates for credit limits upto Rs. 25,000 was prescribed at 12.0 per cent per annum and for credit limits of over Rs. 25,000 and upto Rs.2 lakh, a ceiling rate of 13.5 per cent per annum was fixed. In order to remove any disincentive to the flow of credit to small borrowers, effective April 29, 1998, it was stipulated that the interest rates on credit limits of Rs.2 lakh and below should not exceed prime lending rate which is available to the best borrowers of the concerned banks. It was also announced in April 1998 policy statement that advances against domestic term deposits would be at an interest rate equal to PLR or less. Following reduction in the Bank Rate from 10% to 9%, a number of scheduled commercial banks revised downwards their PLR by 0.5-2.0 percentage points. In August 1998, with a view to maintain orderly conditions in forex market following volatility in exchange rate, a number of monetary measures were taken. These, inter-alia, included an increase of 300 basis points in the fixed rate repos from 5.0 per cent to 8.0 per cent and a hike of CR from 10 per cent to 11 per cent. PLR of major scheduled commercial banks remained in the range of 12.75-14.50 per cent with PLR of most of the major banks ranging in a narrow band of 13.0 -13.5 percent. Some banks announced separate Prime Term Lending Rate (PTLR) which was generally lower than the PLRs by 0.25-0.50 percentage points.

Domestic deposit rate

With a view to providing greater freedom to banks in respect of deposit mobilisation, the minimum period of maturity of term deposits was reduced from 30 days to 15 days in April 1998. Following the reduction in the Bank Rate in April 1998, the domestic deposit rates of banks came down considerably at the shorter end of maturity spectrum as compared with the rates prevailing in March 1998.

Consequent to the measures undertaken in August 1998, a hardening of deposit rates was observed in private sector banks. Since then divergent revisions are taking place in bank deposit interest rates on shorter maturity. On longer maturity, some private sector banks have reduced interest rates. The domestic term deposit rates of major scheduled commercial banks are in the range of 5.0 - 12.50 per cent. The banks are now permitted to determine their own penal interest rates for premature withdrawal of domestic term deposits. Restriction on banks that they must offer the same rate on deposits of the same maturity irrespective of the size of such deposits was withdrawn and the banks can now offer differential rate of interest for the same maturity for deposits of Rs. 15 lakh and over. The deposit rates are higher on such large deposits by 0.25 - 3.0 percentage point than on deposits of less than Rs. 15 lakh, depending upon the size of the deposits.

Selective credit control

The agricultural commodities except buffer stock and the unreleased stock of sugar of sugar mills are, for the present, exempted from any of the selective credit control measures. In the case of sugar effective October 22, 1997, minimum margins of 10 per cent for levy and 15 per cent for free sale sugar against stock held by mills/processing units have been prescribed. However, there are no restrictions on the level of credit or interest rate chargeable on the credit facilities extended by banks.

Certificates of deposit (CDs)

During the financial year 1998-99 upto September 25, 1998, outstanding amount of Certificates of Deposits (CDs) issued by scheduled commercial banks showed a downward trend. These outstanding declined from Rs.14.296 crores (2.5 per cent of aggregate deposits) as on March 27, 1998 to Rs.5,686 crores (1.1 per cent of aggregate deposits) as on September 25, 1998. This declining trend in outstanding CDs during 1998-99 may be attributed to the improved liquidity position of banks. Typical discount rate on primary issues of CDs with a maturity of 3 months declined from 13.0 per cent to 11.0 per cent per annum during the above period, while that for CDs with one year maturity declined from 15.5 per cent per annum to 12.5 per cent per annum.

DRI scheme

The DRI scheme introduced in June 1972 by the Government of India is meant to cater to the credit requirements of the weakest among the weak by assisting them in their efforts to improve their economic conditions through small productive endeavours. Banks have to lend 1% of their aggregate advances as at the end of the previous year under the scheme and 40% of which should go to SC/ST Under the scheme, credit upto Rs.6,500/- is to be made available to eligible borrowers at an interest rate of 4%. In addition, eligible borrowers belonging to SC/ST can get housing loan to the extent of Rs.5,000/- in each individual case under the scheme. Further, under DRI Scheme, physically handicapped persons are eligible to avail of loan for acquiring aids, appliances and equipments to the extent of their actual cost but not exceeding Rs.5,000/-. This assistance is independent of production loan of Rs.6,500/- available under DRI Scheme.

Data on implementation of DRI Scheme by public sector banks for the last two years is as under :

(Accounts in lakhs and amount Rs. in crores)

Year ended March	*Total DRI advances*		*Of which to SC/ST*		*% of adv. to SC/ST to total DRI adv.*	*% of total DRI adv. to total adv. of previous year*
	No. of A/cs.	*Amount O/s.*	*No. of A/cs.*	*Amount O/s.*		
	1	2	3	4	5	6
1997	15.81	648.95	7.52	413.08	63.65	0.35
1998	14.07	575.79	6.47	384.47	66.77	0.30

Commercial paper (CP)

Commercial Paper (CP) market recorded a strong growth during the financial year 1998-99 (upto November 1998). The outstanding amount of CPs increased from Rs.1500 crores as on March 31, 1998 to Rs.5534 crores as on

November 30, 1998. The typical effective discount rates on CP declined from the range of 13.60-15.75 per cent per annum as on March 31, 1998 to 9.35 -13.00 per cent per annum as on November 30, 1998.

Swarna jayanti shahari rozgar yojana (SJSRY)

The SJSRY Scheme is in operation from 1.12.1997 in all Urban and semi-urban town of India. Among other components, the scheme has two sub-schemes where bank credit is involved namely Urban Self Employment programme (USEP) and Development of women & Children in Urban Areas (DWCUA).

The beneficiaries are identified by the Urban local bodies on the basis of house to house survey. Under the scheme, women are to be assisted to the extent of not less than 30%, disabled at 3% and SC/STs at least to the extent of the proportion of their strength in the local population. The scheme is funded on a 75:25 basis between central and the state. Under USEP underemployed and unemployed urban youth whose annual family income is below the poverty line and who are educated upto ninth standard and who have been included in ULB list are to be assisted with bank loans. Projects costing upto Rs.50,000/- are to be' financed by banks. Subsidy would be provided by government at 15% of the project cost subject to a maximum of Rs.75,000/-. The borrower has to bring in 5% of the project cost as margin money. Partnership are also permitted. Under DWCUA, women beneficiaries may take up self employment ventures in group. DWCUA group should consist of at least 10 urban poor women. The group is entitled to a subsidy of Rs.1,25,000 or 50% of the project cost whichever is less. In addition the group may set itself up as a thrift and credit society.

The performance of banks during 1997-98 and 19918-99 upto June 1998 are given below:

(Rs.Lakhs)

	Sanction		Disbursement	
	No.	Amount	No.	Amount
1997-98 (March 98)	2086	440.90	1177	251.67
1998-99 (June 98) (Prov)	1042	278.93	606	151.29

Prime minister's rozgar yojana- performance during 1996-97 and plan for 1997-98

The scheme was launched on 2.10.93 and will be in operation during the IX Five Year Plan. The scheme is implemented throughout the country with effect from 1.4.94 consequent on merger of SEEUY Scheme with PMRY. The objective of the scheme is to provide sustained employment to about 10 lakh educated unemployed youths in Micro Enterprises. All viable and bankable schemes including partnership ventures can be financed under the scheme. The project cost is limited to Rs.1 lac per borrower of which 5% will be brought in by borrower. Subsidy at 15% subject to a maximum of Rs.7500/- is provided. Government allocates the statewise targets annually which are divided among the banks at the state level. So far target allocated stands at 1616128 including the target of 361350 under programme year 1998-99. Banks were permitted to exceed their target by 20% during 1998-99. The performance of banks during the past 2 years is as under:

Year	Target	Sanction		% of Sanction to target	Average size of loan
		No.	Amount (Rs. lakhs)		
1997-98	345000	266275	159072.57	77.18	59740
1998-99	*361350	57075	32005.08	15.79	56075

The scheme is monitored at District, State and National Level through various committees set up under the scheme. At the instance of Government of India, a Cell to monitor the progress of PMRY and IRDP has been set up in RBI under the chairmanship of Deputy Governor. The Cell has been constituted to monitor the progress of the scheme on a continuing basis.

Flow of credit to minority communities

At present, the following five communities have been categorised as minority communities by the Government of India:

i) Sikhs

ii) Muslims

iii) Christians

iv) Zoroastrians

v) Buddhists

Under the present arrangements, banks have to ensure that credit is made available to the members of minority communities in an adequate measure not only in the 41 districts identified by the Government of India as having concentration of minority communities, but also in the country as a whole. However, no sub-target has been earmarked in the priority sector credit for the minority communities. Although there is no special earmarking of targets for minority communities, available data indicates (as shown below) that the flow of credit to these, communities is steadily increasing.

Priority sector credit to minorities in all the districts in the country

Period year ended March	*No. of A/cs (in lakhs)*	*Balance outstanding (in Rs. crores)*
1996	64.44	7916.24
1997	62.28	8670.85

Priority sector credit to minorities in 41 identified districts

Period year ended March	*No. of A/cs (in lakhs)*	*Balance outstanding (in Rs. crores)*
1996	12.71	1313.31
1997	13.23	1558.19

Financial assistance to the persons affected by natural calamities, riots & disturbances

Reserve Bank of India has issued standing guidelines to banks vide circular RPCD.No.PS.BC.6/PS.126-84 dated 2 August 1984 to be followed by them for providing relief in areas affected by natural calamities/riots etc. without waiting for instructions from RBI on occurrence of such incidents. The above guidelines have been issued to enable banks to take uniform and concerted action expeditiously, particularly to provide the financial assistance to agriculturists, small scale industrial unit, artisans, small business and trading establishments affected by natural calamities. These guidelines envisage, inter alia, conversion of short-term production loans into medium term loans; rescheduling/postponement of existing term loan instalments, provision of additional need-based crop loans/working capital and relaxation in security and margin norms.

Reserve Bank of India has issued modified guidelines to banks vide circular RPCD.No.PLFS.BC.128/05.04.02/97-98 dated 20 June 1998 for relief measures to persons affected by natural calamities giving discretion to the banks to decide the quantum of fresh loans to be granted to the affected borrowers, taking into account among other, the extent of crop loss/scale of finance and their repaying capacity. As per the revised guidelines, in extreme cases i.e. three successive crop failures and debt burden being found beyond repaying capacity of the borrowers, conversion for longer period upto a maximum period of 9 years can be considered by banks in consultation with Task Force/State Level Bankers Committee.

Central interest subsidy scheme for november 1984 riot affected borrowers

Government of India decided to extend relief in deserving cases by way of reduction of interest on bank loans to 6% p.a. in the case of borrowers affected by November 1984 riots. Accordingly, a "Central Interest Subsidy Scheme" for November 1984 riot affected borrowers, was prepared and circulated to banks on 17 September 1990. Under this scheme claims for Rs.22.68 crores were received upto 31.3.1992 from the banks and an amount of Rs.21.50 crores was released to the banks.

To give them further relief a "Revised Central Interest Subsidy Scheme" for November 1984 riot affected borrowers was formulated. This Scheme is meant for borrowers who are not covered by the Debt Relief Scheme of Government of India i.e. where total loans by way of principal from all the banks exceed Rs.25,000/-. Under this Scheme banks have been advised to charge interest at one per cent (simple) per annum on all eligible bank loans outstanding on the effective date for the period from 1 November 1984 to 31 March 1992. The above scheme was circulated to banks for implementation on 1 September 1993.

Debt relief scheme (revised) for november 1984 riot affected borrowers

Government of India formulated "Debt Relief Scheme (revised) for November 1984 riot affected borrowers" which was circulated to banks by the Government on 29th December, 1997. Under the scheme riot victims whose aggregate of eligible loans from all banks upto and inclusive of Rs.50,000/- as principal, granted on 1

November 1984 or afterwards together with outstanding interest, has to be written off by the banks.

Housing finance under priority sector

Housing finance by commercial banks as under is treated as priority sector lending.

(i) Direct finance

(a) Loans upto Rs.5 lakhs for construction of houses granted to all categories of borrowers except to own employees of the bank.

(b) Loans upto Rs.50,000/- for repairs to damaged houses granted to all categories of borrowers except to own employees of the banks.

(ii) Indirect finance

(a) Assistance given to any government agency for the purpose of construction of houses where the loan component does not exceed Rs.5 lakhs per housing unit.

(b) Assistance given to any government agency for slum clearance and rehabilitation of slum dwellers where loan component does not exceed Rs. 5 lakhs per housing unit.

(c) Assistance given to a non-governmental agency, approved by the National Housing Bank (NHB) for the purpose of refinance, for construction of houses for slum clearance and rehabilitation of slum dwellers where loan component does not exceed Rs.5 lakh per housing unit.

Rate of interest

As per existing RBI Directives on interest rates, the interest on loans upto Rs.2 lakhs should not exceed the Prime Lending Rate which is available to the best borrower of the concerned bank.

As regards loans over Rs.2 lakhs, banks are free determine the rate of interest.

For loan upto Rs.5,000/- to SC/ST borrowers satisfying the DRI criteria, rate of interest would be 4% per annum.

As per the latest data available financing for housing under priority sector is as under:

As on last Friday of March 1997

(Amount Rs. in Lakhs)

	Direct Finance		*Indirect Finance*		*Total*	
	No. of a/cs	*Amount (Rs. in lakh)*	*No. of a/cs*	*Amount (Rs. in lakhs)*	*No. of a/cs*	*Amount (Rs. in lakhs)*
i) All public sector banks	136402	109639.52	60636	136684.71	197038	246324.23
ii) All scheduled Commercial Banks	158116	133483.99	128144	182558.74	286260	316042.73

In F.M.'s budget speech on March 15,1995, a Scheme under which the banking system would provide Rs.1000 crore on a consortium basis to the Khadi and Village Industries Commission (KVIC) which would on lend to viable khadi and village industrial units either directly or through State Level Khadi and Village Industries Board (KVIBs) had been announced. Accordingly, a consortium of select public sector banks was formed (in June 95) to provide credit to KVIC. The credit provided by the banks to KVIC under this scheme is reckoned as their indirect lending to SSI under the priority sector. These loans are being provided at below the average prime lending rates of 5 major banks in the consortium. So far, Rs.601 crores has been disbursed (as at the end of November 1998) by the consortium to KVIC and an amount of Rs.539 crore is outstanding there against.

National Housing Bank's (NHB's) activities and operations

Resources

(i) The share Capital of NHB which is fully subscribed by the Reserve Bank of India (RBI) stood at Rs.350 crore as on June 30, 1998. A sum of Rs.25 crore was raised through issue of Government Guaranteed (SLR) Bonds during March 1998 and the cumulative amount raised by NHB was Rs.450.50 crore as on June 30, 1998. An amount of Rs.300 crore was mobilised by issue of Priority Sector Bonds (both tax-free as well as taxable) on private placement basis. The cumulative amount raised by the Bank under Priority Sector Bonds stood at Rs.800.00 crore, as on June 30, 1998. The total borrowing from LIC stood at Rs.1167 crores as on June 30, 1998 including an amount of Rs. 100 crore borrowed during the year.

(ii) The Asian Development Bank (ADB) had sanctioned a loan of US $ 100 million during the year, out of which the Bank drew the first instalment of US $ 20 million. Under a structured arrangement the Bank availed counter part rupee funds of Rs.100 crore through issue of special series priority sector bonds to Bank of India, on private placement basis.

Disbursements

(i) During the year 1997-98 (July-June) refinance assistance extended by NHB to all eligible primary lending institutions stood at Rs.524.15 crore as against Rs.445.35 crore last year.

(ii) The cumulative financial assistance provided by NHB as on 30th November 1998 stood at Rs.3878.27 crores enabling construction of 671486 dwelling units (excluding the number of units constructed under the line of credit to HUDCO and under Land Development and Shelter Project (LID & SP)/Rental

Housing Projects). Agency-wise the break-up of financial assistance provided by NHB indicates share of HFCs as Rs.3007.48 crore (77.55%), Cooperative sector institutions Rs.671.72 crore (17.32%) and scheduled banks Rs.199.08 crore (5.13%).

Agency-wise Refinance Disbursements by NHB during 1997-98 and 1998-99 (upto 30 November 1998)

(Amount in Rs. crore)

Agencies	*1997-98*	*1998-99*
Banks	8.45	0.25
Co-op. Sector	138.08	96.45
HFCS	377.62	154.58
Total	524.15	251.28

Project finance

NHB has upto 31 st December 1998 sanctioned 253 projects with a total project cost of Rs.782.84 crores and loan component of Rs.611.41 crores. A cumulative amount of Rs.248.41 crores had been disbursed till 31 st December, 1998.

Direct Lending

(i) During the year 1997-98, NHB has sanctioned 4 land Development and Shelter Projects of Madhya Predesh Housing Board, Goa Housing Board, Rajasthan Housing Board and Tamil Nadu Housing Board with a project cost of Rs.33.55 crores and loan component of Rs.29.47 crores. NHB so far has sanctioned 7 projects with a total project cost of Rs.65.55 crores and loan component of Rs.52.91 crores upto 31st December, 1998

(ii) During the year 1997-98, NHB has disbursed a sum of Rs.2.35 crores to Tamil Nadu Housing Board for its LDSP located at Chennai. During the year 1998-99, as on 31 st December, 1998, NHB has disbursed a sum of Rs.7.03 crores to Tamil Nadu Housing Board, Rajasthan Housing Board and Madhya Pradesh Housing Board for its various projects.

Slum redevelopment scheme

Under this Scheme, Rs.14.74 crores has been released till 31st December 1998, NHB, till 31st December, 1998 had sanctioned 28 projects for Slum Redevelopment and Low Cost Housing, with a total project cost of Rs.58.15 crores and loan component of Rs.39.28 crores. Out of this 28 projects 18 projects have been sanctioned to APUDHC under the direct lending window with a project cost of Rs.21.40 crores and loan component of Rs.1 5.97 crores. The remaining 10 projects have been sanctioned to HUDCO under refinance scheme to finance Karnataka Slum Clearance Board for its projects. These projects have a total cost of Rs.36.75 crores and loan component of Rs.23.30 crores.

Home loan account scheme (HLAS)

Under the Scheme, the designated banks and the recognised HFCs are reported to have collected an estimated amount of Rs.209.60 crores as on 31st March, 1998. A sum of Rs.13.63 crores has been utilised by the implementing agencies so far.

Interest rates on bank's refinance scheme

NHB , during the year, revised the interest rates on its refinance schemes,. There were no major changes in the existing loan slabs, apart from minor reschedulment in the loan slabs.

Housing Finance Companies (NHB) directions:

During the year, amendments were made in the I Housing Finance Companies (NHB) Directions. :On and from September 17, 1997, Registration with NHB has been made compulsory for every HFC accepting deposits :and having a minimum net owned fund of twenty five lakhs rupees. The definition for net owned fund has also been modified to make it in line with the definition provided in guidelines for prudential norms. The requirement for maintenance of liquid assets also got modified through this amendment. According to the amendment, every HFC accepting deposit is required to keep 5% of deposits as liquid assets in an account with a scheduled bank or in deposits with NHB or by way of subscription to NHB bonds. In addition, the HFC is required to invest a minimum of 5% of deposits in unencumbered approved securities. For ensuring compliance with the above provision, HFC are required to furnish a quarterly return on liquid assets. HFCS are also liable to pay to the NHB, penal interest in case of shortfall in the maintenance of liquid assets. The amendment also stipulates creation of a reserve fund by HFCs and transfer therein a sum not less than 20% of its net profit every year.

With effect from January 1, 1999, housing finance companies (HFCs) having net owned fund (NOF) of Rs.25 lakhs and below or housing finance companies having NOF of Rs.25 lakhs and above but credit rating below 'A' are prohibited from accepting fresh deposit or opening new deposit account.

Further, the ceiling limit on the overall borrowings of housing finance companies have been reduced. The revised ceiling will also include loans or other assistance received from NHB. While the ceiling limit in respect of borrowings in respect of HFCs having NOF upto Rs. 10 crores has been retained at 10 times of the NOF of the company, in respect of HFCs having NOF above Rs. 10 crores but below Rs.20 crores and Rs.20 crores and above the ceiling limits have been reduced to 11 and 12 times of their NOF from the earlier levels of 12.5 and 15 times, respectively In addition, within the overall borrowing limit, a sub limit of upto 5 times the NOF has been prescribed for public deposits.

In respect of HFCs holding a~ at the commencement of business on January 1, 1999 deposits in excess of the revised ceiling as mentioned above, they have been advised to accepting fresh deposits and not to open any new deposit account. Further, they are advised not to renew the existing deposit after September 30,2000 or where the deposits are received under any recurring scheme, receive instalments under any such scheme after the expiry of the scheme period. Similarly, in case of a down gradation of credit rating to any level below 'A', the HFCs should stop with immediate effect accepting any fresh deposit and repay the amount of excess deposit within a period of one year or such further period as may be prescribed By NHB.

The HFCs have been allowed to reimburse expenses to any broker in respect of public deposits collected by or through him on the basis of relative vouchers/bill produced upto 0.5 per cent of the deposits so collected.

It has also been decided to increase the minimum percentage of liquid assets to be maintained by HFCs from 10 per cent to 12.5 per cent with effect from April 1, 1999. Consequently, the percentage of liquid assets to be maintained in unencumbered approved securities is also being increased from 5 per cent to 6 per cent with effect from April 1, 1999.

Prudential norms for HFCs

NHB during the year, issued a clarification in Guidelines on Prudential Norms with respect to interest income recognition in response to the requests received from various HFCs. It has been clarified that income recognition norms on Government Guaranteed loans will be the same as applicable to any other loan assets. The income in respect of such assets even though backed by Government Guarantees shall be recognised only when the same is actually realised and not on accrual basis. Consequent on the amendment of Housing Finance Companies (NHB) Directions with effect from January 1, 1999, the paragraph relating to credit rating has been deleted from these guidelines. Further, these guidelines have been made applicable to HFCs having net owned funds between Rs.25.00 and 50.00 lakhs with effect from January 1, 1999.

Regulation and supervision

The total number of HFCs under the regulatory ambit of NHB stood at 377 as on 30th June, 1998. Of these, 102 HFCs including 26 NHB approved HFCs, have submitted Statutory Return showing their financial position as on 31 st March, 1998. During the year, 14 HFCs including 11 HFCs with NOF of Rs.20 lakhs and above were inspected by NHB.

Golden jubilee rural housing finance scheme

The Golden Jubilee Rural Housing Finance Scheme was launched during the year 1997-98 with a target of financing 50,000 houses by various primary lending institutions viz., the Scheduled Commercial Banks, the State Coperative Banks, the Apex Cooperative housing Federations (ACHFS), the Agriculture and rural Development Banks (ARDBs), the Regional Rural Banks (RRBs) and the Housing Finance Companies (HFCs). The target was successfully achieved. Further, the Hon'ble Finance Minister in the budget announcement for the year 1998-99 has enhanced the target under the captioned scheme to 1,00,000 loans from the previous year's target of 50,000 housing loans in rural areas. Till 30th September 1998, 29,118 loans have been disbursed under the scheme.

National bank for agriculture and rural development (NABARD)

As an apex development Bank in the country, the National Bank for Agriculture and Rural Development (NABARD) has been given the responsibility of providing credit for the promotion of agriculture, Small Scale Industries, Cottage and Village Industries, handicrafts and other rural crafts land other allied economic areas with a view to promoting integrated rural development and securing prosperity of rural areas and for matters connected therewith or incidental thereto. In order to achieve the objective NABARD provides short term and medium term credit for agricultural production to State Cooperative Banks (SCBs) and Regional Rural Banks (RRBs). It also provides investment credit under refinance for agriculture and allied activities to all types of banks. Further, under Rural Infrastructure Development Fund (RIDF), NABARD provides loans to State Govt. and State owned corporations to complete on-going projects relating to major, medium and minor irrigation, soil conservation and other projects of rural infrastructure like rural roads and bridges.

During 1997-98 (July - March), NABARD has provided aggregate credit limits of Rs.5169 crores to SCBs for short term agricultural operations as compared to Rs.5185 crores in 199697. This credit limit is inclusive of Rs.673 crore, Rs.34 crore and Rs.213 crore sanctioned to SCBs for implementing Oilseeds Production Programme (OPP), National Pulses Development Programme (NPDP) And Development of Tribal Population (DTP) respectively. Further, State Cooperative Banks were sanctioned Rs.743 crore and Rs.29 crore for financing production/ procurement and Marketing activities and trading in yarn of weavers' cooperative societies as against Rs.759 crores and Rs.29 crores respectively sanctioned during 1996-97. In addition, SCBs were sanctioned Rs.17 crores for financing industrial Cooperative societies in their areas.

The RRBs were sanctioned Rs.872 crores during 1997-98 as compared to Rs.794 crores during 1996-97 for the purpose of financing short term agriculture operations. These limits included Rs. 188 crores for OPP.

Under Credit Authorisation Scheme, NABARD had granted authorisation for an amount of Rs.351 crores covering 42 proposals of 8 SCBs & 6 DCCBs for providing block capital finance and Rs.3926 crores covering 247 proposals of 15 SCBs and 52 DCCBs for providing working capital in 1997-98 as against Rs.553 crores and Rs.2653 crores respectively during 1996-97.

NABARD had also provided Medium Term limits of Rs. 0.51 crores to SCBs and Rs. 0.10 crores to RRBs during the year 1997-98.

For the purpose of strengthening the share capital base of cooperative credit institutions, NABARD had sanctioned Rs. 150 crores to 16 State Governments covering 8 State Cooperative Agriculture and Rural Development Banks, 198 Primary Co-operative Agriculture and Rural Development Banks, 5 SCBs, 201 DCCBs and 8256 Primary Agriculture Co-operative Societies.

As far as commercial banks are concerned, NABARD provided them refinance facility under schematic lending. NABARD had provided Rs. 725 crore during 1997-98 as against Rs. 601 crores during 1996-97 for schematic lending to commercial banks. The total disbursement to all banks during 1996-97 and 1997-98, purpose-wise, is given below:

(Rs. crores)

Purpose	1996-97	1997-98
Minor Irrigation	592	524
Land Development	44	59
Farm Mechanisation	871	1099
Plantation & Horticulture	149	186
Poultry	119	105
Sheep/Goat/Piggery	85	94
Fisheries	41	33
Dairy Development	241	353
Bio Gas	1	1
Forestry	9	11
Storage/Market Yards	14	14
IRDP	513	611
NFS	645	616
SC/ST Action Plan	96	112
Others	123	104
Total	3523	3922

The agency-wise details of refinance disbursed during 1996-97 and 1997-98 are given below:

(Rs. crores)

Agency	Disbursements	
	1996-97	1997-98
SCARDBs	1895	2100
RRBs	654	668
SCBs	373	429
CBs	601	725
Total	3523	3922

Rural infrastructure development fund

A fund with initial corpus of Rs.2000 crores (RIDF-I) was

made available to NABARD during 1995-96 from the contribution from scheduled commercial banks excluding foreign banks operating in India to the extent of shortfall in Agricultural lending [in the priorities sector target subject to maximum of 1.5% of net bank credit. Subsequently, RIDF-II with corpus of Rs. 2500 crore was given to NABARD during 1996-97. The cumulative disbursements aggregated Rs. 1501.39 crore covering 20 States against the sanction of Rs. 1794.86 crores. This covers Minor and Major Irrigation projects, rural bridges, rural roads and watershed management schemes. Under RIDF-II, the cumulative disbursement to 16 states aggregated Rs. 1139.75 crore against the total sanction of Rs. 2616.89 crores, as on 30 November, 1998. The operative period of RIDF-II is for three years from 1996-97. Considering the need of state governments for these purposes, the Union Budget for 1997-98 further allocated a corpus of Rs. 2500 crore to the RIDF-III. The further pronouncements made in the Union Budget for 1998-99 has given a further fillip to the efforts in creating sustainable rural infrastructure by adding a fourth tranche of Rs. 3000 crore for the year 1998-99 as RIDF-IV. NABARD has sanctioned 14,454 projects under RIDF-III totalling in amount of Rs. 2668.31 crores. As on March. 1998, the cumulative total amount sanctioned under RIDF scheme was Rs. 7034.63 crores.

Integrated rural development programme (IRDP)

Integrated Rural Development Programme (IRDP), which is recognised as a major Poverty Alleviation Programme for the upliftment of weaker sections of the society was introduced in selected areas of the country in 1978 and was subsequently extended to the whole of the rural India with effect from 2.10.1980. During 1997-98, 16.97 lakh borrowers with total credit of Rs. 1990.67 crore were financed as against 18.87 lakh borrowers with total credit of Rs. 1953 crore during 1996-97.

R.V. Gupta committee

The One Man High Level Committee of Shri R.V. Gupta, former Deputy Governor, Reserve Bank of India had suggested in its Report several procedural modifications in regard to agricultural advances which include simplification of procedures regarding application agreements, etc., rationalisation of internal returns of banks, delegation of more powers to branch managers, introduction composite cash credit limit to agricultural farmers, introduction of new loan products with savings components, cash disbursement of loans, dispensation of No Due Certificate, discretion to banks on matters relating to margin/security requirements for agricultural loans above Rs. 10,000/- etc. RBI has issued necessary instructions to banks advising them to implement these recommendations.

Kisan credit cards

In pursuance of the Budget Speech for the year 1998-99, National Bank for Agriculture and Rural Development (NABARD) had formulated a model scheme for issue of Kisan Credit Card (KCC) by all public sector and co-operative banks to farmers on the basis of their holdings. The scheme aims at adequate and timely support from the banking system to the farmers for their cultivation needs including purchase of inputs such as seeds, fertilisers, pesticides, etc. and draw cash for their production needs in a flexible and cost effective manner. All public sector banks have launched the scheme of Kisan Credit Card and over 6 lakh cards have been issued so far.

One time settlement of chronic dues

In pursuance of last year's budget speech where it was indicated that farmers should not be forced to go to jail or commit suicide for default in repayment of loans, Reserve Bank of India had issued instructions to all scheduled commercial banks to provide appropriate relief to chronic defaulting farmers who are unable to repay the principal amount together with accumulated interest due to circumstances beyond their control, banks may consider the possibility of settlement of overdues in respect of such farmers on merit of each case, as a measure of relief. The banks were also asked to consider providing appropriate relief on accumulated interest in deserving cases. 9 Public sector banks have already formulated schemes on the above lines and have since started settling cases. Remaining banks are also likely to formulate similar schemes.

Appointment of non-workman directors

During the year 1998-99 fresh appointments of Officer Employee Directors were made in 15 public sector banks. Action has been initiated to appoint fresh Officer-Employee Directors on the Boards of the remaining public sector banks, where the position of Officer-Employee Director is presently lying vacant or the tenure of the present incumbent has already expired but he is continuing as a Director Pending the appointment of his successor.

Committee on banking sector reforms

The Committee on Banking Sector Reforms, headed by Shri M. Narasimham to suggest measures to strengthen the banking system, submitted its Report in April, 1998. It contains recommendations on several issues like capital adequacy, prudential norms and disclosure requirements, asset quality, up-gradation and human resource development, structural issues and regulation and supervision of banks. The recommendations contained therein form a valuable input in the on-going efforts of Government and the Reserve Bank of India to make the banking system more efficient and competitive.

Task force on non-banking finance companies

The Task Force on Non-Banking Finance Companies, headed by Special Secretary (Banking), submitted its Report in October 1998. The recommendations made by the Committee include, inter-alia, minimum capital requirement for NBFCs, stipulation of CRAR, stipulation regarding investment of a portion of their reserves in marketable securities, limit of public deposits, increase in the liquid asset ratio, appointment of depositors grievance redressal authorities, setting up of Cells at State and District level for redressal of depositors's grievances, nature of advertisements, setting up of a separate regulatory and supervisory body for NBFCs under the aegis of RBI, enabling the NBFCs' access to loans other than public deposits etc.

Expert committee on legislative proposals

The Committee on Banking Sector Reforms in its Report submitted in April, 1998 has, inter-alia, recommended the setting up of an Expert Committee, comprising amongst others, representatives from the Ministry of Law, Banking Division, Ministry of Finance, RBI and some outside experts to formulate specific legislative proposals to give effect to the suggestions made by the Committee, which need making wide ranging changes in the legal framework affecting the work of the financial sector. The Expert Committee has been set up. Further action in the matter shall be taken after the Committee submits its report.

Panner selvam committee

The Government had appointed a Committee headed by Sh. Panner Selvam, Chairman IBA and Chairman & Managing Director, Union Bank of India to look into the problems of NPAs of the Public sector banks and to suggest measures to bring down the NPAs in the banks to acceptable levels. The major recommendations of the committee are as under:

- Changes in legislation for facilitating smooth mergers/ acquisition and appropriate legislation for recovery of banks' dues.
- Revival of capital markets.
- Setting up of Asset Reconstruction Fund (ARF).
- Ensuring that governments honour guarantees when invoked by banks.
- Strengthening of credit appraisal, credit monitoring credit risk rating, and monitoring of standard assets to arrest fresh NPAs.
- Review of doubtful and loss assets.
- Improvement in functioning of BIFR by constituting more Benches and adequate infrastructure.
- Statutory powers under Section 29 of SFCs Act to be extended to the banks empowering banks to seize assets both movable and immovable and sell the same by incorporating a suitable provision in the BR Act.
- Separate Bench of civil Courts for dealing with recovery/ cases of banks/Financial Institutions at all levels, for expeditious recoveries of dues.
- Compulsory arbitration through former Senior Supreme Court/High Court Judge, ex-ED/Chairman & Managing Director of banks/FIs, in disputes between banks or banks and FIs.

The above recommendations are under examination of the Government.

Insurance division

Organisation & role: Insurance Division is administratively concerned with the activities of both life and non-life segments of the Insurance industry, which is wholly nationalised. The functions of the Division include policy formulation and administration of the Insurance Act,

1938, the Life Insurance Corporation Act, 1956 and General Insurance Business (Nationalisation) Act, 1972 and other related Acts; constant review and monitoring of the performance of the Insurance companies, framing of rules and regulations in respect of service conditions of employees of insurance companies; coordination of vigilance activities in the insurance industry; and appointment of Chief Executives and Directors on the Boards of Insurance Companies. The Division has a Special Secretary, Joint Secretary, two Directors and three Under Secretaries.

Life Insurance Corporation of India, General Corporation of India and its four subsidiaries are wholly Government owned financial institutions. They are subject to the provisions of the Insurance Act, to the extent applicable. In addition, the Life Insurance Corporation of India is subject to the provisions of the Life Insurance Act, 1956. The General Insurance Corporation of India and its for subsidiaries are subject to the provisions of the General Insurance Business (Nationalisation) Act, 1972.

Human resource development Director (I) attended a training programme on various aspects of general insurance industry at Munich, Germany between ...1998. Director (II) attended seminar on Insurance Regulators organised by College of Insurance, NewYork between... Under Secretary (II) attended three months course on Human Resource Development organised by Australian Government at Sydney, Australia between April-June, 1998. The above course was also attended by PPS to SS(I).

Progressive use of official language The LIC, GIC and subsidiary companies have continued to progress in the implementation of the Official Language Policy of the Government.

To accelerate the use of Official Language in the Offices of Corporation, LIC organised a conference of Official Language Implementation Officers and Language Assistants of all the Zonal Offices. The percentage of correspondence originating in Hindi in the offices of Corporation located in 'A', 'B' and 'C' regions was 93,76.9 and 19.29 respectively during the year. All the 3 Zonal Offices, 33 Divisional Offices and 706 Branch Offices in 'A' region, Central Office, one Zonal Office, 24 Divisional Offices and 461 Branch Offices, in 'B' Region and 3 Divisional Offices alongwith 46 Branch Offices in 'C' Region have been notified under Rule 10 (4) of the Official Language Rules, 1976. During the year training in Hindi was imparted to 695 employees, 41 typists and 33 stenographers in Hindi typing and Hindi stenography. All the 28694 employees/ officers working in the off ices in 'A' Region and 22355 employees/ officers working in 'B' Region and 19780 employees/ officers out of 42163 working in the offices in 'C' Region have acquired training in Hindi. Bilingual word processors have been provided at 86 places. Besides, the management development Centre at Gurgaon, Zonal Training Centres at Mumbai and Bhopal and Branch Office at London have been provided with bilingual processors.

In GIC and its four subsidiaries 2862 Offices have been notified under Rule 10(4) of Official Language Rule, 1976. In these Offices more than 80% employees have working knowledge of Hindi. Official Language implementation committees have been set up in 2730 Offices. It conducted 300 workshops in which about 6000 employees obtained training for conducting day to day work in Official Language. Hindi Day and Hindi Week celebrations were organised by all the Offices of the industry. For encouraging the employees to do more work in Hindi, cash incentive schemes has been introduced. Further Chairmen and Managing Directors

Raj Bhasha Shields are awarded to companies/ departments with best performance in Hindi implementation. An All India Bima Raj Bhasha Sammelan covering all insurance companies was held at Bangalore.

Lic

Category class of employee	*Total No. of employee*	*Total No. of Sc*	*ST*
A(CLASS-I)	14520	2169	673
B(CLASS-II)	18832	2564	888
C(CLASS-III)	80061	12496	5637
D(CLASS-IV)	12206	3403	970
TOTAL	125619	20632	8168

Company	*General*	*SC*	*ST*	*OBC*	*Total*
GIC	538	124	38	6	706
NATIONAL	14357	3936	849	935	20077
NEW INDIA	18337	4589	1049	1092	25067
ORIENTAL	14088	4108	1055	1477	20728
UNITED	17203	4053	1239	149	22644
TOTAL	64523	16810	4230	3659	89222

Welfare of scheduled castes& scheduled tribes: GIC/ LIC and its four subsidiaries have appointed separate Liaison Officers for the Welfare of SC/STs and Backward Class employees. Vacancies have been reserved and filled up for SC/ST and Backward Class candidates in the recruitment as per the brochure provision and they have also been offered concessions/ relaxations in age, educational qualifications, payment of application fees etc. Reservation for SC/STs is also provided in the promotions within the clerical and subordinate cadre and for promotions to the lowest rung of the Officers cadre as per guidelines. Pre-promotion training is provided for SC/ST candidates for promotion to the cadre of Record

Clerk, Stenographers and Officers (AAO). SC/ST candidates are also provided reservation in allotment of residential accommodation. The Liaison Officers of GIC conducted inspections of rosters regularly.

Representation of scheduled castes/scheduled tribes in LIC/GIC and its Subsidiaries. The Table indicates representation of Scheduled Castes/Scheduled Tribes in LIC, GIC and its four subsidiaries viz., National Insurance Co. Ltd.; New India Assurance Co. Ltd.; Oriental Insurance Co. Ltd.; and United India Insurance Co. Ltd. as on 31.3.1998.

Vigilance in Insurance Industry: Insurance Division keeps a close watch on The working of LIC, GIC and its subsidiaries. Each of the Insurance Corporation and company has its own Vigilance Machinery headed by the Chief Vigilance Officer. Director in the Insurance Division, who is also working as Chief Vigilance Officer of the Insurance Industry, undertakes reviews in the Insurance Corporations and Companies. During the year Board level reviews were also conducted in LIC, GIC and its subsidiaries. Cases of corruption and irregularities reported to Insurance Division were forwarded to the competent authority for further investigation. Complaints received from Anti Corruption Cell formed in the Prime Minister's Office were also sent for thorough investigation and prompt disposal. Monitoring of such cases are done periodically and reports there on are sent to the Prime Minister's Office as well as to DOPT every fortnight. In addition, enquiry reports of vigilance cases referred to these companies earlier were received by the Division and after examination, appropriate action was initiated wherever necessary. During the year special focus was given to reducing tendency in vigilance cases and on preventive aspect of the vigilance. Efforts were also made to have better integration in between the management on the one hand and vigilance cell on the other in the insurance industry. During the year a number of review meetings to clear pending vigilance cases were convened in which senior officers of the insurance industry alongwith vigilance/ enquiry/ presenting officers and officers from Central Vigilance Commission were present.

Redressal of public grievances: Insurance Division receives grievances of policy holders, from the public, VIPs and Directorate of Public Grievances in the Cabinet Secretariat. The division co-ordinates with LIC, GIC and its subsidiaries in all the matters relating to public grievances and monitors the grievance disposal system. Individual grievances received by the division are taken up with insurance companies for speedy redressal. Directorate of Public Grievances also takes periodic meetings of insurance companies for redressing the public grievance cases, in which the insurance division also participates and monitors the progress of these cases. The division also participates in the region wise meetings undertaken by Directorate of Public Grievances. LIC, GIC and its subsidiaries have been holding regular workshops on public grievance so as to examine the procedure of settlement of claims and simplify the complicated procedure wherever necessary. The continuous emphasis has been to dispose of grievances expeditiously. During the year under review, a total of 247 public grievance cases were received from DPG and out of these 231 cases were disposed of. Further, during the year 1997 98, out of a total of about 21.67 lakh claims received by the subsidiaries of GIC, 21.63 lakh claims were settled. Joint Secretary (Ins) is taking weekly meeting with aggrieved parties for redressal of public grievances.

Reforms in insurance sector: In pursuance of announcement of the Finance Minister made in his

Budget Speech 1998-99, the Insurance Regulatory Authority Bill, 1998 was introduced in the Lok Sabha on 15th December, 1998. The Bill seeks to establishing a statutory Insurance Regulatory Authority to protect the interest of holders of insurance policies and to regulate, promote and ensure orderly growth of the insurance industry. It also seeks to amend Life Insurance Act, 1956, General Insurance Business (Nationalisation) Act, 1972 and consequential provisions in Insurance Act, 1938 with a view to cease the exclusive privilege of LIC and GIC in life and non-life business respectively. The Bill has since been referred to Standing Committee on Finance.

Steps have also been taken to strengthen and improve the competitiveness of the nationalised insurance companies. These companies are being given full autonomy to meet the competition. The management of these companies have been given adequate powers of investment and now they are much more Board run companies, autonomous and will be able to meet competition effectively and improve their quality of services.

Reinsurance programme of the general insurance industry: The Insurance Division was also approving reinsurance programme of the General Insurance Industry upto the year 1996 97. Afterwards the powers have been delegated to the management of Insurance Companies to get reinsurance programme approved by their respective Boards and correspond directly with RBI for the release of foreign exchange.

Crop insurance: The total number of farmers covered under the scheme during Kharif 1997 and Rabi 1997-98 was 60.01 Lakhs and the total area covered was 97.40 Lakhs hectares. The sum insured under coverage during the above period was Rs. 2630.50 Crores and the premium income was Rs. 41.49 Crores. Total claims amounting to Rs. 192.24 Crores were paid/payable under the Scheme for the above two seasons. Ministry of Agriculture in coordination with GIC is formulating Modified Crop Insurance Scheme (MCIS) which is expected to be in force from Kharif 1999.

Laying of annual reports of GIC & subsidiaries in parliament: In pursuance of Section 619-A of the Companies Act, 1956 the Annual Report of LIC/IC and its subsidiaries for the year 1997-98 were required to be laid in both House of Parliament. These reports have been laid in Lok Sabha on 18.12.1998 and Rajya Sabha on 22.12.1998.

Abatement of pollution and environmental activities: The General Insurance Industry is committed to the cause of pollution control and environmental protection by providing related services to clients. The specially designed insurance policies covering public liability risks and pollution liability risks provide for discounts in premium rates for risk and pollution control measures initiated by clients and also for disaster management system favourable in constraining spread of hazards caused after the occurrence of accidents. This provision of special discounts aims at encouraging safety, minimising risk of pollution and protection of environment, besides ensuring adherence of rules and regulations framed by Government on environment protection.

Inspections by various parliamentary committees

During the year, the Committee on Subordinate Legislation, Rajya Sabha Committee on Petitions, Rajya Sabha Committee on Papers laid in the table of Parliament made a visit to Head Office of GIC at Mumbai. The Committee on Official Language inspected the offices of LIC/GIC and its subsidiaries at Mumbai, Chennai, Madurai and Delhi. The Committee also visited Shimla Division and Puri Branch of LIC of India.

Life insurance corporation of India: LIC was established on 1st September, 1956 to take over the assets and liabilities of the erstwhile insurers and to carry on life insurance business in the country. Over the years its business has grown considerably both in volume and value. The key parameters of its performance in 1997-98 have been stated in succeeding paragraphs. LIC has continued to make efforts to improve the returns to the policy holders through better fund management, reduction in costs, increase in productivity and conservation of business. As a result, LIC has been able to announce as on 31.3.1998, the rates of bonus ranging between Rs. 62 to Rs. 102 per Rs. 1000/- Sum Assured depending upon the Plan and Term of Insurance Policies. Further, the Corporation had also declared Final Additional Bonus between Rs. 35/- to Rs. 1000/- Sum Assured depending upon the duration and the amount of the Sum Assured.

Divisional & branch offices. As on 31st March, 1998, LIC had 100 Divisional Offices and 2046 Branch Offices.

Expenses of management and expense ratio: The expenses of Management, renewal expense ratio and overall expense ratio for the last five years are given in the Table below.

Year	*Expenses of management (Rs. in crore)*	*Renewal expense Ratio (%)*	*Overall expense Ratio (%)*
1993-94	2124.90	5.0	21.8
1994-95	2466.34	6.3	21.4
1995-96	2948.58	7.0	20.8(*21)
1996-97	3503.85	7.1	21.4
1997-98	3953.85	6.1	20.5

Excludes Rs. 644.82 crore being insurance premium contribution towards LIC employees pension.

Premium income and life fund: The year wise position of the total premium income as well as of the Life Fund with the percentage increase over the previous year during the last 5 years is given below:

Year	*Total premium income (Rs. in crore)*	*% increase over previous year*
1993-94	97353.3	21.9
1994-95	11527.8	18.4
1995-96	14181.8	23.0
1996-97	16351.4	15.3
1997-98	19354.7	18.3

Year	*Life fund*	*% increase over previous year*
1993-94	49665.8	21.1
1994-95	59978.9	20.8
1995-96	72780.1	21.3
1996-97	87760.0	20.6
1997-98	105832.9	20.6

Investment: The total book value of investment of the Corporation as at the end of 1997-98 was Rs. 98,947.77 crore as compared to Rs. 82,665.17 crore as at the end of 1996-97.

New business (individual insurances): During the year ended 31st March, 1998 LIC transacted in India, new business of Rs. 63,617.69 crore under 133.11 lakh policies as against Rs. 56,740.50 crore under 122.68 lakh policies during the preceding year. The increase in business was 12.1 % in terms of sum assured and 8.5% in terms of number of policies.

Rural business. The New Business written in rural areas during 1997-98 amounted to Rs. 27,550.69 crore under 68.40 lakh policies as against the business of Rs.

24,278.73 crore under 60.33 lakh policies during the preceding year. This represents 43.3% of the total business on sum assured basis and 51.4% on number of policies basis as against 42.8% and 49.2% respectively during the preceding year.

Group insurance business. During the year ended 31st March, 1997, new business under Group Schemes issued and renewed was to the tune of Rs. 75,148.22 crore providing cover to 227.18 lakh lives against Rs. 62,691.88 crore providing cover to 223.78 lakh lives during the preceding year.

Social security schemes: The Social Security Fund (SSF) was set up in 1989-90 for providing social security through group insurance to the weaker and vulnerable sections of the society. Different Group Insurance Schemes for the approved occupations belonging to these sections are being subsidised from this Fund. These schemes now provide a sum assured upto Rs. 5 ′ 000 on death with accident benefit upto Rs. 25,000. During the year 1997-98 a new group of bread winning women in remote rural hilly areas was approved by the Central Government. With this the number of approved occupational groups as belonging to these sections of the society have become 24. They include among others weavers, rickshaw pullers and auto drivers, primary milk producers, beedi workers, cobblers, hamals, handicraft artisans, handloom and khadi weavers, papad workers attached to SEWA, physically handicapped self-employed persons, tendu leaf collectors and forest workers. A subsidy of 50% of the premium is granted from the Social Security Fund. In additions, group insurance schemes for landless agricultural labourers (LALGI) fully financed from the Social Security Fund and for IRDP beneficiaries are administered by LIC. The number of claims settled by LIC under the LALGI and IRDP schemes during the last five years are given below.

Year	*No. of claims settled under*	
	Landless agricultural Labourers (Lalgi)	*IRDP Beneficiaries*
1993-94	70524	11698
1994-95	58403	9803
1995-96	55149	11251
1996-97	58324	9231
1997-98	52593	8314

Rural group life insurance scheme (RGLIS).- This scheme was launched on 15th August, 1995 to spread the message of life insurance in the rural areas. This is a group insurance scheme and provides a life cover of Rs. 5000 for persons in rural areas for an annual premium of Rs. 60 for those who enrol up to the age of 40 years and Rs. 70 for those who enrol beyond 40 years and upto 50 years. The entry age is restricted to 20 years (minimum) and 50 years (maximum). The exit age is 60 years i.e. deaths occurring after 60 years are not covered. Under the Scheme two types of policies are offered: Type A is available to everyone without any restriction on the number of policies taken, and TYPE B is available only to households below the poverty line and restricted to only one person per household. The scheme is subsidised to the extent of 50% of the premium payable to be shared equally by the Centre and the States. To popularise the scheme, the village level workers (Gram Sevaks) involved in enrolment of the members at the Panchayat level are paid an incentive of Rs. 6 for a new member and Rs. 3 per member for renewal of membership. During the first year from 15.8.1995 to 14.8.1996, a total of 2,48,850 persons were covered out of which 2,33,807 persons were enrolled under the subsidised category and 15,043 persons under the general (non-subsidised category). During the second year (i.e. from 15.8.96 to 14.8.1997) 6,36,211 persons were enrolled as new members and

5,503 persons renewed their membership. Among them, 6,04,568 and 5,256 persons were under subsidised category respectively During the third year (i.e. from 15.8.1997 to 14.8.1998) 3,09,252 persons were enrolled as new members and 73,925 persons renewed their membership. Out of these, under subsidised category 2,98,917 persons were enrolled as new members and 70,183 persons renewed their membership. The scheme is due for review which is under consideration.

Settlement of claims: During the year 1997-98, LIC settled 56.52 lakh claims for a total amount of Rs. 6,674.04 crore as against 49.49 lakh claims for Rs. 5,691.49 crore during the previous year. The percentage of outstanding claims of the claims payable during the last five years is given in the following table:

Year	*% of outstanding claims as at the end of the year to claims payable during the year*	
	%by number	*%by amount*
1993-94	3.05	4.86
1994-95	3.47	5.26
1995-96	3.86	5.99
1996-97	3.13	5.32
1997-98	2.74	4.51

New product development: During the year 1997-98, LIC introduced three new plans namely Jeevan Asha, Jeevan Suraksha (Single premium without life cover) and Jeevan Sanchaya (15 year term)

Valuation: The latest annual valuation was conducted as on 31.3.1998. The simple reversionary bonus rates declared for whole life type of policies are Rs.102 per Rs.1,000 sum assured for policies with date of commencement on or before 31.3.1972, Rs. 98 per Rs. 1,000 sum assured for policies with date of commencement after 31.3.1972 but before 1.4.1977 and

Rs.91 per Rs.1,000/- sum assured for policies with date of commencement on or after 1.4.1977. The rates for endowment type of policies are Rs.62 per Rs.1,000 sum assured for policy term upto 10 years and Rs.69/- per Rs.1,000 sum assured for policy terms 11 to 15 years. The rates for endowment type of policies for a term of 16 to 20 are Rs.71 per Rs.1,000 sum assured. The rates for endowment type of policies for a term of 21 years and above are Rs.74 per Rs.1,000 sum assured. The rates for endowment type of policies are Rs.81 per Rs.1,000 sum assured for policies with date of commencement after 31.3.1972 but before 1.4.1977. The rates for endowment type of policies are Rs.85 per Rs.1,000 sum assured for policies with date of commencement on or before 31.3.1972. Rs. 62 per Rs. 1000 sum assured for 12 and 15 years term policies and Rs. 67 per Rs. 1000 sum assured for 20 years term policies. The rate of bonus for Money Back, Anticipated Endowment and Jeevan Surabhi policies is Rs.62 per Rs.1,000 sum assured for 12 and 15 years term policies and Rs.67 per Rs.1,000 sum assured for 20 years term policies. The rate of bonus for these policies with 25 years term is Rs. 71 per Rs. 1,000 sum assured. For policies with date of commencement after 31.3.1972 but before 1.4.1977 the rate of bonus is Rs. 78 per Rs. 1,000 sum assured. In addition, final additional bonus was also declared at rates ranging between Rs. 35/- to Rs. 1,000 per Rs. 1,000 sum assured in respect of policies other than Anticipated Endowment, Money Back and Jeevan Surabhi Plans depending upon the term and sum assured group which satisfy certain conditions. LIC also declares bonus under individual annuity plans types of policies both for deferred and immediate annuity policies including Jeevan Dhara and Jeevan Akshaya. It also announced bonus under its group annuities. The bonus is payable under both individual and group policies subject to the satisfaction of terms and conditions as laid down in respective policies as per their rules in force from time to time.

General Insurance Corporation of India (GIC): Prior to nationalisation, 107 companies including branches of some foreign companies operated in the country. Under the General Insurance Business Nationalisation Act, 1972 these were amalgamated and grouped into four operating companies viz National Insurance Company Limited, The New India Assurance Co. Ltd., The Oriental Insurance Co. Ltd. and the United India Insurance Co., Ltd. They became subsidiaries of the holding company General Insurance Corporation of India which came into being on January 1st, 1973. The GIC as holding company is responsible for superintending, controlling and carrying on general insurance business. The four subsidiaries carry on the business operations on all India basis and underwrite various classes of general insurance business including reinsurance except for aviation insurance of the national airlines, Hindustan Aeronautics Limited and Crop Insurance. The latter business are directly handled by GIC.

The Gross Premium Income of the General Insurance Industry in India during 1997-98 was Rs.7736 Crores as against Rs.7021 Crores during 1996-97 representing a growth of 10.2% over the premium income of 1996-97. The Net Premium Income of the General Insurance Industry in India during the year 1997-98 was Rs.6725 Crores as against Rs.6041 Crores during 1996-97 representing a growth of 11.3% over the Net Premium Income of 1996-97. The gross profits of the industry during 1997-98 were Rs. 1623 Crores as against Rs. 1084 Crores in 1996-97 recording a growth of 49.7% over the previous year. The net profits of the industry during the year 1997-98 were Rs.1255 Crores as against Rs.719 Crores in 1996-97 representing a growth of 74.5% over the previous year.

Reinsurance: The reinsurance programme of industry aims at optimum retention within the country, consistent with safety and underwriting prudence. The percentage of premium retained in India for different classes of business was 88.4% in 1997-98.

Investment: There has been continuous increase in the investments made by the industry. It was Rs.1 6728 Crores 199798 as against Rs. 14,386 Crores in 1996-97. A substantial portion of fresh accretions of investment goes in the socially oriented sector.

Foreign operations: Indian Insurance companies operate through branches or agencies or associate of the subsidiary companies in 31 different countries of the world. During the year 1997-98, gross premium income written by the four subsidiaries companies through branches or agencies outside India amounted to Rs.382.95 Crores as against 367.05 Crores in 1996-97. The branch net premium income was Rs.343.04 Crores as against Rs.333.33 Crores in the previous year.

Personal accident insurance social security scheme for poor families: The above scheme is operational throughout the country. It covers all the earning members of the poor families in the age group of, 18-60 years whose annual income from all sources does not exceed Rs. 7,200/-. The Scheme provides relief to the dependent by way of compensation of Rs. 3,000/- in the event of accidental death of an earning member of the family. The Central Government bears the entire premium cost in respect of the scheme. During the year 1997-98, a total no. of 9,500 claims involving an amount of Rs.2.85 Crores were settled.

Hut insurance scheme for poor families in rural areas: The above scheme provides fire insurance cover for huts and belongings of landless labourers, small farmers, artisans and other poor families in rural areas whose family income is less then Rs.4,800/- per annum. Under the scheme compensation is provided for an amount not exceeding Rs. 1000/- for a hut and Rs.500/- for belongings in the hut destroyed by fire. The Central Government is bearing the entire premium in respect of the above scheme. During the year 1997-98 a total number of 40,554 claims involving an amount of Rs.4.85 Crores were settled.

Mediclaim insurance policy: Mediclaim Insurance Policy, which was in existence has been revised. The revised policy does away with the sub-limits under the various sub-heads and offers just one sum-insured ranging from Rs.1 5,000/- to Rs.30,000/-. The cover provides for reimbursement of medical expenses incurred by an individual towards hospitalisation/ domiciliary hospitalisation for any illness, injury or disease contracted or sustained during the period of insurance. Premium is calculated on the basis of age of the proposer and the sum insured opted for.

Jan arogya bima policy: The Scheme which is primarily meant for the larger segment of the population who cannot afford the high cost of medical treatment, was introduced w.e.f 12th August, 1996. The limit of cover per person is Rs.5000/- per annum. The premium payable is very low depending on the age of the person covered ranging from Rs.70/- to Rs.140/- per person per year and Rs.50/- per dependent child below 25years of age. The cover provides for reimbursement of medical expenses incurred by an individual towards hospitalisation/ domiciliary hospitalisation for any illness, injury or disease contracted or sustained during the period of insurance.

Overseas mediclaim policy: The existing Overseas Mediclaim Policy offering emergency medical expenses cover to overseas travellers has been extended to include

In-flight Personal Accident cover up to US$ 10,000 and Loss of Passport cover up to US$ 150 from 1st April, 1997. The extended cover will be available without payment of additional premium under Business and Holiday cover and under the Corporate Frequent Travellers cover. A more comprehensive policy with additional benefits has also been devised.

Videsh yatra mitre policy: A new policy called 'Videsh Yatra Mitra' covering supplementary benefits besides providing indemnity for medical expenses during the period of overseas travel, has been introduced by the general insurance industry w.e.f. 1st January, 1998. Two types of policies - one offering limit of benefits up to US$ 250,000 for world wide travel but excluding USA and Canada and the other offering limit of benefits up to US$ 500,000 for world wide travel including USA and Canada are available under the scheme. In addition to medical coverage, the policy also provides coverage for (1) Personal Accident up to US$ 25,000 (ii) Loss of personal baggage up to US$ 1,000 (iii) Delayed baggage up to US$ 100 (iv) Personal Liability up to US$ 2,00,000. The premium under the policy is only 14% more than that under the existing Overseas Mediclaim Policy (OMP), while the medical benefits will be increased five times in addition to supplementary benefits as mentioned above.

Raj rajeshwari mahila kalyan yojana: A new policy called 'Raj Rajeshwari Mahila Kalyan Yojana' offering security to women of the age group of 10 to 75 years irrespective of their occupation was introduced w.e.f. 19th October, 1998. For a premium of Rs. 15/- per annum, the policy provides a cover of Rs. 25,000/- for permanent total disablement of the insured woman. The policy also provides a cover of Rs. 25,000/- for the death of her husband. For the death of an unmarried woman, the policy provides a cover of Rs. 25,000/- which will be payable to her nominee/ legal heir.

Bhagyashree child welfare policy: Another new policy called "Bhagyashree Child Welfare Policy" covering girl child in the age group of 0 to 18 years whose parents age does not exceed 60 years, was also introduced w.e.f. 19th October, 1998. In case of death of the girl child or both parents, an amount of Rs. 25,000/- would be deposited in the name of the girl child with a financial institution. Fixed annual disbursements to the girl child up to the age of 18 years would be made from the amount to her credit, and the balance amount to her credit would be disbursed on attaining the age of 18 years.

Crop insurance scheme: The Scheme was introduced from Kharif 1985 Season and has completed 13 years. The Scheme is implemented in 15 States and 2 UTs. The number of farmers covered was 51.35 Lakhs and 8.66 Lakhs in Kharif 1997 and Rabi 1997-98 seasons respectively. Since inception, the total premium income was Rs. 313.14 Crores as against the total claims amounting to Rs. 1719.00 Crores. The Scheme is being administered by GIC on behalf of the Central Government. The premium and claims are shared by the Central and State Governments in the ratio of 2:1 respectively There are 11 Crop Insurance Cells at State Capitals and UTs under GIC. These Cells maintain close liaison with the State Governments and monitor the implementation of the Scheme. A Modified Crop Insurance Scheme (MCIS) is being formulated by Ministry of Agriculture in consultation with GIC which will replace the present CCIS.

Lok adalat, for motor third party claims: During the year 1997-98, the General Insurance industry has participated in 1691 Lok Adalats and has settled over 65,390 claims and has disbursed over Rs. 268.69 Crores by way of compensation.

Jald rahat yojana: The subsidiaries of GIC have

introduced 'Jald Rahat Yojana' with an objective to expedite payment of compensation to road accident victims. Under the scheme a claimant is not required to go to Motor Accident Claims Tribunal for claiming compensation and he can directly approach concerned insurance company. Non fatal injury claims involving accident victims of 18 years and above are taken. The scheme is in operation in Ahmedabad, Mumbai, Bangalore, Delhi, Kochi, Chennai and Pune. To expedite settlement of Motor TP claims, special in house committees have also been formed.

Ombudsman scheme: One of the major areas of concern of Government has been customer service. As part of this exercise, steps have been initiated to set up Ombudsman for further control over personal line insurance claims of both life and non-life sector. The Ombudsman Scheme has been notified on November, 11, 1998. Under the Scheme, seven Ombudsman who will be persons of eminence in the field of insurance, administration and with judicial expertise, will be appointed. The Ombudsman will be in the rank of Judge of a High Court.

The Ombudsman will have power to recommend or award an amount upto Rs. 20 lakhs in case of claims under personal line portfolio.

Details of draft para

The General Insurance Corporation of India and its four subsidiaries viz. National Insurance Co. Ltd., New India Assurance Co. Ltd., Oriental Insurance Co.Ltd. and United India Insurance Co.Ltd. being Government companies are subject to Audit by Comptroller & Auditor General of India (CAG). During the year 1998, 17 Audit Draft Paras pertaining to GIC/four subsidiaries/ TAC were referred to the Government. Replies in respect of all these Draft Paras (upto 27.1.1999) have been sent to the Audit Board except in respect of 5 Draft Paras.

Action Taken Notes (ATN) on all the Paras relating to general insurance industry appearing in the CAG Audit Reports (Commercial) for the years 1993 to 1998, as prepared by the GIC, have been sent to the CAG for vetting.

Budget division

Budget Division is entrusted with the responsibility of the preparation of, submission to and getting sanction of Parliament, for the Annual Budget and Supplementary and Excess Demands for Grants of the Central Government (other than Railways), and of States and Union Territories with Legislatures under President's Rule. The Division is responsible for monitoring the fiscal position of the Central Government. In this role, the responsibility of this Division also extends to regulating the flow of expenditure of the Government which inter alia includes processing of proposals from other Ministries/Departments for reappropriation of savings in a Grant where prior approval of Finance Ministry is required. The rules regarding New Service/New Instrument of Service laid down on the recommendations of the Public Accounts Committee of Parliament, including their application are also administered by this Division. The Division deals with Public Debt, market loans, ways and means position of the Government, interest rates on Central Government's borrowing and lending, guarantees given by the Government of India and the Contingency Fund of India. The Division also administers small savings schemes and the National Saving Organisation. Matters relating to the Comptroller and Auditor General's (Duties, Powers and Condition of Service) Act, 1971, submission of the reports of the Comptroller and Auditor General of India relating to the accounts of the Union to the President for being laid before Parliament and Government Accounts are also handled by this Division. The Division is also responsible for the work relating to the setting up of the Finance Commission under Article 280 of the Constitution and for obtaining the orders of the Cabinet on the Reports of the Finance Commissions. There is a printing press attached to this Division which prints Budget documents, both sensitive and non-sensitive. It also undertakes printing of a wide range of other documents, reports, special publications, etc. which are brought out on behalf of the Ministry of Finance from time to time like Annual Administrative Reports, Finance Commission's report, etc. One of the Deputy Secretary/ Director in this Division also functions as ex-officio, Treasurer of Charitable Endowment of India under the Charitable Endowments Act, 1890. The Division also deals with matters connected with the National Defence Fund.

Public debt

Open Market borrowing constitutes an important source for raising resources for the Central Government and the State governments.

The overall net market borrowing in 1998-99 was of the order of Rs. 60,047 crore. A sum of Rs. 48,493 crore was actually raised in 1997-98. The details are as follows:

(Rs. in crores)

		Net market borrowings	
		1997-98 Actual	*1998-99 Allocations*
1.	Central Government	40,494	48,493
2.	State Governments	7,193	11,371
3.	Central Guaranteed Institutions	400	-
4.	State Financial Institutions	350	350
5.	State Land Development Banks	56	-
	Total	48,326	60,047

Finance Minister had mentioned in his budget speech for

1994-95 that in order to strengthen fiscal discipline, Government should not be able to finance its deficits by creating money, through unlimited recourse to the Reserve Bank, by issue of ad-hoc treasury bills and that from the year 1997-98 that system would be dispensed with. Accordingly an agreement was signed between the Govt. of India and Reserve Bank of India on 26.3.1997 putting an end to the system of ad-hoc Treasury Bills w.e.f. 1.4.97. The net issue of ad-hoc Treasury Bills in a financial year mainly constituted budgetary deficit. With the discontinuance of the system of ad-hoc TBs, the concept of budgetary deficit lost its relevance from 1997-98. Simultaneously, the system of tap 91 day TBs in which State Govts. and banks were investing their temporary surpluses was also discontinued from 1.4.1997. The outstanding ad-hoc TBs and tap TBs as on 31.3.1997 totalling to about Rs. 50,818 crore were converted into Special Securities carrying interest @ 4.6% p.a. The scheme for sale of 91 day treasury bills on auction basis introduced in January, 1993 is, however, being continued.

With the discontinuance of ad hoc TBs w.e.f. 1.4.1997 the temporary mismatches between receipts and expenditure of GOI are being met under a new scheme called Ways and Means Advances (WMA) from RBI. There will be two separate limits of WMA for the period April to September and October to March, to be decided for each year. WMA in excess of the limit will be treated as overdraft. As a transitional arrangement, it has been decided to allow overdraft beyond 10 consecutive working days, only upto 31.3.1999. The interest on WMA for the GOI will be equivalent to the 'Bank Rate' at par with the rate at which RBI gives WMA to State Governments. The interest on overdraft will be 2% over and above the interest rate on WMA.

As already indicated the 91 tap TBs into which the State Govts. and banks were investing their temporary surpluses was also discontinued from 1.4.1997. However, in order to provide an avenue for investment of temporary surpluses by State Govts. foreign Central banks and other specified bodies with whom the RBI has an agreement by way of investing their surplus funds, a new scheme called 14 day Intermediate TBs was introduced from 1.4.1997. Subsequently, a notification was issued on 20.5.1997 announcing sale of 14 day TBs on auction basis also. The auctions, are held periodically and these can be purchased by any person, resident in India including individuals, firms, companies, corporate' bodies and institutions. State Govts. eligible PFs, and the Nepal Rashtra Bank will be allowed bid in auctions on 'non-competitive basis'.

Of the other important sources through which the Central government raises resources, mention may be made of the following:

(i) *364- day treasury bills:* These treasury bills offer short-term investment opportunity to financial institutions (like banks, etc.) and other parties. The 364- day treasury bills were introduced in 1992-93 to enable development of a market for Government securities. These bills are not rediscountable with the Reserve Bank of India. These bills are periodically offered for sale on auction basis, by the Reserve Bank of India at Bombay.

(ii) *Relief bonds:* 10% Relief Bonds, 1993 was introduced from 15th March, 1993 which replaced the 9% Relief Bonds, 1987. With the general reduction of interest rates the issue of 10% Relief Bonds, 1993 was suspended and a new series of 9% Relief Bonds, 1993 was introduced with effect from 2.9.1993. Subsequently, keeping in view the general increase in interest rates in 1995-96, a new series of 10% Relief Bonds, 1995 was introduced with effect from

4.10.1995. The interest rates on some of the Small Savings instruments were reduced from 1.1.1999. Accordingly, the interest rate on Relief Bonds was also reduced to 9% with effect from 1.1.1999. It is open to investment without limit by individuals and Hindu Undivided Family. Joint holding of the Bonds by individual is permissible. The bonds carry tax-free interest and have a maturity period of 5 years.

(iii) *Market borrowings:* apart from open market borrowing raised through auctions, loans are also raised through other instruments like conversion of 364-day Treasury Bills and 91 -day Treasury Bills sold on auction basis, zero coupon Bonds which do not carry any interest but are sold at a discount, stock for which payment is made in instalments, Floating Rate Bonds, Capital Indexed Bonds, etc.

A total sum of Rs. 80,953 crore (gross) was raised through various instruments of market borrowing upto December, 1,998 during the financial year 1998-99.

Special deposits of non-government provident, superannuation and gratuity Funds.

This scheme was introduced in July, 1975 for a period of 10 years and was further extended from time to time. However, as per the announcement made in the budget speech for 1997-98, the requirement to invest in the scheme was withdrawn from 1.4.1997. The Funds are now required to invest 25% in Central Government Securities; 15% in State Government Securities or securities guaranteed either by the Central government or the State Governments; 40% in Bonds/Securities on Public Financial Institutions/Public Sector Units/the Infrastructure Development Finance Company Ltd. (IDFC) and/or certificate of deposits issued by Public Sector Banks. The balance 20% which the funds were earlier required to invest in Special Deposit Scheme can now be invested in any of the above three categories. In pursuance of the announcement made in the budget speech for 1998-99, the Trustees have also been allowed, subject to their assessment of the risk-return prospects, to invest upto 10% in private sector bonds/ securities which have an investment grade rating from at least two credit rating agencies.

National savings organisation

The National Savings Organisation (NSO), an attached office under the Department of Economic Affairs was set up in the late 1940s. National Savings Organisation is headed by the National Savings Commissioner who is assisted by 01 Joint National Savings Commissioner, 03 Deputy National Savings Commissioners in the Headquarters at Nagpur. 26 Regional Directors on National Savings function from states' Capitals and big cities. Its total sanctioned strength is 1191, out of which 31 are Group "A" Officers. The National Savings Organisation has in all 32 field Offices, all over the country.

Functions of N. S. O

The functions of this Organisation are to assist in mobilisation of Small Savings, its publicity, its coordination with State governments, Post Offices, Banks, etc., compile statistical data, appoint agents, arrange for their training, pay agency commission in respect of certain schemes, etc.

Small savings

Savings is the lifeline for development of a Country. Small Saving collection play a significant role on the mobilisation of the financial resources required for the planned development of our country. Out of the net Small Savings collections, every year loans are advanced to State Governments to meet development expenditure.

Loans are also advanced to Union Territories with legislature, namely, Delhi and Pondicherry against net Small Savings collection from January, 1994.

The following Small Savings Schemes are currently in operation:-

(i) Post Office Savings Account.

(ii) Post Office Time Deposit Account 1 year, 2 year, 3 year and 5 year.

(iii) Post Office Recurring Deposit Account.

(iv) Post Office Monthly Income Account .

(v) National Savings Scheme, 1992.

(vi) Indira Vikas Patra.

(vii) Kisan Vikas Patra.

(viii) National Savings Certificates VIII Issue.

(ix) Public Provident Fund Scheme.

(x) Deposit Scheme for Retiring Government Employees, 1989.

(xi) Deposit Scheme for Retiring Employees of Public Sector Companies, 1991.

Public provident fund scheme: Deposits under the Public Provident Fund Scheme framed under the Public Provident Fund Act, 1968 qualify for tax rebate under the Income-Tax Act. A subscriber can make deposits upto Rs. 60,000 in a year, while the minimum necessary deposit in a year is Rs. 100. These deposits carry a tax-free interest at 12 per cent per annum. Withdrawals from P.P.F are exempt from Income Tax under Section 10 of Income Tax Act. Under the scheme accounts can be opened in the name of individual and on behalf of HUF Nomination facility has been extended to an account opened on behalf of HUF.

Deposit Scheme for retiring government Employees: This Scheme was introduced from 1st July, 1989. The retired/retiring Central and State Government Employees can invest their retirement benefits under the scheme which is being operated through selected branches of State Bank of India and Nationalised Banks. The scheme was extended to the retired Judges of the Supreme Court and High courts from 11.11.1993. The investments under this scheme earn interest at the rate of 9% per annum w.e.f. 01.01.1999 payable half-yearly. The value of deposits is exempt from wealth Tax ' and the interest income is exempt from income tax. The investors have the option to withdraw the deposit after 3 years from the date of deposit.

Doposit scheme for retiring employees of Public Sector Companies: The scheme, which was introduced from 1 st January, 1991 is on the lines of the Deposit Scheme for Retiring Government Employees. The scheme is open to investment by retired/retiring Employees of Public Sector Companies. The investment under this scheme earn interest at the rate of 9% per annum w.e.f. 01.01.1999 payable half yearly.

The net small savings collections during 1998-99 (upto Nov., 1998) were Rs. 19,465.53 crores as against Rs. 11,883.76 crores during the corresponding period of 1997-98.

Three-fourth of net small savings collections, including Public Provident Fund collections in each State/UT with legislature are advanced is long term loans to that state/UT with legislature towards funding the plan outlay. During the year 1998-99, loans to the extent of Rs. 17,115.34 crores have been sanctioned to State. Governments (upto 31.12.1998) as against R$. 11,207.09 crores sanctioned during the same period of last year. Loans to the extent of Rs. 759.67 crores have been sanctioned to the UTs with legislature as against Rs. 490.56 crores sanctioned during the same period of last year.

During the year 1997-98 around 2.12 crores members of Pay Roll savings Group Scheme invested an amount of Rs. 1,134.26 crores. About 3.31 lakhs agents under Standardised Agency System (SAS) have secured collections to the tune of Rs. 19,162.12 crores and about 1.58 lakh Mahila Pradhan Kshetriya Bachat Yojana (MPKBY) agents have secured an investment of Rs. 2,717.10 crores during 1997-98. In the same year 2.15 crore of students who are members of 54,502 Sanchayikas saved an amount of Rs. 89.99 crores. 26876 PPF agents have secured an investment of Rs. 1,592.45 crores during the year 1997-98.

National defence fund

The National Defence Fund was established on 27th October, 1962 for receiving contributions in the form of cash, gold and gold ornaments, silver and silver ornaments, jewellery, precious stones, etc. for defence efforts. The total amount credited to the fund upto Dec.,1998 inclusive of the contributions received in the form of gold, silver, jewellery, etc. was Rs. 242.07 crores including Rs. 124.78 crores paid by government as interest upto Dec., 1998. Withdrawals from the Fund upto the end of 31st Dec., 1998 amounted to Rs. 149.08 crores leaving a net balance of Rs. 92.98 crores.

Hindi branch

All Budget documents are presented to Parliament in Hindi and English. Accordingly budget documents pertaining to two Union Budgets, 1998-99 (interim) and 1998-99 (Regular) were presented before both the Houses of Parliament bilingually. Besides the above mentioned documents Hindi Branch has also prepared Hindi versions of Economic Survey, 1997-98 alongwith document of Economic Classificatory and Status Report on External Debt, which were laid before the Parliament.

The translation of other documents as envisaged in the Official Language Act, 1963 and Rules made thereunder was also undertaken by the Hindi Branch during the year under report. These include all agreements concluded with foreign Governments and International Agencies, Cabinet Notes, Parliament questions/ assurances, notifications, Standing Committee/Public Accounts Committee papers, monthly summary for the Cabinet etc. During 1998-99 Hindi Branch translated 12 agreements.

Capital market and external commercial borrowings division

Capital market branch

Introductory para highlighting the performance and achievement during the year.

Consequent upon the suggestions of High Level Committee on Capital Markets to review the status of the Primary Market an Informal Group on Primary Market was set up under the Chairmanship of Dr. Shankar N. Acharya, Chief economic Adviser in the Ministry of Finance to look into the reasons for sluggishness and recommend remedial steps. The report of the Group was submitted to the High Level Committee on Capital Market on March 12, 1998. Part I of the report consists of a review of the primary market and discusses possible reasons for the slow down in the primary market, while Part 11 deals with the suggestions for improving the market.

Brief para about performance/achievement upto last year

Securities Appellate Tribunal (SAT) was established on 28.7.97 under section 15-T of SEBI Act, 1992 to hear the appeals arising from the adjudicating authority of SEBI relating to the monetary penalties. Office of SAT is located in Mumbai and consists of a Presiding Officer and other supporting Staff.

The Government, through a press release issued on November 16, 1997 decided that the companies floating plantation schemes/Collective Investment Schemes inviting deposits from the public will be brought under the purview of SEBI and that SEBI would be formulating suitable regulations for these schemes under the SEBI Act, 1992. Following this decision SEBI also issued a press release stating that no scheme which is in the nature of a Collective Investment Scheme or plantation scheme can be launched till regulations are framed by SEBI for this purpose. Subsequently, SEBI had also set up a Committee headed by Dr. S.A. Dave to formulate the draft regulations for such schemes.

Information about the performance achievement during the year under review

An informal group on Primary market was set up under the Chairmanship of Dr. Shankar N.Acharya to look into the reasons for slow down in the Primary market and suggest measures to improve it. Some of the main recommendations of the group were introduction of institutional arrangements to compensate investor in the event of broker defaults, standardisation of accounting norms by companies, compulsory market making, popularisation of book building, better credit facilities for brokers, popularisation of scripless trading, introduction of derivative trading and steps to reduce cost of issues. These recommendations are under various stages of implementation.

During 1998-99, the SEBI continued its operations and initiatives in regulating and developing the Indian Securities markets in fulfillment of the twin objectives of investor protection and market development set forth in the SEBI Act, 1992. Throughout its six years of existence as a statutory body, the SEBI has sought to balance the two objectives by constantly reviewing and reappraising its existing policies and programmes, formulating new policies an crafting new regulations to foster development in areas hitherto unregulated and to implement them to ensure growth of the markets with efficiency, integrity and protection of investors' interest.

The SEBI appointed on February 28, 1997 under the Chairmanship of Justice D.R. Dhanuka, a committee to examine areas of deficiency in the SEBI Act, 1992, Securities Contracts Act 1956, Depositories Act, 1996 and Companies Act, 1956 pertaining to the capital market.

The Committee has submitted its report with recommendations in respect of Depositories Act, 1996, Draft Securities Bill 1998 Draft Companies Bill, etc. It has recommended inter-alia amalgamation of SEBI Act, 1992 and SCR Act 1956 into one Act, Single regulatory body for Capital Market, more powers to SEBI etc.

During the year, the following regulations under SEBI Act, 1992 were notified:-

1. SEBI (Stock Broker & Sub-Brokers) Amendment Regulations, 1998.
2. SEBI (Registrar to the Issue and Share Transfer Agent) Amendment.
3. SEBI (Bankers to an Issue) Amendment Regulations, 1998.
4. SEBI (Debenture Trustees) Amendment Regulations, 1998.
5. SEBI (Custodian of Securities) Amendment Regulations, 1998.
6. SEBI (Depositories & Participants) Amendment Regulations, 1998.
7. SEBI (Venture Capital Funds) Amendment Regulations, 1998.

8. SEBI (Portfolio Managers) Amendment Regulations, 1998.
9. SEBI (underwriters) Amendment Regulations, 1998.
10. SEBI (Mutual Funds) Amendment Regulations, 1998.
11. SEBI (Merchant Bankers) Amendment Regulations, 1998.
12. SEBI (Stock Broker & Sub-Broker)2nd Amendment Regulations, 1998.
13. SEBI (Depositories & Participants)2nd Amendment Regulations, 1998.
14. SEBI (Mutual Funds) Amendment Regulations, 1998-CORRIGENDUM.
15. SEBI (Substantial Acquisition of shares & Takeovers) Amendment Regulations, 1997-CORRIGENDUM.
16. SEBI (FII) Amendment Regulations, 1998.
17. SEBI (FII)2nd Amendment Regulations, 1998.
18. SEBI (FII)3nd Amendment Regulations, 1998.
19. SEBI (Substantial Acquisition of shares & Takeovers) Amendment Regulations, 1998.
20. SEBI (Buy-back of securities) Regulations, 1998.

Stock exchange section

Introductory para highlighting the performance and achievements during the year: The report of the Committee on "Regulatory Framework for Derivatives Trading in India" under the Chairmanship of Dr. L.C. Gupta, was approved by the SEBI Board in May, 1998. The Board also approved the suggestive Bye-laws proposed by the Committee covering the operational aspects for regulation and control of trading and settlement of derivative contracts. The regulatory frame work for derivatives trading in India was laid down by

SEBI on June 16,1998. However, the derivatives trading could commence only after necessary amendments to the Securities Contracts (Regulation) Act, 1956 are made to enable derivatives instruments to be treated as 'securities'. A Bill amending the Securities Contracts (Regulation) Act, 1956 to provide for trading in derivatives of securities is under consideration of the Parliament. Trading in dematerialised securities have seen tremendous growth. As reported by National Securities Depository Ltd., the first depository in the country, by the end of December, 1998, 291 securities have been admitted for dematerialisation and the total value of securities in dematerialised form is around Rs. 70,000 crores. To popularise the concept of dematerialisation steps are being taken towards spreading depository awareness among the various sections of the investing community across the country. Approval has been granted for setting up a second depository, the Central Securities Depositories (Pvt.) Ltd. (CDS), which is being promoted by the Stock Exchange, Mumbai. The Depositories (Appeal to the Central Government) Rules, 1998 was notified under Section 24 of the Depositories Act, 1996, on 28th July, 1998. Following this, any person aggrieved by an order of the SEBI Board under the Depositories Act, 1996 or the Regulations made thereunder may prefer an appeal to the Central Government under Section 23 of the Act. A new stock exchange, the Inter-Connected Stock Exchange of India Ltd. (ISE), promoted by 15 regional stock exchanges in the country, has been set up at Mumbai. The ISE provides a member-broker of any of these stock exchanges an access into the national market segment, which would be in addition to the local trading segment available at present.

A brief pare about the functions/working of organisation and set up of the division including its various advisory boards and councils in a brief and concise form. This division is headed by a Joint Secretary. The Division has two branches viz., the Capital Markets Branch and External Commercial Borrowing Branch. The Capital Markets Branch consists of two sections viz. the Capital Market Section and the Stock Exchange Section. The main functions of the Capital Market Branch relate to evolving policies for the orderly growth and development of the Capital Market, monitoring the movement of indices of share prices and supervising the overall functioning of the Unit Trust of India and the Securities and Exchange Board of India.

A brief para about the achievements performance upto last year: Based on the recommendations of the Varma Committee set up by the Securities and Exchange Board of India to review the Revised Carry Forward System (RCFS), the following significant modifications were made to RCFS: (i) the twin track system whereby carry forward transactions are segregated at the time of execution of the trade would continue. However, trades identified for carry forward would attract a daily margin of 10% instead of the daily margin of 15%. 50% of this 10% daily margin would be collected upfront either in cash or in the form of bank guarantee. The margin requirement of 7.5% on transactions marked for the delivery for Type I members (members doing carry forward business) was withdrawn. These daily margin requirements are the minimum requirements and stock exchanges would be free to impose more rigorous requirements based on their risk perceptions. (ii) Limit of 90 days for carried forwarded transactions would continue. However, the stock exchanges were advised to ensure that no roll over the transactions take place beyond 90 days. (iii) Overall carry forward limit was enhanced to Rs. 20 crores per broker. per settlement. (iv) Limit of Rs. 10 crores for a financier was withdrawn.

Shares received by Vyaj Badla financiers would continue to be deposited with the clearing house. The stock exchanges would arrange for proper insurance cover for aggregate value of shares lying in the clearing house. The Committee's recommendations regarding strict enforcement of capital adequacy and other prudential safeguards and effective monitoring and Surveillance system and that the scripts chosen for carry forward should have sufficient floating stock and high liquidity were also accepted.

In order to expedite the process of dematerialisation, settlement of trades in the depository was made compulsory from January 15, 1998 for all institutional investors in respect of shares of 8 Companies. In view of the availability of facilities like depository system and the stock lending scheme, rolling settlement (T+5) was introduced in respect of trading in the dematerialised segment of all companies with effect from January 15, 1998. A notification was issued on 6th November, 1997 under the provisions of Section 16 of the Securities Contracts (Regulation) Act, 1956 through which 19 non bank entities were allowed to enter into reverse ready forward contracts provided that all transactions are put through the Subsidiary Ledger Account with the RBI in treasury bills of all maturities issued by the GOI and in such dated securities of GOI as approved by the RBI in consultation with the Central Government. Another notification was issued on March 18, 1998 further amending GOI notification dated June 27, 1969 for extending the facility of ready forward transactions to nine RBI registered satellite dealers in the government securities market.

Information about the, performance/achievements during the year under review: Based on the report of the Committee on regulatory framework for Derivatives Trading in India under the Chairmanship of Dr. L.C.

Gupta set up by the Securities and Exchange Board of India (SEBI), the following major recommendations of the Committee were accepted: (i) There should be phased introduction of derivative products and the stock index future should be the starting point for equity derivatives in india. (ii) Definition of 'Securities' under Securities Contracts (Regulation) Act be expanded by declaring derivative contracts based on index of prices of securities and other derivative contracts as securities. (iii) Existing stock exchanges be permitted to trade derivatives provided they meet the eligibility conditions which would, inter-alia include adequate infrastructure facilities, online trading and surveillance system and minimum of 50 members opting for derivative trading. The derivative market should have a separate Governing Council with representation of trading/clearing members of the derivative segment limited to 40%. The Chairman of the Governing Council shall not carry on any trading or clearing business on any Exchange during his tenure as Chairman. Further, no trading/clearing member shall be allowed to simultaneously be on the Governing Council of derivative segment and the underlying securities market. (iv) Initial margin requirements related to the risk of loss on the position and capital adequacy norms shall be prescribed. (v) Annual inspection of all the members operating in the derivative segment would be undertaken by the stock exchanges. (vi) The Exchanges would disseminate information about trades, quantities and quotes in real time over at least two information vending networks. (vii) The clearing corporations/house to settle derivative trades would have to meet certain specified eligibility conditions and the clearing corporation/house must interpose itself between both legs of every trade, becoming the legal counter party to both or alternatively provide an unconditional guarantee for settlement of all trades. (viii) There would be two tier membership i.e. the trading member and clearing member and the entry norms for the clearing member would be comparatively more stringent. The clearing member should have a minimum networth of Rs. 3 crores and shall make a deposit of Rs.50 lakhs with the exchange/clearing corporation in the form of liquid assets. (ix) A model Risk Disclosure Document would be prescribed and the Exchange would monitor the broker dealer/client relationship. The sales personnel working in the broker dealer office would need to pass a certification programme. (x) Corporate clients/financial institutions/ mutual funds should be allowed to trade derivatives only if and to the extent authorized by their Board of Directors/ Trustees. Mutual Funds would need to make necessary disclosures in their offer documents if they opt to trade derivatives. For the existing schemes they would require the approval of their unit holders. The minimum contract value would be Rs. 1 lakh which would also apply in the case of individuals. (xi) The issue of accounting and disclosure norms for derivatives should be taken up with the Institute of Chartered Accountants of India so that proper accounting and disclosures are made in the annual reports of the corporates and others.

Further, the Board approved the suggestive Bye-laws proposed by the Committee covering the operational aspects for regulation and control of trading and settlement of derivative contracts. The regulatory frame work for derivatives trading in India was laid down by SEBI on June 16, 1998. They are mainly as follows: (i) The Governing Council of the derivatives exchange will have representation of trading members to the extent of 40% only. (ii) The derivatives trade should be settled by a separate clearing corporation/clearing house. (iii) The definition of networth for the clearing member has been prescribed by SEBI, which inter alia would require a clearing member to maintain a liquid capital of Rs. 300

lakhs as a risk containment measure. (iv) The minimum value of the derivative contract shall not be less than Rs. I lakh and the Exchange would seek prior approval of SEBI before start of trading in the derivatives contract. (v) SEBI would also prescribe the initial margin requirement, exposure limits linked to capital adequacy and margin demands related to the risk of loss on positions. (vi) The exchange or clearing corporation willing to start derivatives trading or clearance and settlement of derivatives trades respectively, may apply to SEBI for approval. However, the derivatives trading could commence only after necessary amendment to the, Securities Contracts (Regulation) Act, 1956 are made to enable derivatives instruments to be treated as 'securities'. A Bill amending the Securities Contracts (Regulation) Act, 1956 to provide for trading in derivatives of securities is under consideration of the Parliament.

Trading in dematerialised security have seen tremendous growth. As reported by National Securities Depository Ltd., the first depository in the country, by the end of December, 1998, 291 securities have been admitted for dematerialisation and the total value of securities in dematerialised form is around Rs. 70,000 crores. 76 depository participants have commenced operations and are offering their Services from 610 centres in 160 cities across the country. The number of investor's accounts opened with these depository participants was about 1,70,000 by the end of December 1998. By 15th February, 1999, dematerialised trading will be compulsory for institutional investors in 304 scrips. In respect of 31 specified scrips trading by all investors has been made compulsory in the dematerialised form from January 4, 1999. Further, any investor who would have a net delivery obligation of more than 5000 shares, in any of 24 specified scrips in any settlement commencing from

January 4, 1999 could only do so in dematerialised form. The widespread network of bank branches are being utilised in order to extend depository services. Those banks which are connected with their branches electronically can offer this facility to the customers of different branches by connecting the depository participant computer system in their office with their central computer. To popularise the concept of dematerialisation steps are being taken towards spreading depository awareness among the various sections of the investing community across the country. The SEBI Board has accepted the recommendations that primary issues should be compulsorily made through the depository mode after a specified date. Approval has been granted for setting up a second depository, the Central Securities Depositories (Pvt.) Ltd. (CDS), which is being promoted by the Stock Exchange, Mumbai.

The Depositories (Appeal to the Central Government) Rules, 1998 was notified under Section 24 of the Depositories Act, 1996, on 28th July, 1998. Following this, any person aggrieved by an order of the SEBI Board under the Depositories Act, 1996 or the Regulations made thereunder, may prefer an appeal to the Central Government under Section 23 of the Act.

Several measures have been initiated to protect the integrity of the market and to make it more transparent and safe. The measures include an elaborate margining system, implementation of circuit filters and uniform intra day price bands etc. Institutional arrangements have also been strengthened for protecting small investors from defaults and financial failures of brokers and other market intermediaries with the setting up of Investors Protection Funds to compensate investors in case of default by brokers. Guidelines have also been issued by SEBI to all stock exchanges for setting up a Trade

Guarantee/Settlement Guarantee Fund in Stock Exchanges to provide for necessary resources in case of a default by a member broker in fulfilling his pay-in liabilities for ensuring timely completion of settlements. In order to bring about certainty in settlement of trades and thereby encourage long term investors, rolling settlement has been introduced in the dematerialised segment. Banks have been allowed to extend loans to corporates against shares held by them to enable such corporates to meet the promoters' contribution to the equity of new companies in anticipation of raising resources.

A new stock exchange, the Inter-Connected Stock Exchange of India Ltd. (ISE) has been set up, with its headquarters at Vashi, Mumbai, The ISE is promoted by 15 regional stock exchanges in the country and provides a member-broker of any of these stock exchanges an access into the national market segment, which would be in addition to the local trading segment available at present.

Details of audit objections pending in the Division for inclusion of the said report to enable the Department to fulfil the requirements of Public Account Committee contained in their 169th, Report: Nil

Economic Officer

A small write up on the action taken to implement the policy statement for the abatement of pollution as well as other environmental initiative taken by the Division: Nil

External commercial borrowing

Functions/working and set-up of the ECB division

The ECB Division headed by the Joint Secretary (ECB & CM) deals with examination and sanction of all external commercial borrowings proposals including commercial bank loans, buyer credit, suppliers credit, securitised instruments such as floating rat(notes and fixed rate bonds etc., credits from official export credits agencies and commercial borrowings from the private sector window of multilateral financial institutions such as International Finance Corporation (Washington), ADB, AFIC, CDC etc.

External Commercial Borrowings are being permitted by the Government for providing an additional source of funds for India Corporate for financing expansion of existing capacity and as well as for fresh investment, to augment the resources available domestically and at the same time, to take advantage of the relatively lower interest rate prevailing in the International market. External Commercial Borrowings are approved within annual ceiling, consistent with prudent debt management, keeping in view the balance of payments position and level of foreign exchange reserves.

Review of ECB guidelines for 1998-99

The existing ECB policy was further reviewed for 1998-99 in the light of the South East Asian Financial crises Economic Sanction and their impact on international markets and requirements of different sectors. The requirement of having a longer maturity for larger borrowing, cap on borrowing cost and restriction of end-use of ECB have helped in avoiding the difficulties, which some of the South East Asian countries are currently facing.

In view of the importance of infrastructure and export sectors in the overall economy, they would continue to be thrust areas in regard to ECB allocations for financial year 1998-99. After a careful review, the following changes have been made to the existing ECB guidelines.

(i) In case the company is not going for financial closures and the loan agreement is not taken on record within the validity period, the cooling off period for making a fresh application for ECB was reduced from 6 months to three months w.e.f. 30.4.98. Subsequently, this has been further reduced to one month with effect from 10.7.98.

(ii) It has been decided to permit ECB for project related rupee expenditure in all sectors subject to the following conditions:

(a) ECB raised for project related rupee expenditure must be brought into the country immediately.

(b) ECB raised for import of capital goods and services should be utilised at the earliest and corporates should strictly comply with RBI's extant guidelines on parking ECB outside till actual imports. RBI would be monitoring ECB proceeds parked outside.

(c) ECB raised is not permitted for investment in stock market or in real estate.

All other conditions with regard to the ECB eligibility for project finance i.e., exposure limit etc., will remain unchanged.

(iii) The limit under USD 3 million scheme would be raised to USD 5 million and RBI would, as before, be the approving authority.

(iv) The minimum maturity requirement under various ECB scheme has been revised as under:-

(a) USD 5 million scheme - 3 years simple maturity;

(b) ECBs upto USD 20 million - 3 years average maturity;

(c) ECB for 100% EOUs - 3 years average maturity for any amount

(d) ECB above USD 20 million - 5 years average maturity for all other sectors

(v) ECB eligibility under the scheme for exporters is raised to three times from the current two time, the average export performance during the last three years subject to a maximum of USD 100 million.

(vi) Average maturity requirement for ECB under the long term maturity window which are outside the ECB cap is reduced from 10 years to 8 years for ECBs upto USD 100 million and from 20 years to 16 years for ECBs upto USD 200 million for general corporate objectives.

(vii) In order to enable the corporates to hedge exchange rate risks, Domestic Rupee Denominated Structured Obligations would be permitted to be credit enhanced by International Banks/international Financial Institutions/ Joint Ventures Partners.

Status of ECB approvals

The total ECB approvals given to the corporates during 1996-97 and 1997-98 and 1998-99 (as on 07.12.98) under the normal window are as under:-

(USD Million)

Sector	*1996-97*	*1997-98*	*1998-99 (as on 07.12.98)*
Power	1874.529	3013.913	2069.994
Telecom	288.639	1492.530	75.250
Shipping	145.880	209.792	36.480
Civil Aviation	45.598	373.200	0.000
Petroleum & NG	783.109	229.860	40.000
Railways	144.000	179.000	15.000
Financial Institutions	1501.918	795.000	50.000
Ports, Roads etc.		61.590	0.000
Others	3797.076	2357.618	855.521
Total	8580.749	8712.503	3142.245

During 1998-99, the approval under USD 5 million scheme (formerly USD 3 million scheme) implemented vide RBI is USD 223.81 million (as on 31.10.98) and approval by Government under the Long Term Maturity Window (as on 04.12.98) is USD 418 million.

External finance division

Fund bank division

World bank group-IBRD and IDA

IBRD loans though non-concessional are available at relatively more favourable terms than commercial sources. The repayment period is at present 20 years, inclusive of 5 years grace period. The interest rate of IBRD loans is variable and revised semiannually in accordance with the Bank's own cost of borrowing funds. The current rate of interest in single currency loan is 5.5% and 6.18 % in multi-currency loan. The commitment charge on undisbursed balance is at present 0.75%. A rebate of 0.5% is however permitted for timely repayment of World Bank loans.

The total value of assistance extended by IBRD by way of loans for which agreements signed is US$ 20,200million (upto 31/12/1998). The commitments were against projects in various sectors like Agriculture, Irrigation, Power, Oil and Gas, Railways, Urban Development and Water Supply, Transport, Fertilizer, Industry, Telecommunications, etc.

The International Development Association was established in 1960 as an affiliate of the World Bank to make concessional long-term loans. IDA assistance to India began in June 1961 and has been an important component of the external assistance programme. IDA has extended credits to the Government of India for total value of US$ 24,223 million (up to 31/12/1998). This includes assistance in the form of non-project credits for industrial imports and credits for various sectors. The major sectors for which assistance is provided are Irrigation, Agriculture, Education, Health, Rural Development and Poverty Alleviation Projects.

IDA commitments which are known as "Credits" have a ten year grace period and must be repaid over 35 to 40 years depending on the borrowing country's credit worthiness. IDA credits carry no interest charge but a service charge of 0.5% is levied on the disbursed portion of the credit. Commitment charges on undisbursed balances are fixed every year upto a maximum of 0.5%. The credits to India approved upto 30th June 1987 are repayable in 50 years, inclusive of a grace period of 10 years, and those approved from 1st July 1987 are repayable in 35 years inclusive of a grace period of 10 years.

The World Bank assistance has been signed so far for the following projects during year 1998 (upto 31/12/1998): -

S. No.	*Name of the project*	*Amount of Assistance (US$ million)*	*Date of Agreement*
1	2	3	4
IBRD			
1.	States' Road Infrastructure Development Technical Assistance Project	51.50	15.01.1997
2.	Haryana State Electricity Board Reform & Restructuring Project	60.00	16.01.1998
3.	Coal Sector Rehabilitation Project	530.00	19.03.1998
4.	National Agriculture Technology Project	96.80	22.06.1998
5.	UP Diversified Agriculture Support Project	50.00	30.07.1998
	Total :	736.80	

IDA

1.	Third District Primary Education Project	152.00	23.02.1998
2.	UP Second Basic Education Project	59.40	03.03.1998
3.	Coal Sector Rehabilitation Project	2.00	19.03.1998
4.	National Agriculture Technology Project	100.00	22.06.1998
5.	UP Diversified Agriculture Support Project	79.90	30.07.1998
6.	Kerela Forestry Project	39.00	13.08.1998
7.	Orissa Health Systems Project	76.40	13.08.1998
8.	Rural Women Development and Empowerment Project	50.00	14.09.1998
	Total :	558.70	

India's subscription to the capital stock of IBRD

India holds a total of 44,795 shares in IBRD, each share being valued at US$ 120,635.

IDA-11 period has ended on June 30,1998. Estimated total amount for IDA-11 was about SDR 14.5 billion (US$ 22 billion). As far as India is concerned, total subscription for IDA-11 was Rs 2.33 crores. IDA-12 period from July 31,1998 to June 30,2001. Presently it is at discussion stage.

Multilateral investment guarantee agency

Multilateral Investment Guarantee Agency was established on April 12, 1988 with an objective of providing guarantees to encourage the flow of private foreign investment to less developed countries by mitigating political risks associated with projects. India has signed MIGA convention and has become a member of MIGA with effect from January 6, 1994. After subscription formalities, India has become 115th member of MIGA with 3048 shares. Discussions had been going on regarding increase in the MIGA capital in order to address the twin problems of exhaustion of underwriting capacity and problems of liquidity. The board has approved to increase the capital of MIGA by transfer of US$ 150 million net surplus of IBRD.

International finance corporation, Washington DC

The International Finance Corporation, Washington DC (IFC) was established in 1956 as an affiliate of the World Bank, but as separate entity, to promote the growth of private and joint enterprises which would contribute to the economic development of its member countries, Its capital resources are provided by 172 member countries, both developed and developing, which collectively determine its policies and activities. India is one of the founder members of IFC.

At present the total authorized share capital of IFC (W) is US$2.45 billion after the increase of US$ 1 billion in May 1992 and US$ 0.15 billion in December 1992. At the time of increase in the share capital, India was holding 45,976 shares of US$1000 each and was placed at 6th position along with Italy and Canada with voting power of 3.59%. Consequent upon the capital increase, India was allocated 35,366 additional shares, which were fully subscribed by her on 1.8.1997. India is now holding 81,342 shares of IFC. After the completion of subscription of IFC's 1991 capital increase, India's rank has remained the same i.e. 6th along with Italy, Canada and Russia, with a voting power of 3.43%.

IFC (W) provides, without government guarantee, both equity and loan capital to the private/joint sector enterprises in which it participates. The maturity period ranges from 7 to 12 years and interest rate vary from currency to currency and according to the circumstances of a particular transaction.

Earlier, any company seeking IFC investment was not required to seek ECB clearance. In December 1995, a decision was taken to treat IFC investments at par with other foreign investments/ borrowings. As a result, the company seeking IFC investment is now required to obtain the necessary Government of India approval i.e. ECB approvals for debt and /or FIPB/ SIA approval for equity investment (unless it is covered by the Automatic Approval Scheme) as the case may be.

IFC has been investing in Indian companies since 1959. They have, upto 30.06.1998, approved and signed investments in 120 companies for US$ 2.130 billion. The average investment for these 120 companies is not large, being US$ 17.75 million. The investments are mostly in the areas of steel, power, textiles, infrastructure and engineering companies.

During the financial year 1998-99 (1.4.98 to 30.11.98), IFC (W) has approved investment totalling to US$ 29.35 million details of which are given below: -

Approvals in financial year 1998-99 (upto 30.11.1998)

(US$ Million)

S. No.	*Name of the Company*	*Loan*	*Equity/ Quais-equity*	*Syndi-cation/ Underwriting*	*Total*
1.	Global Trust Bank	5.00	5.00	0.00	10.00
2.	IL&FS Ltd.	0.00	3.11	0.00	3.11
3.	Moser Baer	0.00	1.50	0.00	1.50
4.	RPG Communication	9.00	0.00	0.00	9.00
5.	IL&FS Venture	0.00	5.74	0.00	5.74

International monetary fund

The International Monetary Fund (IMF) is an organization of countries that seeks to promote international monetary cooperation and to facilitate the expansion of trade and economic development in all member countries. It was set up by an international treaty, its Article of Agreement drafted at conference of 44 nations held in Bretton Woods, New Hampshire in July 1944.

India is the founder member of the IMF and the Finance Minister is the ex-officio Governor on the Board of Governors of the IMF. India is represented in the IMF by an elected Executive Director who also represents three other countries namely: Bangladesh, Bhutan and Sri Lanka. India's current quota in the IMF is SDR 3055.5 million in the total Quota of SDR 135 billion.

India borrowed from IMF a total of SDR 1351.98 million under Compensatory and Contingency Financing Facility (CCFF), SDR 551.925 million under Credit Tranche and SDR 1656 million under Stand by Arrangement during January 1991 to June 1993.

Repayment terms: The principal amounts of credits drawn under First Credit Tranche Stand-by and CCFF are repayable in eight equal quarterly instalments starting three years and three months from the date of drawl and completed in the fifth year. The credit(s) are subject to a rate of interest (called "charge" in the IMF terms), which is applicable to the use of ordinary resources of the Fund determined from time to time. The rate of charge is comprised of a basic rate which is determined as a proportion (presently 109.6%) of SDR interest rate plus adjustment for burden sharing on account of overdue obligations to the Fund by certain members. The basic rate is determined on a weekly basis while the burden sharing portion is determined once a quarter. The rate of charge with necessary adjustments for burden sharing is payable each quarter. The current rate of charge on an average is about 3.98%.

Our repurchase obligations during 1998-99 are SDR 285.625 million. The balance amount will be paid up to

2000-2001. The charges are to be paid quarterly on the outstanding loan amount.

Interest receipts: During 1998-99 (up to December 1998) India received from IMF an interest of SDR 616,324 (Rs. 3,29,74,902)

G-24, commonwealth finance minister's meeting and annual fund bank meeting

The annual spring meeting of the World Bank and IMF were held on 16th-18^{th}April 1998 in Washington D.C. The Indian delegation was led by the Hon'ble Finance Minister Shri Yashwant Sinha. Other members of the delegation were Dr. Bimal Jalan, Governor, RBI, Shri M.S.Ahluwalia, Finance Secretary, Dr. Shankar N. Acharya, CEA, Shri V.Govindarajan, AS (FB) and Shri. Krishna Saini, PS to FM.

Finance Minister addressed the NRI and private sector on April 14, 1998 at NewYork. In Washington, FM attended the G-24, Interim Committee and Development Committee Meetings. Main issues of the Development Committee were (a) Implementing the major recommendations of the MDB task force, (b) Implementation of HIPC initiative. Besides, there were discussions on the paper on MIGA capital increase, implication of Asian Financial Crisis & WB Net Income Dynamics -with recent trends, in transfer of resources to developing countries. FM also held discussions regarding bilateral issues with his counterparts in Germany, Japan, Russia, USA, Netherlands, UK and France.

Annual Meeting Fund Bank and Commonwealth Finance ministers' and Senior Finance Officials Meeting, 1998 Finance Minister led the delegation attending the Commonwealth Finance Ministers' Meeting (September 21- October 1 1998.) in Ottawa, Canada; the Interim Committee/ Developing Committee and the Annual

Meetings of the IMF/ World Bank at Washington D.C. during October 2-7, 1998. The opportunity was utilised for meeting the NRIs and the potential investors in Toronto, Canada, New York and Boston, besides Washington in USA.

During his visit, besides attending the main meetings, FM also met the President of World Bank, MID of the IMF, President designate of the ADB, President of IFAD, Chief Executive Officer and Chairman of GEF and the Finance Ministers of South Africa, Malaysia, Sri Lanka, Russia, Indonesia, Belo-Russia, UK, Israel and the Deputy Secretary of Treasure of the United States. FM also attended the meeting of Finance Ministers of Group of 22; called by the United States.

Commonwealth Finance Minister's Meeting. The Commonwealth Finance Ministers meeting was held during 30th September - 1st October 1998 in Ottawa, Canada. A meeting of the senior officials on 2911, September 1998 preceded the meeting. In the Commonwealth Finance Ministers meeting, the Ministers of Commonwealth member countries discuss matter of mutual interest and the issues that are likely to come up at the following Interim and Development Committee meetings. The main topic for discussion during this meeting related to the Global Financial crisis, which started in Southeast Asia, and has caught up in several countries including Russia and Latin America. The Finance Ministers discussed the steps required for prevention and containment of the crisis and also the changes required in the International Financial System in the light of the recent events. In addition, issues relating to the Heavily Indebted Poor Countries (HIPCs) and that the steps needed to be taken to alleviate their problems were also discussed. The Commonwealth Finance Ministers approved a Statement on the Global Economic

Crisis-"Ottawa Commonwealth Statement on the Global Crisis" and issued a commonwealth covering various aspects that were discussed during the meeting.

Interim Committee and Development Committee Meeting.-The Interim Committee Meeting of the Board of Governors of the IMF met on October 4, 1998 followed by Development Committee on October 5, 1998. The Interim Committee discussed substantially the matters relating to the current world economic crisis. The actions to be taken for prevention and containment of crisis as also the question of strengthening the architecture of the International Financial System were discussed. The Interim Committee noted that India and China had maintained growth even in the backgrounds of economic crisis in many parts of the World. The most important aspect of FM's speech to Interim Committee was his Seven Point Program for tackling the global crisis. He also outlined on the International Financial Architecture. Annual Meetings of the IMF and the World Bank Governors were held during October 6-8, 1998. The President of the USA delivered the inaugural speech at the Board of Governors meeting on the 6th October 1998. FM spoke on the 7th October 1998.

Global environment facility

The GEF is a financial mechanism that provides grants and concessional funds to developing countries for projects and activities that aim to protect the global environment. India has been a leading developing country participant in the GEF since its inception in 1991 and has played a major role in shaping the restructuring of the GEF The first replenishment of the GEF has over US$ 2.0 billion to its core fund. India has pledged an amount of SDR 6.0 million towards the resources of first GEF replenishment.

So far GEF grant amounting to US$ 43.0 million for

5 projects under its pilot phase and US$ 69.0 million for two projects under first replenishment in India have been committed. The second replenishment of GEF is expected to have over US$ 2.75 billion to its core fund and India has pledged an amount of SDR 6.56 million towards its resources. The amount is payable in four annual equal instalments. The first instalment is payable by 15th January 1999, thereafter the instalments will be payable by 30th November of each year.

India has formed a permanent constituency from the six Asian seats in the GEF Executive Council, and Bangladesh, Sri Lanka, Nepal and Maldives have been grouped in our constituency. Government of India, successfully, hosted the first ever meeting of the GEF Assembly at New Delhi during April 1-3, 1998 which was preceded by NGOs consultation on March 29, 1998 and GEF Council meeting on March 30-31, 1998.

Kerela Forestry Project was signed with the World Bank on 13.8.98 for IDA assistance of US$39 million. The project is likely to be declared effective soon.

International fund for agriculture development

India is one of the original members of the International Fund for Agriculture Development (I FAD), a specialized agency of the United Nations. India is the largest contributor with an amount of US$ 26 million toward the resource of IFAD. Following are the payment made by india in previous instalments:-

Initial	US $	5 million
First replenishment	US $	6.5 million
Second replenishment	US $	6.5 million
Third replenishment	US $	8 million
Fourth replenishment	US $	9 million

The payments are made by the issue of non-negotiable

non-interest bearing rupee securities held in favour of IFAD by RBI. IFAD has so far committed an assistance of US$ 348.86 million for twelve projects in India. Of these 5 projects with an assistance of US$ 182.9 million were committed during 1978-83 and have since closed. The remaining 7 projects representing assistance of about US$ 180.10 million were committed during 1978-98. The one project, which is North Eastern Region Community Resource Management Project for Upland Areas for SDRs 16.55 million ($ 22.9 million) has been signed on 20.5.97. This project is yet to be declared effective.

Power sector

Power Sector is one of the most vital sectors for the development of country's economy. Assistance is provided by the World Bank and ADB for Power Projects in the country, including the projects for reform and restructuring of the state power sector.

The total World Bank, portfolio comprises of 12 projects with a total commitment of US$ 2796.1 million. Likewise the total ADB commitment of seven projects is US$ 1177.98 million.

During financial year 1997-98 disbursement from World Bank for power sector projects was to the tune of US$ 405.716 million and disbursement of ADB assistance was US$ 213.953 million respectively. The disbursements (cumulative) from World Bank/ ADB in power sector has been to the tune of US$ 1931.55 million and US $ 734.762 million respectively upto November 30, 1998.

ADB, Infrastructure, PMU, AC and EC division

Asian development bank

Asian development bank (ADB), an the international partnership of 56 member countries was established in 1966 with its headquarters in Manila, Phillipines. India is its founder member.

The Bank engaged in promoting economic and social progress of its developing member countries in the Asia and the Pacific region with principal functions as follows:

(i) to make loans and equity investments for the economic and social advancement of its developing member countries;

(ii) to provide technical assistance for the preparation and execution of development projects and programmes and advisory services.

(iii) to respond to the requests for assistance in coordinating development policies and plans of developing member countries.

(iv) to responds to the requests for assistance in coordinating development policies and plans of developing member countries.

India's subscription to the Bank's capital stock is the fourth largest of all the member countries. India started borrowing from ADB, Ordinary Capital Resources (OCR) in 1986 with a modest beginning of US$ 250 million. Over the years, the level of borrowing has increased significantly.

The Bank's lending has been to our Energy, Transport and Communications, Finance, Industry and non-fuel minerals, social Infrastructure and multisector. As of December 31, 1998, the Bank has cumulatively approved 41 loans amounting to US$ 7.042 billion. With 22 loans closed, the active portfolio comprises 23 loans, Cumulative disbursements till 31.12.1998 total about US$ 4.39 billion. A statement indicating the projects financed/ being financed by Asian Development Bank is annexed.

During the calendar year 1998 a loan for US$ 250 million was approved by the ADB Board for Rajasthan Urban Infrastructure Development Project. One project in the 1998 pipeline namely Surat Manor Tollway Project ($ 150 million) is scheduled for negotiations with the Bank in the last week of January 1999.

India's disbursement of Bank's assistance has been increasing steadily. During CY 1998, the total disbursement has reached a level of US$ 620.6 million, touching the disbursement level ratio at 32.95% as compared to only 24% during Bank's CY 1997. The improvement is due to continuing efforts of both the Government and the Bank, especially with regard to: improving quality of projects at entry (in terms of project design and readiness for initiating procurement); introduction of new standard bidding documents for tendering on aid-funded projects; rationalisation of the on-going portfolio through loan cancellation for slow moving projects; disintermediation by the Central Government of new loans to Central Public sector entities; advance release of funds to state governments and Bank's review of its imprest account operations.

India has contributed upto the end of 1998 Rs. 435.5 Lakhs in convertible currency to the Technical Assistance Special Fund (TASF) of the ADB. While the first four contributions amounting to Rs. 17 lakhs were wholly tied to their employment of Indian consultants, subsequent contributions until 1997 have been partially untied in as much as the ADB was permitted to use these funds to engage individual consultants from other developing countries, as well keeping with India's general policy towards economic and technical cooperation among the developing countries. The Government reviewed the policy and decided to make further contribution for 1997 and 1998 fully untied removing earlier restrictions for use of the contributions.

The Bank has extended technical assistance to India in addition to loan from its OCR window. The Bank's technical assistance support steadily increased from $ 0.6 m in 1988 to a cumulative Asian Development Bank (ADB), an international Partnership amount of $ 48.5 m as on 31st December, 1998. The technical assistance provided was inclusive of support for institutional strengthening, effective project implemention and policy reforms.

India continues to be well represented in the ADB. There are 49 Indian Professional Staff working in the Bank out of the total of 682 professional staff. Out of these, 9 are holding manager level or higher positions in the Bank. In addition, India continues to hold the position of Executive Director on the Board of Directors of the Bank. The Finance Minister, is India's Governor on the Board of Governors of Asian Development Bank and Secretary, Economic Affairs is the Alternate Governor.

The 31st Annual Meeting of the Board of Governors of ADB was held in Geneva, from 29th April to 1 st May 1998.

Total loans approved by ADB till 31.12.1998 under their public sector operations to India

	Loan No.	*Project*	*Amount (US $ m)*	*Date of approval*
(1)	778	Industrial Credit and Investment Corporation of India (closed)	100.00	3rd April 1986
(2)	798	North Madras Thermal Power1	50.00	18th Nov. 1986
(3)	842	Ports Development (closed)	87.60	24th Sept. 1987
(4)	975	Industrial Finance Corporation of India (closed)	150.00	24th Oct. 1989
(5)	855	Small and Medium Scale Industries (closed)	100.00	3rd Nov. 1987
(6)	954	Second Telecommunications (closed)	118.00	9th Feb. 1989
(7)	1081	Special Assistance (closed)	150.00	4th April 1991
(8)	857	Railways	190.00	10th Nov. 1987

	Loan No.	Project	Amount (US $ m)	Date of approval
(9)	886	Telecommunications (closed)	135.00	4th April 1988
(10)	907	Unchahar Thermal Power Ext.	160.00	29th Sept. 1988
(11)	918	Road Improvement	198.00	10th Nov. 1988
(12)	988	Rayalaseema Thermal Power (closed)	230.00	21 st Nov. 1989
(13)	1016	Second Ports (closed)	129.00	29th Mar. 1990
(14)	1029	Second North Madras Therm Power	200.00	30th Aug. 1990
(15)	1041	Second Road	250.00	30th Oct. 1990
(16)	1072	Second Industrial Credit and Investment Corporation of India Ltd. (closed)	120.00	18th Dec.1990
(17)	1117	Gandhar Field Development (closed)	267.00	14th Nov. 1991
(18)	1140	Second Railways	225.00	5th Dec. 1991
(19)	1148	Hydrocarbon Sector Programme (close)	250.00	17th Dec. 1991
(20)	1161	Power Efficiency Sector	250.00	26th Mar. 1992
(21)	1181	Coal Ports	285.00	27th Oct. 1992
(22)	1208	Financial Sector Programme (closed)	300.00	15th Dec. 1992
(23)	1212	Energy Conservation and Environment Improvement cancelled & closed)	39.30	17th Dec. 1992
(24)	1222	Gas Flaring Reduction (closed)	300.00	30th Mar. 1993
(25)	1274	National Highways	245.00	29th Nov. 1993
(26)	1279	Bombay-Vadodara Expressway Technical Assistance (cancelled and closed)	12.70	2nd Dec. 1993
(27)	1285	Gas Rehabilitation and Expansion (closed)	260.00	7th Dec. 1993
(28)	1343	Industrial Energy Efficiency	150.00	13th Dec. 1994
(29)	1408	Capital Market Program Loan	250.00	28th Nov.1995
(30)	1415	Karnataka Urban Infrastructure Development Project,	85.00	14th Dec.1995
(31)	1416	Karnataka Urban Infrastructure Development project (HDFC Loan)	20.00	14th Dec. 1995
(32)	1405	Power Transmission Sector Project	275.00	16th Nov. 1995

(33)	1465	Renewable Energy Development Private Sector Infras. Facility	100. 00	26th Sept. 1996
(34)	1480	ICICI	150.00	7th Nov. 1996
(35)	1481	IFCI	100.00	7th Nov. 1996
(36)	1482	SCICI	50.00	7th Nov. 1996
(37)	1495	Rural Telecom (cancelled and closed)	113.00	28th Nov. 1996
(38)	1506	Gujarat Public Sector Resource Management Programme	250.00	18th Nov. 1996
(39)	1549	Housing Finance (NHB)	100.00	26th Sept. 1997
(40)	1550	Housing Finance (HUDCO)	100.00	26th Sept. 1997
(41)	1551	Housing Finance (HDFC)	100.00	26th Sept. 1997
(42)	1556	Mumbai Port Trust	97.80	26th Sept. 1997
(43)	1557	Chennai Port Trust	15.20	26th Sept. 1997
(44)	1591	LPG Terminal	150.00	16th Dec. 1997
(45)		Rajasthan Urban Infrastructure Development Project	250.00	3rd Dec.1998
		Total	$7257.600	
		Total Loans 45	Closed 18 Cancelled 4	
		On-going/approved 23		

U.S.A.

USA has been extending economic assistance to India since 1951. US Development Assistance is channelised through US Agency for International Development (USAID). Presently, US development assistance is received in the form of grant and is available as project assistance.

During 1998-99 (upto Sept. 98), five Amendatory Agreements obligating Development Assistance (Grant) of US $ 24.22 million has been signed as compared to US $ 30.70 million obligated during 1997-98.

USAID has disbursed Development Assistance of US $ 25.00 million during 1998-99 (upto Nov. 98) as compared to US $ 27.32 million disbursed in 1997-98. Aid disbursed through budget during the corresponding period of 1997-98 and 1998-99 was US $ 14.00 million and US $ 13.04 million respectively.

Under PL-480 (Title.II) assistance, the US has been donating agricultural commodities as outright grant. Total disbursement (including ocean freight) under Title.II programme during 1998-99 (upto Sept. 98) is US $ 78.09 million as compared to US $ 59.18 million in 1997-98.

Indo-US economic & commercial sub-commission

The meeting of the Indo-US Economic & Commercial Sub-Commission was scheduled to be held at New Delhi during June-July, 1998. However, the meeting could not be held due to lack of response from US side (due to sanctions).

Assistance from ford foundation

The Ford Foundation has been extending grant assistance to various NGOs/institutions in India since 1952. The Ford Foundation's assistance is mainly extended to NGOs/ educational institutions for projects in the areas of health, rural development, water resources, social sector, education and culture etc. Sixty three project proposals involving grant of US $ 9.41 million have been cleared during 1998-99 (upto Dec. 98) as compared to $ 6.97 million of grant cleared in 1997-98.

Assistance from the international development research centre (IDRC) of canada

The IDRC assistance are extended to the Government institutions/NGOs for projects, in the field of agriculture, food, health and family welfare, environmental sciences etc. Seven Project proposals involving grant of C $ 1.407 million have been cleared during 1998-99 (upto Dec. 98) as compared to four proposals involving grant of $ 0.44 million approved in 1997-98.

Rockefeller foundation

During 1998-99 (upto Dec. 98), Sixteen proposals involving grant of US $ 0.67 million of Rockfeller

Foundation have been cleared as compared to eight proposals involving grant of US $ 0.47 million cleared in 1997-98.

Canada

The Canadian assistance is extended entirely in the form of grant since 1st April, 1986. The assistance is provided by Canada through its agency, namely, Canadian International Development Agency (CIDA). There are at present 14 CIDA assisted on-going Bilateral Projects. These include Rajasthan Agricultural Drainage Research Project, Tree Growers Cooperative Project, India Canada Environment Facility Project, Capacity Development of Revenue Administration Project and Energy Infrastructure Services Project. All on-going projects continued to get assistance from CIDA.

A Memorandum of Understanding was signed on 16-101998 for Boiler Emission Upgrade project. A total grant assistance of C$ 2.5 million would be extended by CIDA under this project.

During 1998-99, CIDA disbursed grant assistance of C$ 6.906 million upto 14-09-1998.

Infrastructure section

Description of the infrastructure section

The Infrastructure Section is a newly created Section (vide order dated 14th August, 1995). The Section is headed by a Joint Secretary (INF&ADB) who is assisted by a Director, a Deputy Director and a Section Officer.

Broad Function

Infrastructure Section has the sectorial charge of Railways, Telecommunications, Roads, Ports and Civil Aviation. It examines and processes policy issues on these sectors in consultation with other Divisions and Departments in the Ministry. It also handles Cabinet/COS notes, Telecom-Commission papers and PIB/EFC proposals pertaining to these sectors.

Roads

India has the third largest road network in the World. Out of the total road network the National Highways account for 38,445 Kms.. The National Highways Act has been amended to enable levy of a toll on selected sections of National Highways so that private participation in road construction on a Build-Operate-Transfer (BOT) basis is facilitated. Also, guidelines on private sector participation in the road sector has been announced.

Recently Government of India has constituted Task Force on Infrastructure under the Chairmanship of Deputy Chairman, Planning Commission. The Task Force has been mandated to evolve strategies for implementation of six lane expressways of 7,000 Kms. length having North-South and East-West corridors and four-laning of National Highways.

Moreover, the Model Concession Agreement for four-laning highway projects on BOT basis would soon be finalised by NHAI/ MOST

Civil aviation

Ministry of Civil Aviation have announced National Policy on airports. The major issues of this sector include restructuring of Indian Airlines and upgradation of airport infrastructure. Recently constituted Task Force on Infrastructure has also been given the responsibility to identify and implement five World Class International Airport. A Sub-committee has also been constituted to examine the various aspects of a comprehensive airport policy with a view to establishing World Class International Airports with 100% private participation.

Telecommunication

India has a telecommunication network of over 22,53(telephone exchanges, with a capacity of 189.1 lakh lines and 158.1 lakh working connections as on 31.12.1997. In pursuance of the National Telecom Policy 1994 DOT has permitted entry of private sector in manufacturing basic/ cellular mobile telephone services and other value added services. In order to ensure fair competition and to protect the interests of consumers, Government has set up a statutory Telecom Regulatory Authority of India. Recently, Government of India has constituted a Group on Telecommunications (GOT) under the Chairmanship of Deputy Chairman, Planning Commission. The GOT would recommend on proposed New Telecom Policy, issues relating to the existing licenses of basic and cellular services and issues relating to TRAI.

Ports

India has 11 major ports, which handle around 90 percent of the sea borne trade. These are managed by Port Trusts under the Central Government. As against the total capacity of 217.3 million tonnes on March 31, 1997, major ports handled 227.3 million tonnes in 1996-97. Guidelines have been issued regarding private investment in the port sector. A Tariff Authority for Major Ports (TAMP) set up under the Major Port Trusts Act, 1963 to fix and revise various port charges to be collected by private providers of port facilities has started functioning from April, 1997.

Railway

Indian Railways have a network of 62,725 Km. Electrified p networks of 13,517 Km. length account for 21.5% of the total route kilometer. The Railways employ about 16 lakh employees. Overall resource stringency has led to a decline in capital from the Gene Exchequer to the Railways from 42 percent of the outlay in the Seventh Plan to 23 percent during the Eighth Plan.

Project management unit

Power Management Unit is concerned effective monitoring of the progress of implementation of the externally aided project (EAPs). It undertakes regular review d disbursements and deals, interalia, with measures for adequate -provisioning for externally aided projects, release of Additional Central Assistance (ACA) as 100% additionally, advance release of ACA to the States and procurement related issues.

During the current year (as on 31.12.1998), the total aid utilisation (provisional) on Govt. & Non-Govt. account was Rs.8199.73 crore against the corresponding figure of Rs.7042.78 C crore during the last year. As regards the ACA to the States/UTs Rs.3089 crore was released upto 31.12.1998, against the corresponding figure of Rs.3346 crore during the last year. In addition, during 1998-99, an advance ACA of Rs.775 crore was released to the State.

To disseminate world Bank procurement procedures in India, four two week seminars on procurement for officials from State/Ministries/project Authorities have been conducted during 1998-99. Seminars on 'Procurement of Goods' were held at National Institute of Financial Management, Faridabad in May, 1998 & November-December, 1998 and seminars on 'Procurement of a Works' were held at Administrative Staff College of India (ASCI) in April 1998, June 1998 and October, 1998.

In order to encourage better quality bids and to educate bidders/suppliers on World Bank Procurement & Consultant guidelines & Standard Bidding documents a seminar was organised c through ASCI at Chennai in May, 1998.

In order to operationalise the External Assistance Monitoring Information System (EAMIS) in the 9 select State (Andhra Pradesh, Karnataka, Madhya Pradesh, Maharashtra, Orissa, Rajasthan, Tamil Nadu, Uttar Pradesh and West Bengal) and project Monitoring Cells

(PMCs) in select Ministries (Agriculture, Health & Family Welfare, Power, Surface Transport and Urban Development), the State and Ministry sites were in the process of being connected to the Master DEA Server. For proper data capturing and data transmission, training courses on the EAMIS were conducted at NIFM, Faridabad in September 21-24, 1998 & November 16-19, 1998 and at ASCI, Hyderabad on December 28-31, 1998.

UNDP assistance to india

UNDP-background

United Nations Development Programme (UNDP) is the largest source of development cooperation in the UN System. It has 136 offices worldwide and each office is headed by a Resident Representative, who is also designated by UN Secretary-General as the United Nations Resident Coordinator.

The policy making body for UNDP is 36 member-UNDP Executive Board that came into being in 1994. India is one of the elected members of Board and has been elected Vice-President for the year 1)98. Before that, there was a Governing Council in place of Executive Board.

Funds Allocation

UNDP derives the funds from voluntary contributions from various donor countries. India contributes approximately US $ 4.38 million per year to UNDP since 1993. GOI in 1997 made an enhanced contribution of US $4.45 million. For 1998, we have pledged the contribution of US $ 4.5 million. India is the largest single contributor to UNDP core resources from amongst the 'developing countries.

UNDP's approach to development

The UNDP's approach has shifted and as per UN mandate, UNDP assistance should be based on the sustainable human development which encompasses a variety of dimensions including poverty elimination, good governance, building equity, employment, empowerment and environmental regeneration.

UNDP assistance to india

India has been a net recipient of UNDP assistance, which increased from US $ 50,000 in the first cycle (72-76) to US $ 156 million in the fifth cycle (92-96). With this allocation of US $ 156 million, India was the third largest beneficiary of UNDP assistance after China and Bangladesh during the fifth programming cycle.

UNDP has now changed its approach from project to programme. Instead of several scattered projects across the country, UNDP will now concentrate on few programmes. According to the new allocation, 60% of the core resources will be allocated to the countries at the beginning of the programme cycle. Further allocation which may vary from 0% to 100% of the initial allocation may be provided after monitoring the progress and quality of implementation of the programmes.

At present, there are 67 operational projects and two programmes totaling US $ 153 million. Around 72% of this is under National Execution followed by UNDP which is executing 13% of the total programmes and UNDDSMS which is executing around 6% of the programme. National Execution appears to have come of age in India and the NEX implementation rates has stabilized at around the same level as those for the agencies (viz., 60%). The areas in which UNDP assistance has been received range from research and development in science & technology to agricultural cooperation, transport and communication, environment, industry etc.

Programme development for CP-V

The Government of India, in close cooperation with

UNDP Country Office, has formulated the CCF (1997-2001). In India, it is felt that there is a strong case for approaching UNDP's SHD mandate through building on past or ongoing programme initiatives especially in the area of technology management, which has been delivering good results. Interventions should as far as possible, focus on areas where there is a stated demand among end users.

Since 1994, when SHD was adopted as the main goal of UNDP a process has been underway to re-orient the Country Programme in accordance with this new mandate and the needs and opportunities in this regard in the country. A series of high-level programmes and policy review meetings during the last two years has prepared the base for more SHD oriented programmes under the Country Programme/Country Cooperation Framework (1997-2001). CCF-I focuses on growth with equity with poverty alleviation and human development as central concerns. The CCF-I goals are to be achieved through the following ten mutually reinforcing programmes in the thematic areas of employment and sustainable livelihood, access to basic services, management of development and sustainable development with a focus on technology upgradation and capacity building as a means to achieving the objectives.

The ten programmes are:

Food and Nutrition Security Programme	-	US $ 13.5 million
Primary Education Support Programme	-	US.$ 9 million
Health Support Programme	-	-
Economic Reforms Support Programme	-	-
Capacity Building Programme	-	-
Community-Based Pro-Poor Initiatives	-	US $ 13 million

Technology Programme - US $ 10.5 million

Energy Programme - US $ 4.2 million

Environment Programme - US $ 9 million

PSD on Leather - US $ 7 million

PSD on Fibers & Handicrafts - US $ 7 million

PSD on Village & Small Industries - US $ 5.5 million

UNDP Executive Board has approved CCF-I document in its second Regular Session in March, 1997. The total resources likely to be available for CCF-I Programme cycle (1997-2001) will be in order of US $ 167 million.

Under CCF-I, so far we had signed four programme support documents, viz., Technology management Support Programme, Community-based Pro-poor Initiatives, Food & Nutrition Security Support and Environment Support Programme and Energy programme. Besides these 3 PSDs on Leather, Fibres and Handicrafts sectors and Village & Small Industries have been signed under the Umbrella Programme of Small Industries Development & Employment (SIDE). We have also signed 12 sub-programmes so far.

Exchange Control (EC)

Overseas investment by Indian Companies

Reserve bank has been empowered to consider proposals for Indian direct investment abroad in all countries under its Fast Track Route where such investment does not exceed USD 15 million. In the case of rupee investment in Nepal and Bhutan, the ceiling has been raised to Rs.60 crores. In case of investment in the field of Software by Indian software companies whose cumulative foreign exchange earnings for previous three years have been more than USD 25 million. Blanket approval by Reserve Bank of India will be given to investment abroad upto 50% of their forex earnings.

Foreign investments in India

General permission has been granted in respect of investment by NRIs/OCBs in priority industries under 100% scheme as also under 24% and 51 % schemes.

EEFC accounts

Exporters and other recipients of foreign exchange have been permitted to retain upto 50% of their foreign exchange receipts (70% in the case of 100% Export Oriented Units and Units in Hardware/Software Technology Parks) in their Exchange Earner's foreign Currency (EEFC) accounts with banks, which can be utilised by the account holders for all trade and business related purposes as also for certain other approved purposes.

Exports

Exporters have been given general permission to accept advance payment from their overseas customers and in case they failed to meet the contracted obligation they can refund the advance without approaching the Reserve Bank.

Hedging through International commodity exchanges

It has been decided to allow Indian Corporates having genuine underlying exposure to access International Commodity Exchanges for hedging of their commodity price risk.

Advance payments against imports

Authorised dealers have been permitted to allow advance remittances towards cost of imports upto USD 15,000/-.

Forward contracts

ADs have been permitted to provide forward cover to FIIs for their investment in equity and debt instruments. NRIs/OCBs for their equity investment and to NRIs for their FCNR/NRE balances.

International Credit Cards (ICCs)

Residents in India have been permitted to hold international Credit Cards which can be used by them either in India or abroad subject to drawals of foreign exchange to the exchange entitlement of the card holder for travel abroad for various purposes or for making personal payments. Full-fledged money changers have also been permitted to sell exchange for travel purposes against ICC.

Credit by Indian Banks abroad

Indian banks have been permitted to extend buyer's credit/ acceptance finance to overseas customers of Indian exporters to provide a boost to export of goods and services from India. Indian banks have also been permitted to extend fund/non-fund based facilities to joint ventures and wholly owned subsidiaries abroad of Indian companies.

EEC division

Functions and organisational set up of EEC division

EEC Division deals with bilateral assistance from European countries. The division is also territorially in charge of all European countries except the CIS countries. Germany, UK, European Commission, Netherlands, France, Italy, Sweden, Denmark, Switzerland and Belgium offer official development assistance to India. The division acts as a nodal agency for coordinating work relating to development cooperation right from the stage of identification of projects to the final stage of utilising the assistance extended for these projects. The work involved includes framing targets for disbursements made by donor agencies, negotiating aid packages at inter governmental talks leading to the conclusion of aid agreements, allocation of aid to Central/State Departments. Public Sector Undertakings, monitoring technical assistance projects including training programmes and initiating procedural reforms relating to bilateral development cooperation when required.

Performance

As against a disbursement target of Rs. 1212.92 crores (RE 1997-98): the EEC Division achieved a disbursement of Rs. 1407.42 crores during 1997-98. The amount routed through the Govt. budget was Rs. 1069.88 crores. The Revised Estimate for disbursement for 1998-99 is Rs. 1116.99 crores (through budget -Rs. 757.99 crores and the non Govt. portion Rs. 359.00 crores)

Netherlands

1. Netherlands has been extending economic assistance to India since 1962-63 in the form of General Purpose Credits, debit relief assistance, suppliers credits (Financial Export Credits) and grants. Grant is extended mainly for local cost expenditure and technical assistance.

2. The major sectors in which the Netherlands assistance is received are Environment, Drinking Water Supply, Irrigation and Water Transport.

3. The Netherlands Govt. provides assistance under an annual cashceiling. Upto 1991, this commitment amounted to Dfl 200 million, which was divided into loans and grants on roughly, 50:50 basis. The loans were repayable in 30 years with 8 years, grace period and carried an interest rate of 2.5% per annum. From; 1992 onwards, the Netherlands assistance is completely in the form of grants and balance against earlier loan commitments will be disbursed out of grant funds. In the past the amount available for disbursements annually was DFL 130 million.

4. The disbursement during 1997-98 was Dfl 64.42 million (equivalent of Rs. 122.23 Crores approx.) including Gujarat Health Care Project (ORET) of DFL 14.94 million. During 1997-98 and 1998-99 the Netherlands Govt. has not extend macro-economic support During 1998-99 (April - December) the disbursement has been DFL 22.426 million (equivalent Rs. 48.47-crores).

5. The Netherlands Govt. also provides ORET grants to Govt. of India to subsidises costs of import of selected capital goods from the Netherlands upto 40% of the total cost. There is a similar scheme called MILJEV which can be used while importing items that have a positive contribution to projection of environment.

European community (EC)

1. The EC has been extending economic assistance to India, since 1976. The EC assistance to India is entirely in the form of grant and can be used to finance the rupee as well as foreign exchange cost of identified projects. In the area of Development Cooperation, the cumulative total of EC's financial and technical' assistance since 1976 is around ECU 1.60 billion.

2. Presently, EC assistance is being provided to projects in the sectors of Watershed Management, Irrigation, Forestry, Education and Health. There is an ongoing Education Sector Programme (District Primary Education Project) with a total contribution of ECU 150 million. In 1996-97, a commitment of ECU 200 million, approximately Rs. 900 crores has been made for the Health sector programme.

3. During the Indo-EC Sub commission meeting held in, Nov., 97 it was agreed that beneficiaries should

be deprived groups and that projects should work with the involvement of the NGOs. Reinforcing the policies in the social sector through sector programmes and working with NGOs in individual projects would constitute the new EC development strategy.

4. The EC has also given assistance under EC food aid for Operation Flood III and other programmes. The food aid was, provided in the form of butter oil and skimmed milk powder for Operation Flood III.

5. The disbursement of EC assistance in respect of ongoing development cooperation was ECU 70.761 million during 1996-97 and. ECU 52;984 million.

Belgium

1. Belgium has been extending financial assistance to India since 1962-63. The assistance was in the form of supplier's credit upto 1965-66. Since 1966-67, Govt. to Govt. credits in the form of project and non-project assistance for import of capital goods and commodities were also made available. Since 1985, the Belgian assistance has been on mixed financing pattern.

2. In February, 98 Belgian Government have agreed to extend assistance for the installation of a Medical Cyclotron in Calcutta. The soft loan will cover 45.17% of the total project cost Rs. 31.8 crores.

U.K.

India is the largest recipient of British development assistance. The bilateral assistance from 1975 onwards comes fully in the form of Grants. The aid agency of the U.K. is Department for International Development which is a part of the Foreign & Commonwealth Office and is headed by a Minister for Overseas Development.

The aid from U.K. is used for mutually agreed projects in various sectors viz. Education, Slum Improvement, Health and Family Welfare, Coal, Energy Efficiency (Power) and Forestry. The assistance comes in the following forms :-

(a) Tied Grant Assistance:- for goods and services of British origin for specific projects.

(b) Local Costs Grant:- which are given at present mainly for poverty alleviation and environment improvement programmes.

(c) Technical Assistance Grant:- through which project related and general consultancies, training and imports are financed.

(d) Assistance under Aid and Trade Provision (ATP) Scheme :- which helps British companies to win contracts in developing countries and

(e) Commonwealth Development Cooperation (CDC) separately invests in India on the lines of IFC (W) and DEC.

The bilateral development cooperation, with UK is based on genuinely liberal principles guiding ODA assistance which has as its major objective alleviation of poverty. U.K. is our largest grant donor and in increasing part of this aid goes for local cost expenditure in social sector projects.

During 1998-99 Grant agreement worth Pds. 15 min. was i signed for Haryana Power Sector Reforms under Technical Cooperation.

France

French Credit is in the form of mixed credit of treasury loan and export credit of OECD consensus rates of interest. The assistance is tied to projects which involve imports of French goods and services. The total French

Assistance from April 1968 to March 1998 amounted to FF 15216.17 in the form of grant and mixed

Achievements/performance upto last year:

In 1997-98 (April 1997 to March'98) the indo-French Financial Protocol 1997 was signed on 25.1.1998 between the two Govts. Through this Protocol the French Govt. has committed to finance FF 125 million (Rs. 92.63 crore) in the sectors of mines, infrastructure, health, agriculture, water supply etc. The interest rate of @ 0.47% p.a. on the soft treasury loan is an all time low as compared to the earlier Protocols signed. The Finance Minister visited France on 2-3 September, 1997 and subsequently, the French Finance Minister visited India on 6th January, 1998. The exchange of high level visits has enhanced the level of cooperation and understanding between the two countries. Total disbursements in respect of French external assistance (mixed credit & grants) routed through Govt. of India account during FY 1997-98 were Rs.199.12 crore against the revised target of Rs. 182.62 crore.

Performance/achievements during the year under review

The Indo-French Financial Protocol, 1998 was signed on 23.11.1998 for an amount of FF 68.8 million (Rs. 51 crore Approx.) This Protocol was signed between MOS (Finance) and the French Minister for Foreign Trade during the latter's visit to India. Priority sectors identified by the French Govt. for future Protocols are water, Railway equipment, Agro-food projects and Environment. As regards disbursement of 1998-99 (upto Dec. 1998) an amount of FF 52.592 million (Rs. 37.76 crore) has been disbursed against the revised estimates of FF 63.80 million (Rs. 45 crore).

Denmark

Danish aid at present is mainly in the form or grant available for tied imports related to specific projects and also-for local cost projects. Upto March 1998 a total of DKK 5774.74 million has been committed by Denmark which included loan as well as grant.-

Achievements/performance upto last year :- During 97-98 (April 97 to March'98) Govt. of Denmark has committed to provide DKK 158.12 million grant (Rs. 87.22 crore) through new agreements that were signed in the field of health, non-conventional energy sources and agriculture sector. Total disbursements on account of Danish external assistance (loans & grants) routed through Govt. of India account during the FY 97-98 were Rs. 36.65 crore as against the revised target of Rs. 3.6.73 crores.

Performance/achievements during the year under review :Upto Dec. 1998 Govt. of India have signed one grant agreement with Govt. of Denmark in the Health Sector (Eradication of Leprosy, Phase III) for DKK 76.4 million (Rs. 43.89 crores). Against a revised estimate of Rs. 13 crore for 98-99, disbursements to the tune of Rs. 12.62 crores have been received upto Dec'98 from Govt. of Denmark in the GOI account.

Italy

Italian assistance is available for specific projects and is generally tied to the financing of Italian goods and services.

During the Indo-Italian cooperation meeting of June 1996, the Italian side committed soft loan upto an overall amount of Lire 100 billion out of which Lire 50 billion would be devoted towards establishing an open credit line with NSIC for financing supplies of capital goods and related technical assistance for the development of the Indian small and medium enterprises. The remaining amount can be used for financing projects in the priority sectors of (a) and Water Treatment, (b) Environmental

Protection and Infrastructure with positive Environmental Impact and (c) Medium Enterprises Development. The soft loan will be highly concessional (80% grant element).

Under the general Technical Cooperation Agreement concluded in 1981, Italy had also agreed to provide technical assistance grants on tied basis. However, due to a substantial reduction in the Italian funds legislated by the Italian Parliament, no significant resources are being made available for financing projects through grants.

Switzerland

1. The Government of Switzerland has been providing assistance to India since 1964. Currently, Swiss aid is available both for capital goods imports and for local costs/technical assistance. The former is being funded through a mixed financing line and the latter through grants which are channelised through the Swiss Agency for Development Cooperation (SDC).

2. The line of mixed financing, the agreement for which was signed on 24.6.91 has a Swiss Government contribution of 40% grant and 60% export credit given by a consortium of Swiss Banks and provides 100% coverage of the contract value. It was valid upto June, 1998 but is likely to be extended to accommodate Neriyamanglam Hydroelectric project.

Swedish assistance

India has been a recipient of Swedish assistance since 1964 although Sweden joined the Aid India Consortium as a full member only in 1969. The terms of Swedish assistance have become progressively softer over the years. After 1976, Swedish assistance is in the form of a 100% grant and is mainly focused on the social sector and the energy sector. In addition to grant assistance, Swedish Government, has extended soft loans, for large power sector projects. Earlier, Sweden used to allocate 0.91 per cent of its GDP for development cooperation. This was reduced to 0.7% of its GDP in the last year. The aim, however, is to restore the level to 1 percent of the GNP as soon as the Swedish economy so permits. Despite the cut in the Swedish aid budget, taking into account SIDA grant aid concessional credits available from other Swedish Organisations, India becomes the largest recipient of Swedish assistance not only among the Asian countries but also among African and Latin American countries.

Future Strategy for Indo-Swedish Development Cooperation (1997-1999) : Future strategy for Indo-Swedish Development Cooperation in three year period of 1997-1999 covered by the new Development Cooperation Agreement dated 28.11.96 focuses on poverty alleviation and infrastructure :-

(a) The broad areas of Swedish assistance are :-

(i) poverty oriented projects and programmes in the primary education and health sectors;

(ii) environment, including natural resources management and the modern/industrial/urban sector;

(iii) energy saving and other areas of importance to more efficient use of energy resources;

(iv) consultancy fund;

(v) activities aimed at encouraging sharing of experiences and expertise between India and Sweden.

(b) Since there is a high level of skills and knowledge that are to be found in both India and Sweden, it was agreed that a gradually increasing amount should be used to stimulate the exchange of experiences and joint development of know-how between India and Sweden. This can be done within the framework of research cooperation, exchange of experts, contract financing, courses, and through cooperation between India and Swedish NGOs. The Indian side emphasised that they would like the maximum amount to be allocated under the country frame for projects where the funds are roted through the Government of India budget, especially for local cost projects.

(c) Sweden primarily concentrates its assistance in the States of Rajasthan, Tamil Nadu, Orissa and Himachal Pradesh. During the negotiations held in November, 1996 the India side indicated that Swedish support should be extended as far as possible to more number of States. This was again discussed during Annual Review Meeting held in February, 1998 and it was agreed that a certain geographical spread would be considered by Embassy while initiating and identifying new projects.

(d) Since the strategy for Swedish assistance was finalised only in November, 1996, no new projects were being considered by the Swedish Government for the last 2-3 years. Now that the strategy has been finalised, project proposals have been called from the various administrative Ministries/Departments and State Governments.

Allocations and disbursements during 1997-98

For the year 1997 and 1998 IDF pledge was of the order of SEK, 300 million per year. During 1997-98, however, total, disbursement of SIDA funds through GOI budget was of the order, of Rs. 45.23 crores, as against a budget estimate of As. 65 crores. Disbursement upto Dec.,98 (as in the current Financial year 98-99) is Rs. 30/28 crores.

Norwegian assistance

Assistance extended by the Norwegian Government is through the Norwegian Agency for Development Cooperation (NORAD). Norwegian assistance is in the form of a grant.

Areas of cooperation

Earlier Norwegian assistance was concentrated in the social sectors. In 1990, the Norwegian Government took a decision to gradually reduce aid to India and to shift their focus on the industriai sector. They continue to give priority to issue relating to the development of women and environment.

Norwegian aid policy for India

The policy of the Norwegian Government on Aid to India has undergone radical change since 1991-92. Previously, approximately 60 per cent of the aid allocated to India was oriented towards social sectors and for eradication of poverty. However, they have now taken a decision to with draw from these sectors and only concentrate, on institutional cooperation and promotion of their industrial sector. They would, however, continue their assistance in the environment, sector and for the development of women. The volume of Norwegian aid to India has shrunk to almost one third of what it used to be in, 1990. As compared to NOK 140 million in 1990 it was NOK 45 million in 1995. Under Norway's new aid policy India no longer enjoys the status of a programme country after 1995. From 1996, no allocations are being made for India under the country programme. All commitments made by the Norwegian Government under the country programme on projects for which agreements, have already been signed will be fulfilled.

Norway is moving away from the country framework i.e. they will not earmark funds country wise but will have global funds which can be accessed by all countries with suitable projects.

Recently, we have been informed by the Norwegian Government that with regard to the new guidelines for Development Cooperation with adopted by Norwegian Parliament, Education, Child labour India and Environment will be the priority areas. Allocations to India, would be financed by NORAD's Regional Fund for Asia. Productive Sector Projects will be gradually phased out. The global fund for Industrial Development Cooperation will be open for India comprising of financing of mixed credit schemes and Investment support.

Allocations And disbursements during 1997-98

No amount was pledged at the of since 1996. However, NOK 30.923 million was disbursed in 1997-98 through the Budget of GO$ in DEA for local cost expenditure. The rest was disbursed directly under the country programme.

Disbursement upto Dec'98 (as in the current financial year 98-99) is 11.36 crores.

Federal republic of germany

Germany is India's largest bilateral European donor. For the year 1997-98, the German Govt. had committed an amount of D 862.5 M as bilateral assistance (including technical assistance The German Govt. has not yet made any commitment for financial assistance during 1998-99 as the German Govt. cancelled the A Talks scheduled in May 1998 in response to India's nuclear test Recently the German Govt. has committed an amount of DM 22.5 M for technically assisted projects for 1998.

The total aid disbursement during 1998-99 till December 1998 is DM 244.58 million (excluding TC). This amount also includes DM 135.34 M which has been disbursed directly to the implementing agencies by KFW in respect of disintermediated projects. The aid disbursement (excluding TC) during 1997-98 was DM 261.28 (Rs, 554.17 crores) against a target of DM 186.98 M.

The following project agreement for which commitments were made in the past by the German Govt. have been concluded during the current financial year

		Amount	*Dt. of Sign in*
(i)	Fertiliser Sector programme	DM 70 M	11.9.98
(ii)	Adivasi Dev. Prog. (NABARD)	DM 28 M	24.11.98
(iii)	Minor Irrigation Prog. Maharashtra	DM 45 M	30.12.98
(iv)	HDFC-III	DM 30 M	24.11.98

F.T. division

Functions of FT division

The main function of this Division is to render advice to the Government of India in particular to the Ministry of Commerce on matters relating to Foreign Trade. It is, however, directly involved in questions of Bilateral Trade Agreements with East European countries, since in these cases there are special rupee payment agreements. This Division is also responsible for matters relating to grant or economic assistance and export credits to other Countries as also Indian ventures abroad. In addition, matters relating to import of petroleum and African Development Bank are handled in this division. FT Division also looks after the work connected with bilateral technical assistance either received from Foreign Countries or extended by India to other countries (including Bangladesh).

This Division is also handling all Bilateral Trade and

Economic matters concerning Asian & African countries. Work Trade Organisation is also being dealt with. This division is also responsible towards policy matters related to multilateral trade blocks like SAARC, SAPTA, Bangkok Agreement, ASEAN, APEC etc. They are the nodal point for colombo Plan, CFTC (Commonwealth Fund for Technical Cooperation) and all technical training coming from DFP, Singapore, FRG, TASC and BCD (British Council Division).

African development bank/African development fund

India became a member of the African Development fund in 1982 and African Development Bank in 1983. Membership of these two organisations will enable India to cooperate more closely with developing Countries of the African continent. Indian exporters are also enable to bid against tenders for procurement of goods and services for various Development Projects in Africa that are financed and Co-financed by these organisations.

India has so far contributed Rs.9851 lakhs towards the various replenishment of the African Development Fund and also paid Rs.540.30 lakhs towards the paid up portion of the Capital Stock of the African Development Bank. India has been alloted 3000 shares (375 paid up shares and 2625 callable shares) of the African Development Bank. Negotiations for VIII Replenishment of the African Development Fund have also started.

There is a proposal for increasing the Capital Stock of the Bank through GCI-V. Negotiations on GCI-V have concluded recently. As per the tentative estimate, India has been allocated 1893 shares under GCI-V. Out of these, 114 shares are Paid-up and remaining 1779 shares are callable. Paid-up portion will amount to UA 11.40 lakhs (Rs.592-lakh) which will be paid in 8 equal Annual instalments (from 1999 to 2006 years).

India's cumulative procurement of goods and services in the projects assisted by the Bank stood at Rs.32,360 lakhs and Rs.22,771 lakhs in the projects assisted by the Fund and Rs.18 lakhs in the projects assisted by Nigerian Trust Fund as at 30.6.1998.

Technical cooperation agreement

India has signed Technical Cooperation Agreement with African Development Bank and African Development Fund on 27th July, 1998. Under this Agreement India shall provide to the Bank Group a grant of Rs.15 crore in three annual instalments for acquisition of the services of consultants and consulting firms for Project related activities in the territories of the Regional members of the Bank and training of professional and technical staff of the Bank of India.

West asian credits

Abu Dhabi Fund for Arab Economic Development, OPEC Fund for International Development, Kuwait Fund for Arab Economic Development (KFAED) and Saudi Fund for Development (SFD) have been extending Credits for various Projects in India. They charge interest at small rates and Repayment period ranges from 15 to 20 years. The total loans extended/committed by these West Asian Sources commencing from 1975-76, amount to US $ 770.8 million. So far Abu Dhabi Fund has extended a loan of Dinar 68.0 million (US $ 15 million) against one Project, OPEC Fund has extended total loan of US $ 218.8 million against 14 Projects, Saudi Fund has extended loan of SR 769.2 million (US $ 210.0 million) against 4 Projects and Kuwait Fund has extended KID 92.3 million (US $ 327.0 million) against 8 Projects.

At present there are following 7 Projects under implementation:-

1. Kalinadi Hydro Electric Project Stage-II (KFAED).

2. Raichur District Hospital Project (OPEC).
3. Kerala Rainfed Farming Development Project (OPEC).
4. Rewa Hospital Project (OPEC).
5. Basti District Hospital Project (OPEC).
6. Shimla Sewerage Project (OPEC).
7. Koraput Rayagada Railway Project (SFD).

A loan of US $ 10 million for Tripura School Education Project is likely to be received form OPEC Fund.

World trade organisation

India is a founding member of World Trade Organisation, India ratified the Agreement establishing the World Trade Organisation on 30th December, 1994. Opening up of Trade in Services was one of the areas which was negotiated in the Uruguay Round. The outcome in this area is embodied in the General Agreement on Trade in Services (GATS) which covers the multilateral framework, sectorial annotations and the schedules of market access. Offers in Financial Services constitutes one of the areas under GATS.

In India, Ministry of Commerce has been assigned the role of Nodal Office for WTO and related matters. We in the Ministry of Finance are mainly concerned with Financial Services under WTO regime.

On the conclusion of negotiations in Geneva, Agreement on Financial Services was arrived at on 13th December, 1997. India made an improved offer. India made the following commitments:-

(i) The MFN exemption taken earlier in the areas of Banking, Non-banking Financial Services (including Insurance) were withdrawn in response to all the important trading partners undertaking a similar MFN obligation.

(ii) In Banking, the number of new Bank branches bound for both existing and new Foreign Banks was increased from Eight to Twelve per Year.

(iii) In Insurance, status quo was maintained. In the area of re-insurance the existing binding has been aligned to the market. Earlier, the Indian Insurance Companies were obliged to cede a minimum of 10% of the overall premium abroad after retaining the statutory percentage with the domestic Insurance Companies. The above 10% limit has now been removed to allow Indian Insurance Companies to exercise their commercial judgement in deciding the premium to be ceded abroad.

The overall bindings are well within the actual liberalisation being permitted in each area. In allowing the limited Improvement in Financial Services, the intention of the Government of India has been to increase the confidence level of Foreign Investors in the Indian Financial Sector in particular and the Economy in general. This is expected to have a positive impact, both qualitatively and quantitatively, on the inflow of Foreign Investment know-how into India. The Agreement on Financial services will come into force with effect from 30th Jan., 1999.

With a view to effect speedy reconciliation between the two sets of data on merchandise trade, comiled by DGCIS, Calcutta and the Reserve Bank of India and also keeping in view the recommendations of the technical group constituted for the purpose, Rule 6 sub-rule (1) of the Foreign Exchange Regulation Rules, 1974 has been amended vide notification no 1(11)/98-CIE(l) dated 31 st December, 1998 making provisions for replacement of declaration form 'GR' by 'SDF' form in the case of specified customs offices wherein specified categories of shipping bills are processed electronically.

Credits extended to foreign governments

A fresh Line of Credit (LOC) to Myanmar has been extended by Government of India this year and a formal agreement in this regard was signed on 29th March, 1998 at Yangon between the Government of India and Government of Myanmar. Another LOC to the Government of Iraq for US $ 25mn. has also been approved 'in principle' but signing of the proposed credit agreement is yet to take place due to certain difficulties in view of UN embargo against Iraq. An amount of Rs.36.79 crore has been disbursed in the current financial year against the credits of the GOI to the Government of Vietnam (1996) and Government of Sri Lanka (1997).

Efforts towards recovery of our blocked funds overseas have been continuing and some progress have been made with respect to Vietnam. Efforts are also continuing to recover the dues from Ugands, Tanzania and Mozambique.

Under Colombo Plan/Bilateral, training courses are offered by UK, Netherlands, Germany, Thailand and Singapore. The training courses can broadly be divided into two categories:

(a) Project specific - which like in the case of UK relates to ODA funding of a particular project.

(b) General courses, which cover areas of Public Administration, Science& Technology. Rural Development, Agriculture, Science and Technology, Economics, etc. for example are being offered by Governments of UK, Netherlands, Germany, Thailand and Singapore.

United kingdom

The trainings in UK form a major part of training under the Colombo Plan and its is broadly categorised into (a) project-related training: and (b) Non project training.

Germany

The FRG Offers 20 long term and 40 short term trainings in the field of S&T, Agriculture, Education, Railways, Labour, Environment and Forests, Water Resources, HRD, Industry, Commerce and Surface Transport etc.

Singapore

Training in Singapore under Singapore-Colombo Plan Training awards covers different areas like communication, education, finance, urban development, health, information technology, Port activities and Social activities, Public utilities etc. There are about 100 slots available for 35 different courses.

Netherlands

Netherlands Fellowship Programmes are offered annually in the field of science & technology, agriculture, management and development oriented studies, media etc. There are approx 140 slots for 70 different courses. There is a provision made for tailor-made training programmes for national from developing countries.

Thailand

The courses in Thailand are received through MEA in the field of agriculture, civil aviation, health, development and forestry, etc. Approx 22 training courses are available in different areas.

India aid section

Indian Aid Section provides technical assistance in the form of training facilities and services of experts to member countries in the colombo plan region under Technical Cooperation scheme of Colombo Plan. In 1998-99, 400 training slots in India have been allocated to Colombo Plan countries. This facility has been availed of by these countries in the fields of information technology, computer education, medical sciences, engineering, financial management, insurance, managements of cooperative societies, journalism, rural development, auditing, tool techniques, etc. A budgetary provision of Rs.3.40 crores for meeting expenditure on these trainings has been provided for in the financial year.

Department of Economic Affairs is also the nodal point for Commonwealth Fund for Technical cooperation (CFTC) which extends technical assistance to commonwealth countries. The activities of CFTC cover general technical assistance programme, export market development, industrial development by means of providing services of experts, advisers, consultants and fellowships. India is a major donor to CFTC and has been providing training facilities to the nationals of Commonwealth developing countries in India. India's contribution to CFTC for the year 1998-99 is Pounds Sterling 720,000.

All matters pertaining to the Colombo Plan council, Colombo Plan Staff College, Consultative Committee of the Colombo Plan are handled in IA Section. India contributes annually to the Colombo Plan council and colombo Plan Staff College. The contribution to these organisations in 1998-99 is $ 13,500 and $ 82,932 respectively.

In the financial year 1997-98, as against the target of processing of 400 nominations under Colombo Plan, a total number of 422 nominations were processed. During 1998-99 (upto 15th December, 1998), this figure stands at 450.

Japan division

Japanese ODA to India and Impacts of Economic measures imposed by Govt. of Japan

Japan the largest bilateral donor

Japan is India's largest bilateral donor. The Japanese Aid Pledge for 1997-98 was Yen 132.725 billion as against Yen

132.746 for 1996-97. Japan, therefore holds a pre-eminent position amongst international donors to India.

Trend of credit growth

The table below summarizes the commitment and disbursement profile of ODA Loans on soft terms, administered by the OECF.

Year	*Commitments*	*%age increase*	*(in yen billion) Disbursement*
1986-87	48.44	23.5	48.87
1987-88	68.47	41.4	58.99
1988-89	87.83	28.0	28.19
1989-90	96.71	10.0	36.15
1990-91	104.82	8.4	62.20
1991-92	106.59	1.7	102.82
1992-93	111.91	5.0	53.10
1993-94	119.64	6.9	80.72
1994-95	125.765	5.1	66.52
1995-96	128.774	2.4	77.91
1996-97	132.746	3.1	64.58
1997-98	132.725	-0.015	88.44
1998-99			target 102

Up to 1970, all the Japanese credit was in the form of commodity loans meant for purchase of machinery, equipment and mutually agreed upon commodities. Project loans started coming in from 1970.

In the beginning, the project type loans were restricted to projects in the infrastructure sector like power, fertilizers, telecommunications, gas pipelines, ports and irrigation. In recent years, however, OECF has shown willingness to finance projects in soft sectors like environment and health.

Before 1986-87, the OECF aid to India was meant basically to finance foreign cost components of the projects. It was in 1986-87 that OECF agreed for the first time to cover the local cost of 3 projects. This facility, however, was limited to a ceiling of 30% of the local cost component. Subsequently, the Japanese reviewed their method of financing in 1989-90 and agreed to finance 85% of the total cost covering both foreign and local costs without any fixed percentage for either.

OECF loan package for 1997-98

The Government of Japan made a pledge of Yen 132.725 billion for 1997-98 OECF loan package. The loan agreements were signed on 12th December, 97. All the loan agreements have since been effectuated.

Disbursement for 1997-98 & budgetary estimate 1998-99

Disbursement during 1994-95 and 1995-96 were Yen 66.52 billion and Yen 77.91 billion respectively. However, the disbursement during 1996-97 has been lower at Yen 64.58 billion. The corresponding disbursement ratios for these three years were 13.9%, 11.4% and 10.6% respectively. The failing disbursement ratio was a matter of concern. 'Vigorous steps have since been taken to improve disbursement and step up the pace of implementation of the projects. Our efforts in this direction have resulted the disbursement increasing during 1997-98 to Yen 88.44 billion, the highest amount in last six years and second best in last twelve years. Disbursement ratio rose from 10.6% in 1996-97, which was below the OECF average of 11.9% to 13.1 % in 1997-98, which was above the OECF average of 11. 1 %. For 1998-99, we targeting a disbursement of Rs.2800 crores.

Impact of sanctions

Consequent to the Pokhran Blast, the Japanese have imposed sanctions. The impact of sanctions imposed by Government of Japan is as under:

(i) The India Development Forum (IDF) meeting scheduled to be held in Tokyo on 30th June and 1 st

July, 1998 did not take place since Government of Japan withdrew its intention to host the meeting.

(ii) Grant aid for new projects has been frozen, except grant aid for emergency, humanitarian and grassroots projects. On July 22, 1998 a grant assistance of Yen 392 million was extended to the Government of India for the Project for Eradication of Poliomyelitis as this project is interpreted as being a humanitarian project.

Yen-loan program for new projects has been frozen. However, all ongoing projects will continue unaffected. Sanctions could have a significant effect on new project approvals. Disbursement for the ongoing projects (both loans and grants) continue. During the, current year, there will be no impact on disbursements. Disbursements would be affected from 1999-2000, if sanctions continue in place.

Second and subsequent tranches for the ongoing projects are to be committed by the Government of Japan on a case to case basis. Out of the 9 short-listed projects in the 1998-99 loan package, 6 projects need additional loan tranches. Former Finance Secretary has written to Japanese Ambassador regarding this. Finance Secretary also raised the issue with Mr.Utchida, Vice President of OECF when the latter called on him in Delhi on 16.10.1998. Mr. Utchida indicated that they were awaiting clearance from the Japans Ministry of Foreign Affairs.

(iii) The Government of Japan will "cautiously examine the loans extended to India by international financial institutions". This seems to imply that the Japanse will follow the US example in multilateral fora.

(iv) The technical co-operation programme implemented by the Japan International Co-operation Agency

(JICA), like despatch of experts, and training of Indian personnel in Japan, has not been affected.

VI OECF loan package for 1998-99

36 projects were posed by us to the Government of Japan for assistance under OECF 1998-99 loan package. Govt. of Japan fielded a Fact-Funding Mission in January/February, 1998 to assess these projects. A Japanese Government Mission further visited India during 6-7th April, 1998 to further discuss the short-listed projects. Appraisal of these projects by OECF have since been completed. The IDF meeting scheduled to be held in Tokyo in June 1998 could not take place consequent to the Pokhran blast (details in para VI below). No loan commitments have therefore been made for this year.

The details of the six projects for which second or subsequent trenche is required are given below:

(1) *Bakreshwar Thermal Power Project III, WBPDCL:* To construct 420 MW (210 MWx2) Bakreshwar Thermal Power and associated Transmission System in order b cope with the increase of electricity demand and also to assure stable electricity supply in West Bengal State. A per the OECF's appraisal of the project the total estimate, cost would be Yen 78,780 Million.

This is the third tranche of the project which could not be pledged in the IDF meeting schedule in June, 1998 due to sanctions.

This first two tranches for the project are as under:

(i) ID-P.89 signed on 24.1.1994 for Yen 27069 million to be drawn down by 11.3.1999. Out of which, Yen 24933 million has already been drawn down upto 30.11.1998.

(ii) ID-P.130 signed on 12.12.1997 for Yen 34151 million to be drawn down by 19.2.2003. Out of which Yen

4883.3 million has already been drawn down upto 30.11.1998.

(2) *Bakreshwar Thermal Power project Unit 3, Extension Project 11, WBPDCL :* To construct 210 Bakreshwar Thermal Power Station (Unit 3) in order to cope with the increase of electricity demand and also to assure the stable electricity supply in West Bengal State. As per the OECF's appraisal of the project the total estimated cost would be Yen 24512 Million.

This is the second tranche of the project which could not be pledged in the IDF meeting schedule in-June, 1998 due to sanctions.

The first tranche for the project was ID-P.97 signed on 28.2.1995 for Yen 8659 million to be drawn down by 12.2.2001. Out of which Yen 4355.7 million has already been drawn down upto 30.11.1998.

(3) *Faridabad Gas Based Power Station and Associated Transmission system Project (II), NTPC:* To construct 430 MW Faridabad Combined Power Station and Associated Transmission System in order to cope with the increase of electricity demand and also to assure stable electricity supply in Haryana State. As per the OECF's appraisal of the project the total estimated cost would be Yen 34,881 Million.

This is the second tranche of the project which could not be pledged in the IDF meeting schedule in June, 1998 due to sanctions.

The first tranche for the project was ID-P.90 signed on 24.1.1994 for Yen 23536 million to be drawn down by 11.3.1999. Out of which Yen 3422.2 million has already been drawn down upto 30.11.1998.

(4) *Simdhadri Thermal Power Project (II), NTPC* : To construct a 1000 MW coal-fired Thermal Power

Station in order to cope with growing power demand and to assure stable supply in the State of Andhra Pradesh. As per the OECF's appraisal of the project the total estimated cost would be Yen 122182 Million.

This is the second tranche of the project which could not be pledged in the IDF meeting schedule in June, 1998 due to sanctions.

The first tranche for the project was ID.P.120 signed on 25.2.1997 for Yen 19817 million to be drawn down by 24.6.2007. The disbursement upto 30.11.1998 was nil.

(5) *Western Yamuna HE project, HSEB :* To conduct overhauling works on works on existing power house A, B and C (Stage-I) to extend their service life and enhance generating efficiency of power.

To construct 14.43 MW hydroelectric power house, associated power channel and bypass channel in order to cope with the increase of electricity demand and to assure stable electricity supply in Haryana State (Stage-II). As per the OECF's appraisal of the project the total estimated cost would be Yen 4230 Million.

(6) Afforestation in Aravalli II, Rajasthan Forestry Department:

- To check desertification and to restore the ecological status of the Aravalli hills by intensive reforestation and active peoples' participation.
- To check the soil erosion and thereby improve infiltration of water and bydrological balance.
- To conserve gene-pool and improve the biodiversity of flora and fauna.
- To meet the firewood, fodder, and domestic needs in the area by increased production of fuelwood, grass, timber, fruit and minor forest products.

- To provide employment to the rural/tribal population and improve their socio-econimic condition.
- To improve soil fertility of agricultural land through availability of large quantities of dung presently used for fuel by diverting it as manure.

As per the OECF's appraisal of the project the total estimate cost would be Yen 18117 Million.

This is the second phase of the project which could not be pledged in the IDF meeting schedule in June, 1998 due to sanctions.

The first phase for the project was ID-P.80 signed on 9.1.1992 for Yen 8095 million to be drawn down by 30.3.1999. Out of which Yen 6488.4 million has already been drawn down upto 30.11.1998.

The details of the other three new projects which have been appraised for the year 1998-99 OECF loan package are as under-

(1) *Haryana Transmission Line Project, HSEB :* To strengthen transmission system in the state of Haryana, to reduce transmission and distribution losses and enhance reliability of the system. As per the OECF's appraisal of the project the total estimated cost would be Yen 12360

(2) *Talcher II Power Project, PGCIL*: To evacuate power from the Talcher Thermal Power Plant Stage-II in order to meet the power demand in the Southern Region of India by 2002.

To achieve efficient inter regional power transmission between Eastern and Southern Grid. As per the OECF's appraisal of the project the total estimated cost would be Yen 70741.7 Million

(3) *Renewable Energy Line of Credit, IREDA:* To promote renewable energy development through the

participation of private, public and cooperative sector other than the SEBs (State Electricity Boards) through IREDA's financing schemes. The MOD have not yet been signed. As per the OECF's appraisal the estimated cost of the programme is Yen 10938.2 Million.

Japanese grant assistance to India

Japan also gives grant aid of Yen 3-4 billion per annum approximately. The details of the ongoing grant aided projects are as under:

	Name of the project	*Amount (in million Yen)*	*Date of Closing*
(i)	Construction of Dredger for Fishing Ports	1248	31.3.99
(ii)	Kalawati Saran Children Hospital, 494 New Delhi (Phase-II)	494	31.3.99
(iii)	Cultural Grant Assistance for supply 50 of Video Camera and Video-editing Equipment to Indian Museum, Calcutta	50	31.3.99
(iv)	Increasing Food Production (KR-II)	300	4.3.99
(v)	Eradication of Poliomyelitis	392	21.7.99

In addition, Government of Japan provides debt-relief grant assistant every year amounting to about Yen 0.2-0.3 billion per year. The debt-relief assistance is of non-project tied and can be utilised for import of various items including spares, components and raw materials for Japan aided projects and Indo-Japanese ventures.

Govt. of Japan also extends technical co-operation by providing the services of Japanese experts and project-type technical co-operation. The following are the on-going Project-type Technical co-operation projects:

(i) setting up of collaborative diarrhoeal disease research and control centre.

(ii) Bivoltine Sericulture Technology Development, Bangalore.

In addition to above, the Government of Japan also provide, under the Technical Cooperation programme, with the Colombo Plan training held in Japan. There are about 120 group training courses and seminars that are held in Japan, Usually, one nomination is accepted in each group training course/seminar. There are some courses held in other countries like Malaysia, Singapore-Indonesia. These are funded by JICA and are named Third Country Training Courses.

The Japanese also provide assistance for carrying out development/feasibility studies for various projects based on the GOI's request. The following Development Study projects have recently been concluded:

(i) Master Plan for Bombay Port,

(ii) Rehabilitation of Minor Irrigation Tanks for Rural Development in Tamil Nadu,

(iii) Eleven National Highways By-passes projects in the country.

The grants to ODA ratio is very low compared to other countries. There is a case for a larger share for India in Japan's grant aid and technical co-operation budget and we have submitted proposals for their consideration. However, as the grant aid for new projects has been frozen, except grant aid for emergency, humanitarian and grassroots projects, no new initiative is possible now.

Australian development assistance to india

Australian Development Assistance to India started in the year 1951. The aid, on grant basis, was earlier concentrated in Agriculture and allied sectors. The Australian Aid programme was extensive during the 50s and 60s. During the 70s it varied with the amount of food aid given. Assistance to India under bilateral aid programme was minimal during the early 80s and was deleted altogether in 1986. The highest level achieved was in 1974-75 when it reached Australian Dollars 10.7 million.

2. A new initiative in Indo-Australian bilateral relations was taken in February, 1989, when a Memorandum of Understanding was signed for providing concessional loans to finance development project in India. The objectives of the MOU are to :

   (a) ensure effective procedure for funding projects which have, been agreed as important in India's development programme; and

   (b) facilitate the use of Australian goods and services for the developmental purposes through concessional finance packages.

3. As per the MOU, the Ministry of Finance (DEA) and Australian International Development Assistance Bureau (AIDAB), now AusAID, are to meet at least once a year to discuss and allocate priorities amongst projects and to review the Memorandum and the funds provided by it.

4. In October, 1990, two agreements on bilateral cooperation were signed with the Australian Government. These were : (i) Agreement on Development Cooperation and (ii) MOU relating to the Small Activity Scheme. Australian aid to India is extended under the aegis of the above agreements.

5. Australian Assistance covers the following sectors: (i) Railways, (ii) Telecommunication, (iii) Energy, (iv) Mining, (v) Coal, (vi) food processing (vii) environment, (viii) health and (ix) Transport. The

Small Activity Scheme extends to cover the social sectors also. Under this programme, funds are extended to the NGOs as well.

6. Initially, under the Australian grant aid, an amount of A.$ 35 million (Aus $1=Rs.22) was allocated, which has since been fully committed. Details of ODA expenditure (for previous years) and outlook (current year) are as under:

(in Aus. $million)

Year	*Disbursement amount*
1993-94	15.8
1994-95	20.4
1995-96	24.6
1996-97	21.7
1997-98	20.2
1998-99	19.2 (expected)

7. India-Australia Training and Capacity Building Project is a 3 year project with total allocation of A.$ 12 million. It provides for training of Indian personnel in Australia and India in the fields of HRD, women & Child development, power, environment and forests, health, railways, textiles and revenue. The MOU for the project was signed on 11.12.1997.

8. The Australian Government provides an amount of A $ 1,000,000 annually for its Small Activities Scheme for NGOS.

9. The programme is designed to assist India to help meet our priority development needs while fostering beneficial economic links in areas where Australia has specialist expertise and internationally competitive technology.

PSE division

The Department of Economic Affairs is the nodal Department for the disinvestment programme of the Government of India. The PSE Division within the Department of Economic affairs deals with those matters which are related to Disinvestment of Government's shareholdings in various Public Section Undertakings. It is entrusted with the work of servicing the Core Group of Secretaries on Disinvestment which is headed by the Cabinet Secretary and which gives its recommendations to the Group of Ministers and Cabinet on various aspects of policy as well as implementation of the disinvestment programme. The Division also prepares notes for the consideration of the Group of Ministers and the Cabinet. In actual implementation of the decision of the Cabinet is regard to disinvestment, the PSE Division gets involved at all levels and the Joint Secretary (PSE) or his representative is the member of all the Task Forces/Inter Ministerial Groups formed to carry out the disinvestment of Government's shareholdings in various Public Section Undertakings.

For the year 1998-99, the Government intends to divest its part holdings from the 4 companies viz. CONCOR, GAIL, VSNL & IOC in GDR/domestic markets. The CONCOR issue was successfully completed in the domestic market in which FIIs also participated and an amount of Rs. 221.65 crores was raised from the issue. The process of disinvestment in other 3 companies is in progress and it is expected to be over by the end of the fiscal year.

Government is simultaneously proceeding to disinvest by way of strategic sale, its holdings in 6 Public Sector Enterprises viz. BRPL, BALCO, KIOCL, ITDC, Modern Foods and Madras Fertilizers Ltd. In all these cases the process of disinvestment is on and the global advisers have been appointed by the concerned administrative Ministries for suggesting modes of disinvestment. In addition, it has also been decided that certain percentage of equity held by the Government in Engineers India Ltd., Indian Petrochemicals Corporation of India Ltd. and HTL Ltd. may be disinvested in favour of strategic partners. Disinvestment by ITDC in Ranchi Ashok Bihar Hotel Corporation Ltd. and Utkal Ashok Hotel Corporation have also been approved. All these proposals for disinvestment are likely to materialse during the year 1999-2000.

The PSE Division is headed by Joint Secretary (PSE) who is also looking after the EEC, C&C and Administration Division. The Division also has one full time Deputy Secretary, Under Secretary, Section Officer and supporting staff.

The amount realised through disinvestment during the last 6 years is as under:

1997-98	-	Rs.906 Crores
1996-97	-	Rs. 455 Crores
1995-96	-	Rs. 362 Crores
1994-95	-	Rs. 5078 Crores
1993-94	-	Rs. nil
1992-93	-	Rs. 1913 Crores

IES division

The Indian Economic Service is an organised Central Group A Service with the sanctioned Cadre strength of 516 Officers. The IES division in the Department of Economic Affairs is the Cadre Controlling Authority of the IES. This division as the controlling authority of the IES officers deals with matters relating to personnel management/posting/transfers/Promotions etc.

During the financial year 1998-99 the IES Cadre convened two DPCs for promotion at STS and SAG levels.

As a major step towards improving the quality of personnel, for in-service training programmes were organised at various nodal training institutes of the country.

As recommended by the Fifth Pay Commission ground work was initiated towards the creation of the subordinate Economic Service. As recommended by the Fifth Pay Commission the scales of the Feeder posts holders of IES (comprising of Junior Investigators/Senior Investigators) were upgraded. Several other service issues as recommended by Fifth Pay commission were sorted out with the advise of DOPT/Implementation Cell and Department of Expenditure.

Investment division

During the financial year 1998-99 the following initiatives were taken by this division to further liberalise the guidelines governing foreign investments.

GDRs/ADRs: Modification to the GDR/ADR Guidelines have been announced on 22-05-98. These are:

(i) unlisted companies are also permitted to float Euro issues provided they fulfill the three year track record eligibility requirement and subject to the standard listing requirement of listing in the domestic stock exchanges within three years of having started making profits.

(ii) all end use restrictions on GDR/ADR issue proceeds have been removed. Only the restriction banning investments in real estate and stock markets to continue.

(iii) the 90 day validity period for final approvals for GDR/ ADR has been withdrawn and now final approval would continue to be valid giving greater flexibility to issuing companies on timing of issue.

Press release dated 17-08-98 : Through a Press Release dated 17-08-98 Government had announced that Indian Companies would be permitted to issue GDRs/ADRs, in cases of Bonus or Rights issue of shares, or on genuine business reorganisations duly approved by the High Court. The companies, in all such cases, would be required to apply to the Department of Economic Affairs for obtaining approval for the issue of GDRs/ADRs.

Stock options: Press Release dt. 23.6.98 and 16.9.98: Information Technology Software and Information Technology Services Companies permitted to issue ADRS/GDRs linked stock options to their employees. The issuing company would be entitled to issue options not exceeding 10% of its issued and paid up equity capital to its resident and non-resident permanent employees (including Indian and overseas working directors but excluding promoters and their relatives as defined under the Companies Act).

NRI investment

1. Press Releases dated 11-06-98 & 22-06-98 - Pursuant to the announcement made by the Hon'ble Finance Minister in his Budget speech 1998-99, modifications have been made in the portfolio investment scheme for NRIs enhancing the investment limits for NRIs/PIOs/OCBs for purchase of shares with repatriation benefits in a company through stock exchanges under the portfolio investment scheme as follows-.-

   (a) Investment limit by a single Non-Resident Indian (NRI)/ Persons of Indian Origin (PIOs/Overseas Corporate bodies (owned by such persons to the extent of at least 60 percent) (OCBs) in a company is enhanced from 1% to 5% of the paid up equity capital of the company.

(b) The aggregate limit for all NRIs/PIOs/OCBs investment through the secondary market in a company is raised from 5% to 10% of the paid up equity capital.

(c) In order to avoid NRIs being crowded out by FIIs, the aggregate ceiling for investment by all NRIs/PIOs/OCBs through stock exchanges has been made separate and exclusive of the investment ceiling available, for FIIs.

Press release dated 07-08-98 : Through a Press Note dated 7th August 1998 Government have announced that NRIs/ PIOs/OCBs would be permitted to invest in unlisted companies under portfolio investments scheme in conformity with norms and approval procedures applicable to portfolio investments in listed companies under the portfolio investment scheme. Portfolio investments in unlisted companies by NRIs/PIOs/OCBs would be subject to individual and aggregate investment limits applicable to investments in listed companies.

Press Release Dated 07-08-98 : In order to provide greater flexibility and functional freedom, with a view to attract NRI investment in the health services sector, and to encourage induction of up-to-date diagnostic facilities Government have removed the conditions for proposed NRIs/PIOs/OCBs investments in the health services sector which prescribe that the centres would be equipped as per the norms specified by the Ministry of Health and Family Welfare and 25% of the facilities available in hospitals/diagnostic centres would be provided free of cost-to the poor and needy. But the removal of these conditions is without prejudice to any conditions agreed to by the companies while availing any incentive/concession.

Resurgent India bonds : Input in this regard may be obtained from the Budget Division.

FII investment : The cumulative net FII investments as of 20.11.1998 amounted to US$ 8.616 billion. The number of FIIs registered with the Securities & Exchange Board of India (SEBI) till 20.11.1998 was 545.

Foreign Institutional Investors (FIIs) : The following measures have been taken to facilitate and encourage FII investment inflows:

Foreign Institutions Investors (FIIs) 100% debt funds have been permitted to invest in unlisted debt securities.

FIIs can tender their securities directly in response to open offers for takeovers made in terms of the SEBI (substantial Acquisition of Shares and Takeovers) Regulations, 1997.

FIIs have been enabled to trade in derivative contracts which are traded on a stock exchange without the requirement of taking and giving delivery of underlying securities.

FIIs have been permitted to hedge foreign exchange risk through purchase of forward cover on incremental equity investments.

The overall ceiling of 24%/30% for FII investments will now be operated exclusive of NRIs/PIOs/OCBs investments.

During the current financial year the following developments took place in regard to FDI in so far as DEA is concerned.

(i) Two (2) additional activities were included in the list of permitted activities for foreign investment in the Non-Banking Financial Services sector. These are (i) Credit Card Business and (ii) Money Changing Business.

(ii) It has been decided that foreign investment proposals in the NBFC sector for purely financial consultancy services would not be subjected to the Capitalisation norms as are applicable to the NBFCs subject to the following conditions:

(i) Such a company will not be permitted to set up any subsidiary for any other activity, and

(ii) For purposes of reckoning domestic equity such wholly owned financial consultancy company would not be eligible to provide equity contribution as a domestic partner for any NBFC holding/ operating company.

(iii) For foreign equity investments in the private sector banks where there is a cap of 20% for participation by foreign banking companies or finance companies, including multilateral financial institutions and NRI participation is allowed upto 40% inclusive of equity participation by other foreign investors, it has been decided that in cases of shortfall in foreign equity contributions by NRIs, multilateral institutions would be allowed to contribute foreign equity to the extent of the shortfall in NRI contribution to the equity.

The FDI inflow for the financial year 1997-98 and 199899 (upto October, 1998) as reported by the RBI, are as under:

(in million dollars)

1997-98	:	4407.20
1998-99	:	1354.47 (upto Oct' 98)

Financial Year wise inflows under Various Schemes

(US$ mio)

	1991-92	1992-93	1993-94	1994-95	1995-96	1996-97	1997-98	1998-99 (April Oct 98)	Total
FIPB/ SIA	53.94	256.83	334.21	743.68	1269.37	1950.36	2804.67	1162.53	8575.58
RBI	0.14	44.70	84.50	171.74	168.11	137.70	206.78	102.22	915.90
Sub Total	54.08	301.53	418.72	915.42	1437.48	2088.06	3011.45	1264.75	9491.49
NRI	65.74	64.03	225.90	461.85	594.59	534.60	243.29	46.88	2236.88
FII	0.00	1.46	1718.40	1475.69	1986.19	2114.32	1665.45	485.46	8476.06
GDRs/ FCCBs	0.00	85.83	2368.75	1947.87	145.42	935.81	1152.46	42.84	6678.95
Totals	119.82	452.85	4731.77	4800.83	4163.67	5572.79	6072.65	869.00	26883.38

Conversion Rates	March-93	1 US$ = Rs.29.02
April-93 to	March-94	1 US$ = Rs.31.47
April 94 to	Aug-95	1 US$ = Rs.31.37
Sept. 95 to	July-97	1 US$ = Rs.35.00
Aug. 97 to	Oct.-97	1 US$ = Rs.36.00
Nov. 97 to	Dec.-97	1 US$ = Rs.38.00
Jan. 98	March-98	1 US$ = Rs.39.00
	April-98	1 US$ = Rs.39.73
	May-98	1 US$ = Rs.41.50
June 98	Sep.-98	1 US$ = Rs.42.47

Currency and coinage division

India security press, nasik road

The India Security Press, Nashik Road functionally consists of two units, the Stamp Press and the Central Stamp Depot. The Stamp Press prints postal stationery, postal and non-postal stamps, judicial and non-judicial stamps, RBI/SBI cheques, Bonds, National Savings Certificates, Indira Vikas Patras, Kisan Vikas Patras, Postal Orders, Passports, Promissory Notes and such other security documents as may be required by the Central and State Governments. It has also started printing of MICR cheques etc. The Central Stamp Depot supplies finished products to the indentors.

1. Achievements of the Press during 1997-98 and 1998-99 (upto 31 December, 1998) are as follows:

S.No.	Item	*Production (in crores of Pcs.)* 1997-98	1998-99
1.	Post Cards	50.3000	20.2592
2.	Ordinary Envelopes	14.1120	10.6200
3.	Registration Envelopes	0.5900	0.7400
4.	Inland Letter Cards	3.3900	4.2200
5.	Green Envelopes & Forces letters	0.7300	...
6.	Aerogrammes	2.6900	2.0805
7.	Non-Judicial and allied stamps	18.4610	11.5852
8.	MICR Cheques/IPO/ITRO/Intt. warrants	3.8500	3.4715
9.	NON-MICR cheques	2.2500	1.5527
10.	Misc. Security Items i.e. savings instruments NSC/IVP/KVP/Rly. Warrant.	8.8700	5.5018
11.	Public/Service/Comm. postage Stamps (issue sheets)	5.1121	4.5518
12.	Non Postal Adhesive Stamps (issue sheets)	1.1900	0.5585
13.	Passport-Booklets & Vissa-sheets	0.3900	0.1972
14.	I. Cards/Security Passes	0.0110	0.0142

The India Security Press brought out 47 special commemorative postage stamps during the period 1998-99 (upto 31st Dec. 1998).

Currency note press, nashik road: The Currency Note Press, Nashik Road now prints and supplies currency notes of denominations of Rs. 10/-, Rs. 50/- and Rs. 100/-. During the year 1997-98 the unit produced 3641 million pieces of notes. The actual production for 1998-99 upto 31.12.98 is 2509 million pieces.

Bank note press, dewas: The Bank Note Press

consists of two production units viz., Printing Press and Ink Factory. The Printing Press prints higher denomination bank notes viz.., Rs.20/-, Rs.50/, Rs.100/- and Rs.500/-. The Ink Factory manufactures security inks, meeting partly the requirements of the security/currency printing presses.

During the year 1997-98 the unit produced 1800.638 million pieces of notes . Production during 1998-99 (upto 31.12.98) is 1525.442 million pieces.

The production of the Ink Factory was as follows

	1997-98	*1998-99*
	(In metric tonnes)	
Ink and Intermediaries	293.827	120.549
Finished Ink	256.469	99.107
Varnishes	122.226	48.967

Security paper mill, hoshangabad: The Security Paper Mill manufactures bank note paper as well as other security papers required by other Security Presses. During the year 199798, the Mill produced 3281 metric tonnes of paper and during 199899 (upto 31.12.98) 2124.89 Metric Tonnes.

Security Printing Press, Hyderabad: It produces post cards, Inland Letter Cards, Envelopes, Central Excise Stamps and Non-Judicial Stamps

Production Achievements are as under:-

Achievements

		Production (in crores of pieces)	
No.	Items	1997-98	1998-99
1.	Post Cards	35.14	26.97
2.	Inland Letter Cards	41.18	21.07
3.	Envelopes	11.23	6.67
4.	Central Excise Stamps	37.15	20.89
5.	Non-Judicial Stamps	5.00	4.81

Mints: There are five Government Mints at Mumbai, Calcutta, Hyderabad, Cherlapalli and Noida. The main function of the Mints is minting of coins for the country, gold and silver assaying, medals productions and issue of commemorative coins.

India government mint, mumbai

(a) The targeted production of coins for year 1997-98 was 400 million pieces, against which Mint produced 400.9865 million pieces. The targeted production of coins for the year 1998-99 is 500 million pieces against which Mint has produced 355.6235 Mps upto 31.12.98.

(b) During the year 1997-98 & 1998-99, this Mint produced new coins & Commemorative Coins as under:

Year	*Theme*	*Sets of*	*For Circulation*
1996-97	Sardar Vallabhbhai Patel commemorative coins	Rs.100 Rs.10 &	Rs.2 Rs. 50 Rs.2
1997-98	50th year of Independence Commemorative Coins	Rs. 50 &	50 Paise 50 Paise
1998-99	125th birth anniversary of Shri Aurobindo commemorative coins	Rs. 100, Rs.50, Rs.10 &	Rs.2 Rs.2

(c) *Gold refining:* Mumbai Mint has undertaken gold refining & melting work as detailed below:

	1.4.97 to 31.3.98	1.4.98 to 31.12.98
Refining of Gold	2,588,241.900	942,762.600
Melting	302,957.350	931,728.250
G.B.S. Alligation	11,595,144.900	1,156,332.094
Casting	13,637,282.000	3,157,087.200
G.B.S. Casting	1,438,249.000	494,912.800

(d) In addition to above, the Mint is also engaged in the production of different types of medals, weights and measures.

India government mint, calcutta

(a) The production of coins of different denominations during 1997-98 was 434.1840 million pieces against target of 440 million pieces. The target for 1998-99 is 525 million pieces whereas the actual production (upto 31.12.98) is 361.5750 million pieces.

(b) The Mint manufactured 1,57,746 Medals and delivered 1,51,678 pieces during the period 1997-98 to various departments like Ministry of Defence, Home Affairs etc. The Medals delivered during 1998-99 are 1,17,021 pieces and manufactured 1,45,796 pieces.

(c) During the year 1997-98 the Mint produced Commemorative circulating coins of Re. 1 on "Cellular Jail". During the year 1998-99 the Mint also produced commemorative proof coins of Rs.100, Rs.50, Rs.10 and Rs.2 and circulating coin of Rs.2 in the commemoration of Desh Bandhu Chitranjan Dass.

India government mint, hyderabad

(a) The production achievement of coins of different denominations during 1996-97 was 313.57 million pieces, whereas the production during 1997-98 is 286.35 million pieces. Actual production during 1998-99 (upto 31.12.98) is 255.9045 million pieces.

India government mint, cherlapalli, The Mint was inaugurated on 20.8.97. Production achievements from 1.4.98 to 31.12.98 are as under:-

	(In Million Pes.)
Rs.5/-	0.8580
Rs.2/-	0.1550
Re1/-	42.2225
50 Paise	28.4800
25 Paise	11.9300
Total	83.6455

India government mint, noida: During the year 1997-98, the Mint produced 556.457 million pieces of coins, against the target of 500 million pieces. For the year 1998-99, the Mint produced 555.76 million pieces upto 31 st Dec., 1998 against target of 850 million pieces.

Action taken to implement the policy statement for control of pollution : There is no pollution problem. All sorts of b) Anti pollution measures have been taken in Mints & Presses.

Audit objections pending with this Divisions

(i) Para 5.3 of CAG Report of 1998 - concerning extra expenditure incurred on airlifting of Ink at CNP Nashik. C) Revised ATN is being finalised.

(ii) Para 5.4 of CAG Report of 1998 concerning loss due to under - realisation of electricity charges at IGM, Calcutta. Revised ATN has been sent to Audit for vetting.

(iii) Para 5.5 of CAG Report of 1997 - concerning over payment of incentive at IGM, Calcutta. Revised ATN has been sent to Audit for vetting.

Administration division

Functions: Administration Division is responsible for personnel and office administration of the Department and implementation of official language policy of the Government by the Department and its attached/ subordinate offices.

Staff strength: The staff strength and the strength of Scheduled Castes/Scheduled Tribes employees as on 31.3.1999 is given below:-

Representation of Scheduled Castes/Scheduled Tribes as on 31.3.1999 (Tentatively)

Group	*Total No. of employees*	*Permanent/ Temporary*	*No. of SC employees*	*No. of ST employees*
1	2	3	4	5
Group A (CI.I) Other than lowest rung of CI.I	230	217/13	22	11
Lowest rung of CI.I	235	221/14	14	9
Group B (CI.II)	716	699/17	107	32
Group C (CI.III)	3958	3802/156	674	278
Group D (CI.IV) (Excl. Sweeper)	1010	949/61	296	81
Group D (CI.IV) (Sweeper)	291	264/27	202	11

Position of employment of Ex-servicemen in Group 'C'and 'D' posts as on 31.3.1999 (Tentatively)

Group	*Number of employees*	
	Total	*Ex-servicemen*
Group 'C'	3958	608
Group 'D'	1010	110
Group 'D'	291	5

Use of hindi in official work

During the year under report, progress made in the implementation of various programmes under the Official Language Policy was kept under constant review.

Hindi version of all Budget documents were presented to Parliament during the year under review. All documents specified in Section 3(3) of the Official Languages Act, 1963 as amended, were prepared bilingually. A number of steps, as detailed below, were taken in the Department to propagate the use of Hindi in official work during the year under review:-

(a) Phased programme prepared for training of the officials in Hindi/Hindi Typing/Hindi Stenography continued to be implemented. Officers/Typists /Stenographers of the Department were sponsored for different training courses conducted under Hindi Teaching Scheme of the Ministry of Home Affairs (Department of Official Language).

(b) Annual Programme for the year 1998-99 prepared by the Department of Official Language was circulated to all the Attached/Subordinate Offices including Life Insurance Corporation of India and General Insurance Corporation of India and also among the Divisions/ Sections of the Department. The progress made in achieving the targets under the Annual Programme was reviewed at the meeting of the Official Language Implementation Committee.

(c) Work relating to translation/printing of forms bilingually continues to be pursued in the Department and its Attached/Subordinate Offices.

(d) In order to ensure compliance of the instructions regarding use of Hindi in official correspondence, checkpoints have been set up in R&I Branch of the Department.

(e) Hindi Fortnight was organised from 1st to 15th September, 1998 and Hindi Day was organised on 14th September, 1998 for creating consciousness and for accelerating the use of Hindi for official purposes.

(f) Some of the offices of LIC and GIC and Attached/ Subordinate Offices in the region 'A', 'B' and 'C' have been inspected to see the extent upto which the Official Language Act, the rules made thereunder and the Annual Programme are being implemented and also the extent upto which orders, instructions etc. relating to the Official Language are being complied with.

(g) Official Language Implementation Committee of this Department continued to look after the implementation of Official Language Policy in the Department and its Attached/Subordinate Offices. During the year under review, the meetings of said Hindi Salahakar Samiti and Official Language Implementation Committee were organised from time to time and the progress made in the implementation of Official Language Policy in the Department and its Attached/Subordinate Offices including Life Insurance Corporation/General Insurance Corporation was reviewed.

Vigilance activities

During the year, disciplinary proceedings for major penalties were initiated against two Gr. 'C' Officers, and proceedings were continued against four Group 'A' Officers, two Gr. 'B' officers, four Gr. 'C' officers and one Gr. 'D' Officer.

Penalty of 'Censure' has been imposed on one Gr. 'C' employee and penalty of withholding of one increment for a period of six months has been imposed on one Gr. 'D' employee.

Strict watch was kept on the corruption prone areas in the Department and its subordinate organisations. Security instructions received from Ministry of Home

Affairs were also brought to the notice of all concerned for further tightening of security measures.

Special efforts were also made to dispose off expeditiously. Vigilance/disciplinary cases pending with the Department and its subordinate organisations.

Vigilance Verification Unit conducted physical verification of stocks held by India Government Mints, Security Presses and Security Paper Mill.

Finance library and publication section

Finance Library & Publication Section was established in 1945. Finance Library and Publication Section functions as the Central Research and Reference Library in the Ministry and caters to the needs of Officers of all the three Departments (Department of Economic Affairs, Department of Expenditure and Department of Revenue), Ad-hoc Committees and Commissions set up from time to time and research scholars from the various Universities in India as well as in abroad. There is one more Library i.e. Insurance Division Library which is being controlled by the Finance Library & Publication Section.

Collection

Library has a specialised Collection of more than two lakhs volumes on Economic and Financial matters and receives more than 800 periodicals/ newspapers.

Services

Library provides different kinds of Services viz. Lending Inter-library Loan, Consultation, Reprographic Circulation d Newspapers and Magazines, Reference Service, Current Awareness Service through 'WEEKLY BULLETIN' Distribution 6, Ministry of Finance's publications and Reserve Bank of India's Publications to Reserve Bank of India, State Governments Foreign Governments and renowned Institutions in India as wel[as in abroad.

Publication

Finance library brings out a Documentation List 'WEEKLY BULLETIN', a subject bibliography indexing articles of interest from about 200 Journals/Newspapers and containing list of additions during the week.

Computer application

Finance Library & Publication section has already acquired a PC for generation of House . At present Library is using this computer for official work I brings out Documentation List and for preparing a data-base for up date list of Acts of Parliament.

This Library also serves as the Publication Section of the Ministry co-ordinating the procurement and distribution of official publications, exchange of Government of India's publications with foreign Governments and supply of publications under 'Delivery of Book Act 1954'.

In the Ministry of Finance, there are three more specialised libraries viz. Department of Revenue Library, Tax Research Unit Library and Banking Division Library are being operated under the direct control of respective Departments.

2

Department of Expenditure

Establishment division

The Establishment Division plays a crucial role in the administration of various financial rules and regulations including service conditions of all Central Govt. employees. The Division deals with matters like determination of salary structure and grades, wage policy determination, revision of pay scales, creation of supernumerary posts, basic principles of fixation of pay, House Rent Allowance, Travelling/Daily Allowance, Dearness Allowance and various other Compensatory allowances in respect of Central Government employees including policy relating to pension structure and dearness relief to pensioners. The Division is also, responsible for processing all cases relating to creation of posts at different levels and their continuation. The Division is required to be consulted in all matters where any new facility to Govt. employees by way of service conditions and fringe benefits involving significant recurring financial in Publications is to be given. The Division is actively associated withthe National Council of the JCM in all such matters which have major financial implications and repercussions. The Division is responsible for fixation of terms and conditions of members appointed in different Committies/ Commissions such as retired judges of the Supreme Court and the High Courts. The Division is the nodal point in the Government of India for interpretation, relaxation or amendment of financial rules, viz. Delegation of Financial Powers Rules, General Financial Rules, Staff Car Rules, etc.

This Division is also looking after upgradation/ revision of scales of pay of employees of Central Government as also the autonomous bodies. The attempt of the Division is to maintain comparable relativities amongst various grades of Government Employees with reference to their functions, duties and responsibilities, while deciding upon revision of pay scales, etc.

The Division is closely associated with the principles governing productivity linked bonus and ad-hoc bonus for the Central Government employees. Every year, the upper limit of bonus is decided in consultation with the Ministries/Departments concerned. Orders were issued on 16.9.1998 for grant of ad-hoc bonus for 30 days for the accounting year 1997-98 to the Central Government employees in Group 'C' and 'D' and all non-gazetted employees in Group 'B'.

The Division also serves as Secretariat of the Screening Committee of Secretaries which processes proposals for deputation abroad of officers of the level of Additional Secretary and above.

Establishment Division also services the Committee on Non-Plan Expenditure which scrutinises the proposals of different Ministries/Departments pertaining to various projects/scheme involving expenditure of Rs. 5 crores and above on Non-Plan side.

The Division also formulates and monitors policies instructions and measures in the sphere of management and control of administrative expenditure of the Government. Detailed guidelines were issued on 20.8.98 on expenditure management, fiscal prudence and austerity. In the area of reduction of staff strength as part of the exercise to effect 10% cut therein, around 1.57 lakhs posts have been reduced so far.

A large number of left over recommendations of the Vth Central Pay Commission as well as problems arising out of the implementation of the recommendations of this Commission were addressed during the year. Again, there are a large number of Autonomous/Statutory Bodies under various Ministries/ Departments of the Central Govt. The scales of pay and other service conditions in respect of employees of a large number of these autonomous organisations were considered, revised and successfully implemented.

Administration wing

Administration Wing is responsible for personnel management and office administration, vigilance matters, implementation of the official language policy and redressal of grievances of staff in the Department. It is also responsible for foreign training and assignment of officers of the Department. Office administration and staffing of officer of Finance Minister are also taken care of by this Wing.

It is also the cadre controlling authority for the Indian Cost Accounts Service and the secretarial staff of the office of the Controller General of Accounts.

Administration Wing is also in-charge of cadre administration of C.S.S. (upto the level of Section Officers) for the entire Ministry of Finance. It also functions as a co-ordinating Secretariat for the Departmental Council (JCM) for the Ministry of Finance.

Public grievances redressel machinery

By the nature of work, this Department is not generally grievance prone. The number of grievances received from the public is negligible. However, a Public Grievances

Redressal Machinery with Joint Secy. in charge of administration as the Director of the Grievances is functioning in the Department.

Women cell

A women cell has been constituted in this Department for redressing the grievances of women.

Award scheme

In pursuance of Department of Administrative Reforms and Public Grievances O.M. No. 33011/1/97-O&M, dated 21 st May, 1998, introducing an Award Scheme for the Central Govt. Employees, as well as the members of the public regarding innovative and workable suggestions for improving the quality of service and making it more customer friendly, a Screening Committee has been constituted in this Department under the Chairmanship of Joint Secy.(Per) with Director(A) as Member and Under Secretary(A) as Member Secretary. The suggestions received are under consideration.

National institute of financial management

This institute has been set up to impart Professional Training in Financial Management to the Probationery Officers of Group A services managing Accounts, Audit and Finance functions in various Government Departments and to conduct short term programmes for in service officers of Central Services and All India Services with a view to update their knowledge and sharpen their skill for better management of finances of Government. The objectives of the Institute envisage conducting research and consultancy and to emerge as a centre of excellence in the field of Financial Management.

The Institute started functioning from January, 1994 and has successfully completed training of five batches of Probationers of various Accounts, Audit and Finance Services which is of 10 month's duration. The

Probationers of sixth batch are currently undergoing training.

At the instance of Finance Minister the Institute took the lead in organising a two days seminar for Financial Advisers of various Government Ministries in September, 1997 on issues relating to Budgetary Control, Expenditure Management & Role of FA etc. The seminal inaugurated by Shri C. Ramachandran former Secretary(Expenditure) and was attended by 35 FAs of different Ministries. Persons of eminence like Dr. Suresh Tendulkar, Director, Delhi School of Economics & Shri Prem Chand, Advisor, IMF addressed the participants. The papers presented during the seminar brought out in the form of a book and recommendations of FAs relating to various aspects of their functioning was presented to the Finance Secretary.

The Institute has also been recognised by World Bank as nodal agency for providing training in the area of World Bank procurement procedures. A programme on monitoring of External Aided Projects has been sponsored by Asian Development Bank. The Institute has been co-ordinating with International Agencies like Harvard Institute of International Development, for conducting programmes on Risk Management and with Government of Sri Lanka in training their officers in Computer Application in Financial Management etc.

In addition to the Professional Training Programme, the Institute has also been organizing a number of Management Development Programmes for in service officers.

More than 2500 trees had already been planted in the Institute Campus and more efforts are being made.

Miscellaneous department branch

The Branch functions as an Associated Finance Unit to

the Departments, viz. Prime Minister Office, Supreme Court of India, Ministry of Parliamentary Affairs and Secretariats of the Lok Sabha and the Rajya Sabha, Cabinet, President and Vice President. It deals with all financial matters including the Annual Budget of these Departments.

Pay research unit

The Pay Research Unit was established in 1968 and is mainly responsible for collection, compilation and analysis of data on actual expenditure incurred on pay and various types of allowances as well as the data pertaining to the strength of the Central Government Civilian employees and employees of Union Territory Administration. This Unit brings out an annual Publication entitled "Brochure on Pay and Allowances of Central Government Civilian Employees". The Publication among other things contains expenditure incurred on pay, DA, CCA, HRA etc. of Civilian Employees by the Central Ministries/Departments, group wise number of sanctioned posts and number in position for various Ministries and Departments, disparity ratio i.e. the ratio of the maximum to minimum pay of different State Government Employees. The PRU also works out financial implications of the proposals of the Government and proposals coming before the National Council of JCM etc. and maintains relevant information in respect of minimum and maximum emoluments of State Government employees.

During the year under report, the Unit has brought out the 19th issue of the series of Brochure for the year 1996-97. The work regarding the Brochure for the year 1997-98 is in progress.

Staff inspection unit

The Staff Inspection Unit was set up in 1964 with the object of effecting economies in manpower consistent with administrative efficiency and evolving performance standards and work norms in Government offices and Institutions wholly or substantially dependent on Government Grants. Its officers also serve as Core Member on the Committees appointed to scrutinise manpower requirements of Scientific and Technical Organisations.

Upto 1997, SIU had completed 1246 studies covering 6,46,175 posts out of which 96,099 posts were found surplus. In addition demand for creation of 96,849 new posts was not found justified. During the year 1997, the SIU studied 5,652 sanctioned posts and examined proposals for the creation of 422 posts in 18 offices. The SIU studies resulted in identifying 1241 posts surplus out of sanctioned strength of 5652 posts. The creation of 257 posts against additional demand of 422 posts was also not accepted. The effect of studies would result in net direct economy of Rs.818.56 lakhs after deducting additional expenditure of Rs.152.10 lakhs on account of new posts recommended for creation against additional demand. There was also a preventive economy of Rs. 191.26 lakhs on account of the demand for 257 additional posts not found justified.

During the year 1998, the SIU studied 12,415 sal posts and examined proposals for the creation of 167 posts in 18 offices. The SIU studies resulted in identifying 1735 posts surplus out of sanctioned strength of 12,415 posts. The creation of 117 posts against additional demand of 167 posts was also not accepted. The effect of studies would result in net d; red economy of Rs.1827.81 lakhs after deducting additional, expenditure of Rs.64.00 lakhs on account of new posts recommended for creation against additional demand. There was also a preventive economy of Rs. 131.98 lakhs on account of the demand for 117 additional posts not found justified.

Officers of SIU also represented as Core Members or the study teams/Vetting Committee constituted by the Scientific Organisations. During the year, two studies relating to Scientific organisations were finalised.

Since its inception, the SIU has completed 1264 studies covering 6,58,590 posts out of which 97,834 posts were found surplus. The demand for creation of 96,966 new posts was not found justified.

Use of hindi in official work

In this Department along with the implementation of Official Language Policy of the Government of India, English tc sitHindi and vice-versa translation of all kinds of general Orders, documents required under Article 3(3) of the Official Language Act, 1963, papers to be produced before either House of the to Parliament, Parliamentary Questions and their answers an(to essential reports, Orders, letters received from the Hon'ble Minister is done by Hindi Section. Apart from this, translation of Cabinet Notes, representations, minutes of the meetings of the for nature is also done in Hindi Section.

The instructions given in the Annual Programme and Programmes of Official Language are being implemented in the Department. The Official Language Act in Article 3(3) is being observed completely and all the letters received in Hindi are being replied in Hindi only

In the Department 98.4% Officers/employees have mad the working knowledge/proficiency in Hindi. These Officer/employees are doing from 29% to 75% of their work in Hindi. Typists/Stenographers who do not know Hindi typing/stenography are regularly sent in batches for Hindi training. In this manner 56 employees were nominated for Hindi typing/stenography in last training session and 19 employees were nominated for the training in Prabodh, Praveen and Pragya. Workshops are organised from time to time in this Department with a view to removing hesitation of the Officers/employees who have working knowledge of Hindi. An examination is held after each Workshop and the participating employees are given the Certificates and the employees standing 1 st, 2nd and 3rd are given the Cash awards of Rs.200/-, Rs. 150/- and Rs. 100/- respectively. This year three such Workshops were organised and 40 employees were imparted training in Hindi. Meetings of the Departmental Official Language Implementation Committee are also held regularly.

A short-term Scheme was started in the Department under which employees/officers were honoured by awarding them the 1st, 2nd and 3rd prizes.

First time in the Ministry of Finance, Department of Expenditure, a running Shield Scheme has been introduced from 1st April 98 to 31st March, 99 with the purpose to promote progressive use of Hindi and to encourage Officers/staff of the Department to use Hindi in Official work. Many attractive awards are there in this Scheme.

For the expansion of Hindi in the Department and to create an inclination of the Officers/employees in Hindi a Quarterly Hindi magazine 'Vyay Patrika' is published by Hindi Section and thus the employees/officers of the Department are encouraged to give their original articles to be published in this magazine.

A Hindi fortnight was organised this year also, in which the Additional Secretary (Expenditure) and Chairman, Official Language Implementation Committee guided all the Officers/ employees with his deep studies and experience. Besides Noting & Drafting and Essay Competition, two new Competitions of Hindi typing &

Stenography were also organised on this occasion and the amounts of rewards were raised substantially for those Officers/staff members who stood first, second and third respectively- A meeting of the official Language implementation Committee was also organised under the Chairmanship of Additional Secretary (Expenditure).

Plan finance I division

Plan Financed Division handles matters relating to overall financial position and plan outlays of States. The Division is closely associated with Planning Commission in assessment of financial resources for Five Year Plans and Annual Plans of States. It monitors the ways and means and resource position of States, advises the States to take appropriate action whenever they face problems relating to cash management. If necessary, rescheduling release of funds and other possible measures are planned by this division to help the States tide over their ways and means difficulties subject to Centre's own resource position.

Plan Finance- I Division acts as the disbursement division for Central assistance to States for their States Plans (including externally aided projects, Hill Area Development Programme (HADP), Border Area Development Programme (BADP), Accelerated Irrigation Benefit Programme (AIBP)) on the basis of funding approved by the Planning Commission for States 'Annual Plan. Release of Non-Plan revenue deficit grants and Centre's share to the Calamity relief Fund (CRF) of the States, which are covered by the Finance Commission recommendations is also made by this Division. Funds from "National Fund for Calamity Relief" (NFCR) for natural calamities of rare severity is also released to the States by this Division as per the decisions of the National Calamity Relief Committee (NCRC).

This Division also deals with the matter relating to

Inter State financial relation covering Inter State Council, Zonal Councils and North Eastern Council. As in the past, this Division was actively associated in 1998-99 with the review of resources of the State Governments for their Annual Plans 1998-69 and the assessment of resources of the State Governments for their Annual Plans 1999-2000.

For the year 1998-99, the Latest Estimates of Central assistance to States for their Annual Plans amounted to Rs.27035.86 crores, the details of which are as follows:-

Normal central assistance	14120.00
Additional Central assistance	912.00
Special Central assistance to J&K	850.00
Additional Central assistance to BMS	3358.63
Additional Central assistance to SDS	325.81
Special plan loan	350.00
Advance plan assistance	300.00
Additional Central assistance for EAPs	4750.00
Additional Central assistance for other projects	86.32
Special Central assistance for Hill Areas	490.00
Special Central assistance for Border Areas	200.00
Central loan assistance for AIBP	1200.00
Central assistance for Non-lapsable Pool of Revenues for NE and Sikkim	93.10

The Centre's share to the Calamity Relief Fund of the States amounting to Rs.977.57 crores and Non-Plan Revenue Deficit grant of Rs.258.76 crores are also being given to the States during the year in report.

A total of Rs.1742.12 crores is being adjusted in 1998-99 from the Central assistance to 17 out of 25 State Governments (except Arunachal Pradesh, Goa, Himachal Pradesh, Meghalaya, Mizoram, Nagaland, Sikkim and Tripura) against outstanding dues from the State

Electricity Boards (SEBs)/State Departments to Central Public Sector Undertakings (CPSUs) viz. NTPC, NHPC, NEEPCO, DVC, REC, CIL, BHEL, NEYVELI, and Power grid Corporation. The adjusted amounts are being paid to these CPSUs.

Plan finance II division

Plan Finance II Division deals with matters relating to the Central Plan. These cover the estimates of resources for Central Plan including internal and extra budgetary resources, plan outlays of different Ministries/ Departments of the Central Government, appraisal of Plan projects/schemes before they are submitted to Public Investment Board(PIB)/Expenditure Finance Committee (EFC) etc.

Plan Finance II is also the Secretariat of the PIB. The PIB considers investment proposals of the Central Government Ministries in regard to their Public Sector Undertakings. Under the existing guidelines, Central Sector Projects costing Rs.100 crores and above are considered by PIB. Secretary(Expenditure) is the Chairman of the PIB and Joint Secretary (Plan Finance II) acts as the Secretary to the Board.

Besides its role of an 'appraisal agency" in all Project Schemes considered by PIB/EFCs., Plan Finance Division processes Notes for Cabinet/CCEA for obtaining Finance Minister's concurrence.

During the period between January 1, 1998 to December 31, 1998, 22 meetings of PIB were held and 18 projects with a total capital cost of Rs.33,399.54 crores were recommended for approval. The proposals considered by the PIB for various projects, Ministry/ Department wise, are as follows:-

Ministry/Department	No. of projects Considered	Recommended for approval	(Rs. in crores)
1. Pet. & Natural Gas	8	6	22,385.00
2. Power	8	7	9,585.66
3. Fertilizer	4	3	886.27
4. Surface Transport	3	1	417.39
5. Coal	2	1	125.22
6. Chemicals & Pet. Chem.	2	-	—
TOTAL	27	18	33,399.54

During the same period, the Committee of PIB also considered and approved 3 proposals from different Ministries/ Departments for first stage clearance for the preparation of detailed feasibility reports. As per existing guidelines CPIB has to consider proposals costing Rs.10 crores or more.

Estimation of internal and extra budgetary resources for financing the Annual Plan of the Central Public Sector Undertakings is an important activity of this Division. The Division obtains the details of estimates of receipts and expenditures of different Public Sector Undertakings from the Financial Advisers and in consultation with the representatives of the Administrative Ministries, Planning Commission and Public Sector Undertakings, prepares the estimates of internal resources of the Public Sector Undertakings for finalising their Annual Plan.

Plan Finance II Division is actively associated with the discussions held in the Planning Commission for the formulation of Annual Plans and Five Year Plans of the Central Ministries. Based on the estimates of internal resources prepared by Plan Finance II Divn. and estimates of extra budgetary resources like bonds, ECB/ supplier's credit etc. by the Deptt. of Economic Affairs for the Central Public Sector Undertakings and the annual

Plan discussions held in the Planning Commission, the Annual Plans/ Five Year Plan Outlays for various Central Ministries/Deptts. are finalised.

Plan Finance II also examines, in consultation with the Controller General of Accounts, the proposals received from various Ministries/Departments for Capital Restructuring of sick Public Sector Enterprises including cases which have been referred to BIFR and processes them for finalising the views of the Ministry of Finance.

Central pension accounting office

The Central Pension Accounting Office (CPAO) set up on 1.1.1990 is presently administering the 'Scheme for Payment of Pensions to Central Government Civil Pensioners by Public Sector Banks'. Its functions inter-alia include:

— Preparation of budget under the Grant and accounting thereof.

— Issue of Special Seal Authorities (SSAs) to Public Sector Banks.

— Internal Audit of Banks.

Upto 15th of November 1998 this office had handled approximately 66000 pension cases. Based on these figures, we expect to handle approximately 105000 cases during the financial year 1998-99. This would mark a net increase of over 180% with respect to the last fiscal's figures which stood at 37399 cases. The exponential increase in work is mainly attributable to the implementation of the Fifth Central Pay Commission's recommendations relating to pension and family pension.

The Central Pension Accounting Office administers the pension grant under Grant No.34-Pension. In addition, a test check of pension payments made by 42 branches of various Public Sector Banks has been completed as of 31 st December, 1998. Audit reports in this connection have already been sent to the concerned Public Sector Banks.

2,12,228 authorisations were issued by the Central Pension Accounting Office upto 31.3.98 since its inception in 1990. The number of pension cases handled by this office during the financial year 1997-98 was 37,399.

An Internal Audit Team consisting of one PAO and one JAO/AAO was created on the advice of C&AG of India after getting necessary approval from the Ministry of Finance, Department of Expenditure. Test-check of 88 branches of various PSBs was conducted during the financial year 1997-98.

To avoid financial hardship to pensioners, the procedure for transfer of pension accounts from one Bank to another was simplified after obtaining the concurrence of the RBI and the C&AG.

The third updated edition of the book 'Scheme for payment of Pensions to Central Government Civil Pensioners by Public Sector Banks' was issued in January, 1998 with the prior concurrence of the CGA and the C&AG.

Chief Engineer, NZ-3 and Deputy Director, Horticulture (South) ÇPWD have been requested to provide green cover in the Trikoot office complex.

Controller general of accounts

The Controller General of Accounts is the apex Accounting Authority of the Central Government and exercises the powers of the President under Article 150 of the Constitution for prescribing the forms of Accounts of the Union and State Governments on the advice of the Comptroller & Auditor Genera of India. The Controller General of Accounts is responsible, inter-alia, (a) for the preparation and consolidation of the Union Government Monthly Accounts. A detailed analytical review d the Union Government Accounts is presented to the Finance Minister every month within 4 weeks from the close of the month The review covers major aspects of receipts, expenditure, fiscal deficit, sources of financing, etc. to facilitate during the year tracking at the highest level. A Provisional Account (Unaudited) for the year is also prepared at the end of the financial year. With effect from October, 1998, select accounting data are also released v the INTERNET every month at the web site addresses (1) htp: www.indiagov.org and (ii) htp:// www.meadev.gov.in. (b presentation to Parliament of the Annual Appropriation Accounts (Civil) and Finance Accounts of the Union Government. These accounts for 1996-97 were laid before Parliament during the Budget Session on 5th June, 1998 along with the Report of the Comptroller and Auditor General of India. (c) ensuring a sound and effective internal audit and pre-check system in the Civil Ministries (C enabling prompt and accurate accounting (e) ensuring effective and close monitoring of Receipts of the Government of India especially those relating to Income Tax, Customs and Cent" Excise (f) enabling the effective utilisation of accounts as a tc of management by constant upgradation of the quality (accounts, leading to improved financial control within Government.

The organisation of the Controller General of Account is also responsible for government disbursements and banking arrangements of various Ministries/Departments of the Government of India. The Controller General of Accounts closely monitor the extant system by means of periodical interaction with the Reserve Bank of India and Public Sector Banks on an ongoing basis.

The Controller General of Accounts also brings out every year, a booklet entitled "Accounts at a Glance", bringing out broad and significant features of Government Receipts and Expenditure.

The Controller General of Accounts is looking after the computerisation of Government Accounting functions in all the Civil Ministries. It has already implemented five accounting packages - IMPLROVE for Voucher Level Computerisation in PAOs; CONTACT for Consolidation of Accounts in Principal Accounts Offices; GAINS for Consolidation of Accounts in CGA's Office; SCT for collecting annual accounts data from field offices and FINEACT for preparing Annual Finance Accounts of the Government of India.

All Principal Accounts Offices are only using CONTACT for consolidation of accounts. Besides, some of the PAOs have also discontinued manual compilation of accounts. Efforts are being made to progressively extend the coverage of computerisation to all offices.

A new comprehensive software for Principal Accounts Offices CONTACT (with several new features) on ORACLE platform is nearing completion. This will be installed in the Principal Accounts Offices in place of the existing CONTACT

The Institute of Government Accounts and Finance (INGAF) was set up in February, 1992 with a view to imparting intensive induction and in-service training in accounting, budgeting, financial management, expenditure control, internal audit, administrative-cum-establishment matters and initial and advanced level training in development and use of Computer applications to officials working in various Central Government Ministries, etc. The Institute has established its regional Centres in Calcutta, Chennai and Mumbai. The Institute has the credit of imparting training to more than 6643 officers and members of the staff belonging to various Accounting Organisation, Drawing and Disbursement Officers and other Central Government Undertakings. The Institute has also been approved by the Ministry of External Affairs for imparting training to the officers of developing countries under the ITEC programmes. Courses have been conducted for officers of the Governments of Sri Lanka during 15.11.98 to 4.12.98. Officers of the Indian Civil Accounts Service are being imparted a high level of professional training at this Institute after their initial training at the National Institute of Financial Management.

Finance commission division

The Finance Commission Division of Department of Expenditure is concerned with the implementation of the recommendations of the Finance Commission. The Tenth Finance Commission was constituted by the President on 15th June, 1992. The Commission submitted its Report for the period 1995-2000 on 26th November, 1994., The report together with an explanatory memorandum as to the action taken on the recommendations of the Commission was laid on the table of both Houses of Parliament on 14th March, 1995. The Government accepted the recommendations of the Commission regarding devolution of Income tax, Union excise duties, Additional duties of excise in lieu of sales tax, grants in lieu of tax on railway passenger fares, grants-in-aid to cover non-plan revenue gap, grants for financing relief expenditure, grants for Upgradation and Special Problems, grants for local bodies and debt relief to States.

Upgradation and special problem grants

The Tenth Finance Commission in its report has recommended grants-in-aid for upgradation of standards of administration and special problems of States. Under upgradation, the Finance Commission has selected the following areas:

District Administration

i) Police
ii) Fire Services
iii) Jails
iv) Record rooms
v) Treasuries and Accounts

Education

i) Promotion of girls' education
ii) Additional facilities for Upper Primary Schools
iii) Drinking water facilities in Primary Schools.

The Tenth Finance Commission has not recommended upgradation grants for those States which have been assessed to have an overall non-plan revenue surplus before devolution. The Finance Commission has observed that in their view it is not only desirable but also necessary and possible for these States to give from their own resources priority allocation to the areas needing upgradation. The States failing in this category are Gujarat, Haryana, Karnataka and Maharashtra.

The Tenth Finance Commission has recommended upgradation grant amounting to Rs.1362.50 crore under the District Administration and Education Sectors. In addition the Commission has also recommended Special Problem Grants amounting to Rs. 1246 crore. Though the recommendation of the Tenth Finance Commission are for a period of five years 1995-2000, the Commission recommended the upgradation and special problem grants payable to States over a period of four years viz. 19962000 as the Commission felt that the first year of the period covered by their recommendation would be required for working out the details of the scheme. The

Inter-Ministerial Empowered Committee (IMEC) in its nine meetings held so far has considered the Action Plans (on various programmes) of different States and has approved Action Plans amounting to Rs.2391.20 crore (excluding the amount of Rs.77.51 crore recommended by the Tenth Finance Commission for Police Telecommunication which is being implemented and monitored by the Ministry of Home Affairs). During 1996-98 an amount of Rs.474.86 crore was released to the States under Upgradation and Special Problem Grants. During 1998-99, so far, another Rs.407.67 crore has been released to the States. Thus, a total grant of Rs.882.53 crore has been released to State Governments for upgradation and special problems.

Local bodies grants

In consonance with the purpose, intent and spirit underlying the 73rd and 74th amendments to the Constitution, the Tenth Finance Commission has recommended ad hoc grants to the States to supplement the resources of Panchayati Raj Institutions (PRIs) as well as for the Urban Local Bodies (ULBs). For PRIs the Commission has recommended an ad hoc provision of Rs. 4380.93 crore and for the ULBs a provision of Rs.1000 crore. As per Commission's recommendations, these grants are payable during the four-year period of 1996-2000. During 199698 Rs.1676.34 crore was released for Panchayati Raj Institutions and Rs.365.26 crore for Urban Local Bodies of different States. During 1998-99, so far an amount of Rs.437.51 crore and Rs. 109.86 crore respectively has been released for Panchayati Raj Institutions and Urban Local Bodies of States.

Debt relief to states

The TFC has assessed the debt position of States as on 31 st March, 1994. The Scheme of Debt Relief has two parts:

i) a scheme for general debt relief for all States linked to fiscal performance; and

ii) specific relief for States with high fiscal stress, special additional debt relief from the Central Government to the tune of category States and States with debt problem warranting Rs.10.39 crore under this scheme. No such proposal has been special attention.

As an incentive to better fiscal management the TFC have designed a scheme which links debt relief to the fiscal performance of a State. The improvement in fiscal performance has been measured by comparing ratio of revenue receipts to total revenue expenditure in a given year with the average of corresponding ratios in the three immediately preceding years. Accordingly, each State would be considered against its performance in the past. The Commission has recommended that generalised debt relief may take the form of a certain percentage of repayment (maximum allowable level is 10%) failing due in each year of the period of its recommendations being written off. Based on the scheme designed by the TFC during 1998-99 an amount of Rs.46.81 crore was written off as general debt relief to the States of Arunachal Pradesh, Bihar, Jammu & Kashmir, Karnataka, Kerala, Meghalaya, Pubjab, Tamil Nadu and Tripura.

Under specific debt relief for States with high fiscal stress, i.e. Orissa, Bihar and Uttar Pradesh and special category States, the Commission has recommended writing off of 5% of repayment due with respect to fresh Central loans given during (1989-95) and outstanding on 31st March, 1995. Accordingly, the specific debt relief to be given to the States during 1995-2000 is as under:-

Period	*Amount to be written off (Rs. crores)*
1995-96	28.44
1996-97	36.96
1997-98	44.22
1998-99	51.09
1999-2000	58.11

Special loans to punjab

The Commission under debt relief also recommended that one third of the repayment of principal falling due during 1995-2000 on the special term loans advanced to the State of Punjab to fight militancy and insurgency be waived. Based on the recommendations of the Commission, the sanction for write off of special term loans amounting to Rs.495.22 crores during the period 1995-2000 have been issued by the Plan Finance-I Division.

In addition, the Commission has also recommended a scheme for encouraging retirement of Central Debt from the proceeds of disinvestment of equity holdings of the State Governments. For those States who disinvest upto 20% of their aggregate equity during the award period of Tenth Finance Commission from the State Level Public Sector Enterprises and utilise the proceeds of such disinvestment for retirement of debt owed to the Central Government, the Commission has recommended that the Central Government should additionally write off debt equivalent to the debt retired by the State limited to 20% of the equity investment of the State as on 31 st March, 1995. During 1996-97 only the Government of Tamil Nadu availed of additional debt relief from the Central Government to the tune of Rs. 10.39 crore under this scheme. No such proposal has been received from any other State in this regard.

Cost accounts branch

Cost Accounts Branch of Ministry of Finance (Department of Expenditure) renders professional assistance to different Ministries and other agencies of Central Government in studies relating to costing, pricing tariff fixation and other related aspects. The Chief Adviser (Cost) as head of the Indian Cost Accounts Service (ICAS) assists the Department of Expenditure in matters relating to the cadre administration. This office also looks after the training requirements of the ICAS Officers. The Officers of the Branch also serve in different inter-Ministerial Committees.

During the period from January 1998 to December 1998 the following major studies were completed by this Branch:

1. Supply of Ayurvedic/Unani Medicines to CGHS by Indian Medicine Pharmaceutical Corporation Limited (IMPCL) -Vetting of prices.
2. Cost of production and fair price of Tear Smoke Munitions and guns supplied by Border Security Force, Tekanpur.
3. Fixation of fair prices for insecticides supplied to NMEP by two Public Sector units.
4. Cost price study regarding revision of Bench Mark Price for Natural Rubber.
5. Reimbursement of deficit of the State Trading Corporation on account of the import of Fatty Acid.
6. Evolving a suitable price variation formulae for Traction Electrics manufactured and supplied by BHEL to Indian Railways.
7. Report on the revision of the Rate Structure of Advertisement for Directorate of Audio Visual Publication (DAVP)

8. Cost/Price study of Multilingual Character Generate System supplied by M/s C-DAC, Pune to Doordarshan.
9. Subsidy payable for catering at Parliament House, Parliament House Annexe and Prime Minister's office to Northern Railways.
10. Costing of Pricing of various types of Digital Product produced by Survey of India for use of Governmental Semi Governmental /Non Governmental Agencies.
11. Fixation of storage charges payable by Food Corporation of India to Central Warehousing Corporation from 1.4.9 onwards.
12. Revision of the rates for Special Parties hosted b, Ministries/Members of Parliament and Rajya Sabha an Lok Sabha Secretariats in Railway Catering Units I Parliament House and Parliament House Annexe.

3

Department of Revenue

General

Department of Revenue exercises control in respect of matters relating to all the direct and indirect Union taxes. The department administers the following Acts:

1. Income Tax Act, 1961
2. Wealth Tax Act, 1956
3. Gift Tax Act, 1958
4. Interest Tax Act, 1974
5. Expenditure Tax Act, 1987
6. The Benami Transaction (Prohibition) Act, 1988
7. The Estate Duty Act 1953
8. The Super Profits Tax Act, 1963
9. The Companies (Profits) Sur-tax, 1964
10. The Compulsory Deposit (income Tax Payers) Scheme Act, 1974.
11. The Hotel Receipts Tax Act, 1980
12. The Central Excise and Salt Act, 1944 and related matters.
13. The Customs, Act, 1962 and other related matters.
14. The Central Sales Tax Act, 1956
15. Narcotic Drugs and Psychotropic Substances (NDPS) Act, 1985.
16. Smugglers & Foreign Exchange Manipulators (Forfeiture of Property) Act, 1976. (SAFEM (FOP)A)

17. Indian Stamps Act, 1899 (to the extent failing within jurisdiction of the Union).
18. Conservation of Foreign Exchange and Prevention of Smuggling Activities Act, 1974 (COFEPOSA).
19. Foreign Exchange Regulation Act, 1973 (FERA).

The administration of Acts mentioned at S.No.7 to 11 above is limited to cases pertaining to the period when these laws were in force.

The Department looks after the matters relating to the above Acts through the following field/attached/ subordinate offices supervised by the Headquarters Administration :

1. Central Board of Excise and Customs (CBEC)
2. Central Board of Direct Taxes. (CBDT)
3. Central Economic Intelligence Bureau (CEIB)
4. Enforcement Directorate (ED)
5. (a) Narcotics Control Bureau (NCB)
   (b) Central Bureau of Narcotics (CBN)
   (c) Chief Controller of Factories (CCF)
6. Appellate Tribunal For Forfeited Property. (ATFP)
7. Settlement Commission (income Tax and Wealth Tax)
8. Customs, Excise & Gold (Control) Appellate Tribunal(CEGAT)
9. Authority For Advance Rulings, (AAR)
10. Competent Authorities (CA)
11. National Committee for Promotion of Social and Economic Welfare.

Collection of direct and indirect taxes taken together showed an upward increase over last year as indicated below

S.No.	*Nature of Taxes*	*Taxes collected in Financial Year (Rupees in Crores)*		
		1998-99 (upto Jan'99)	*1997-98 (upto Jan'99)*	*%age growth over last year*
1.	Corporation Tax	17054.20	14188.29	20.20
2.	Interest Tax	13940.61	12295.59	13.38
3.	Interest Tax	644.79	591.90	8.94
4.	Central Excise	39720.82	37246.75	6.64
5.	Customs Duty	32870.25	33395.43	(-)1.57
	Total	104230.67	97717.96	6.66

An organisation chart of the Department of Revenue given on the next page

Central board of excise and customs

Organisation and functions

CBEC essentially deals with the task of formulation of Policy concerning and collection of Customs and Central Excise duties, prevention of smuggling and administration of matters relating to Customs, Central Excise and Narcotics (to the extent under CBEC's purview. The Board is headed by a Chairman and has five members.

In the performance of its administrative and executive functions, the Board is assisted by the following attached and subordinate offices :

i) Various Commissionerates.

ii) Directorate General of Inspection & Audit

iii) Directorate General of Revenue Intelligence

iv) Directorate General of Anti Evasion;

v) National Academy of Customs, Excise and Narcotics;

vi) Directorate of Organisation & Management Services;

vii) Directorate of Statistics and Intelligence;

viii) Directorate of Preventive Operations;
ix) Directorate of Publicity and Public Relations;
x) Directorate General of Vigilance;
xi) Central Revenue Control Laboratory
xii) Directorate of Valuation;
xiii) Directorate of system; and
xiv) Directorate of Service Tax

The functions of the above offices are indicated in Annexure.

The Commissionerates of Customs and Central Excise which are spread over the country perform the executive f unctions entrusted by the Board. There are 59 Commissionerates concerned mainly with Central Excise. There are four major Customs Houses (at Mumbai, Chennai, Calcutta & Cochin) and 20 custom Commissionerates at international aiports and other places mainly handling Customs work. There are 20 Appellate Commissionerates situated in the metropolitan cities and other industrially important places.

Statement showing the sanctioned strength as on against which the 1.7.98 in various grades in CBEC.

Group	Sanctioned Strength
Group A	1951
Customs Department	
Group 'B	2685
Group 'C'	12785
Group 'D'	7056
Central Excise	
Group 'B'	5954
Group 'C'	29445
Group 'D'	10384
NC & CCF	
Group 'B'	88

Group 'C'	1113
Group 'D'	1378
Others (Directorates & CRCL)	
Group 'B'	183
Group 'C'	1369
Group 'D'	394
Total	74785

Computerisation of customs and excise operations

The computerisation of Customs operations has been undertaken at major ports, air cargo complexes and ICDs across the country The implementation involves initial site preparation followed by hardware installation and establishment of connectivity using UTP, Fibre and Radio links. Export process are first automated followed by import operations. Import and export operation have already been computerised in nine customs stations in Delhi, Mumbai, Chennai, Bangalore, Vishakhapatanam and Hyderabad. Work in several other customs stations is in progress.

Computerisation is accompanied by new procedures formulated to reduce the number of stages in document processing. The Department is actively working on a proposal to introduce EDI at major customs stations which will be able the trade to file their documents and monitor them to physically come top to the Customs office.

A strategy for upgradation of existing systems in Central Excise is under formulation. The new systems would involve upgradation of both hardware and software. The year 200 problem has been addressed by the latest version of the Excise application software released in Aug., 1998. Following the reorganisation of Commissionerates and Divisions a new coding scheme is being finalised for identifying Ranges and assesees with respect of the changed jurisdiction.

Custom duty

Revenue from custom duties for 1996-97 and 1997-98 is given below :-

1996-97		*1997-98*	
Budget Estimate	Actual Realisation	Budget Estimate	Actual Realisation
44435.00	42889.96	52550.00	40536.76

Major changes proposed in budget 1998-99 highlights

- A special Additional Duty @ 4% has been proposed on imports with certain exemption to provide a level playing field for domestic procedures.
- Anomalies in duty structure have been rectified.
- Import duties on goods used in the Information Technology sector has been reduced significantly.
- Full exemption has been provided on import of specified life saving drugs.
- Free baggage allowance for income passengers has been raised from Rs. 6000/- to Rs. 12,000/-.
- In order to provide adequate protection to the domestic industry, import duties have been increased by 5% on certain items and import duty of 5% has been imposed on glazed newsprint.
- In order to improve the cost competitiveness of domestic industry, import duties on many items have been reduced to the extent of 5% to 25%.
- To promote health care and to give relief to people suffering from AIDS and thallassaemia, full exemption has been provided on medicines such as Lamivudine for AIDS and Maltol for manufacture of Deferiprone which is used as drug for Thallasaemia.
- To encourage investment in the information technology sector, import duty on 75 specified machinery has been reduced from 25% to 15%. Basic

import duty has been reduced to a level of 5% advalorem on Silicon, ICs of value exceeding Rs. 1000 per piece. Cathode ray tubes for colour monitors for computers, detection components for such colour monitors, Hard disk drive, Floopy disk drive and CID Rom drive.

- As per GATT obligations customs duties on a number of specified items have been reduced to be within the band rates.

Post budget scenario

- Special Additional Duty (SAD) of 8% in imports as proposed in the budget was reduced to 4%. Items of import under export promotion schemes have been exempted from SAD.
- Complete exemption of Customs Duty granted to all software used in information technology Sector.
- Full exemption of duties on CD - Roms containing educational material, newspaper, magazines etc.
- Basic Customs duty on edible oils for manufacture of Vanaspati reduced from 20% to 10% ad valorem.

Excise duty

Revenue from Union Excise Duties (excluding cesses not administred by Department of Revenue) during 1996-97 and 1997-98.

Budget estimate for 1998-99 (excluding cesses not administred by department of Revenue) is Rs.57425.00 crore as against which the collection upto end of January, 1999 has been Rs. 39720.00 crore.

Major changes proposed In budget 1998-99

- The full excise duty exemption limit for small scale units was raised from Rs. 30 lakhs to Rs. 50 lakhs.
- Tax base has been widened by imposing new levies.

- Rationalisation of duty rates.
- Increase in the specific rates of duty on Cigarettes.
- Imposition of additional excise duty @ Rs. 1 per litre on motor spirit.
- Provision for the setting up of a Settlement Commission to settle certain types of customs and excise disputes.
- Kar Vivadh Samadhan Scheme
- Simplification of excise procedures.
- Excise duty at a nominal rate of 8% adv. was imposed on a number of items which were hitherto exempt from duty.
- In order to rationalise the duty rates, excise duty on a number of products which were attracting a low rate of duty was raised. The increase in duty was 5 percentage point.
- Excise duty was reduced on a number of items such as pagers, cellophone, diesel engine sets upto 10 HP, surgical and medical examination gloves and matches.
- In order to give relief to the construction sector, a number of products used in construction has been exempted from excise duty.
- The full excise duty exemption limit for units working under the general SSI excise duty exemption scheme has been raised from Rs.30 lakhs to Rs.50 lakhs. Clearances in excess of Rs. 50 lakhs but not exceeding 100 lakhs attract a concessional rate of duty of 5%.
- The procedure for collection of excise duties have been significantly rationalised and simplified with a

view to minimise the interface between the tax collector and the tax payer.

- A new scheme called Kar Vivadh Samadhan Scheme has been introduced to provide for a quick and voluntary settlement of customs and excise duties outstanding as on 31 st March, 1998 by offering waiver of a part of the arrears of taxes and interest and providing immunity against institution of prosecution and imposition of penalty.

Post budget scenario

During the consideration stage of the budget, excise duty exemption was provided to a number of items such as packaged tea in retail packs upto 100 gms., branded food and dairy products, branded spices, rubberised coir mattresses, spectable lenses etc. Full exemption from excise duty was also provided on certain anti-TB drugs. Excise duty was reduced on fire works from 18% to 13%, on medical furniture from 13% to 8% and on motor spirit from 35% to 32%.

The coverage of service tax was widened to cover 12 more services such as services rendered by architects, interior decorators, management consultants, chartered accountants, cost accountants, Company Secretaries, Credit rating agencies, market research agencies, under writers, private security/detective agencies, real estate agents and consultants, and mechanised slaughter houses.

Notifications

Information on number of Customs & Central Excise notifications issued during the year 1997-98.

Simplication of central excise duty

During 1998-99, a number of measures were taken for further simplification and liberalisation of Central Excise rules and procedures especially for the small scale sector and exporters.

Small scale units

(i) Consequent upon full exemption limit for SS units having been enhanced from Rs.30 lakhs to Rs. 50 lakhs, full exemption from registration upto the value of clearance to the tune of Rs. 50 lakhs was provided.

(ii) SS units will be required to file declaration only once and not every year. No declaration is required to be filed by SSI exemption from registration upto the value of clearance of Rs.40 lakhs. (Notification No. 22/98-CE (NT) dated 4.6.98).

(iii) Audit only once in two years (Executive Instructions).

(iv) SS Units cannot be visited without the permission of Assistant Commissioner (Executive instructions)

Liberalisation & Simplification In the Export Sector

(i) The following two categories of manufacturer-exporter have been extended special facility in respect of examination, certification and sealing of export goods.

(a) Those who have paid Central Excise duty exceeding Rs. 10 crores in the preceding financial year.

(b) Those who have been accorded the status of Super Star Trading House, Star Trading House, Trading House or Export: House under EXIM policy, (Notification No. 36/98-CE(NT) dated 2.9.98

(ii) A special ware-housing facility has been provided to Super Star Trading House or Star Trading House and the foreign Departmental Stores of repute for storage of excisable goods and export there from without payment of duty subject to finishing of necessary bond.

The warehouse can be established and registered in Ahmedabad, Bangalore, Calcutta, Chennai, Delhi, Hyderbad, Jaipur, Kanpur, Ludhiana & Mumbai.

The exporters can now export from their factory situated in any part of the country through any of the above place without having the need to have separate office at all places. (Notification no. 26/98-CE(NT) dated 15.7.98).

Miscellaneous

Central Excise rules have been amended so as to dispense with (i) large assessees from authenticating invoices, under rule 52A, (ii) filing of quarterly return under rule 55, (iii) intimation of principal raw material under rule 173D (iv) intimation under rule 55F(4) and 575(ii), (v) filing of declaration under rule 57T(4) and (5); and (vi) permission for removing non-excisable goods under rule 50.

Permission' under rule 57(F) and 173M have been substituted by intimation. Period for return of goods sent for job work has been extended from 60 days to 180 days.

Court cases - central excise

1. Legal Cell in the Board's Office handles court cases in the Supreme Court. It is also, in consultation with the Ministry of Law, attending to appointment of Counsels including Sr. Public Prosecutors to represent the Department in various courts through out the country.

2. The comparative position of cases relating to Central Excise pending in Supreme Court and High Courts as on 31.12.97 and 30.11.98 is given below. During this period, there was an addition of 331 cases involving Rs.93.12 crores as duty in Supreme Court and 1971 cases involving Rs. 382.66 crores in various High Courts. However, there has been a

disposal of 499 cases involving Rs. 21.19 crores at the level of Supreme Court and 1247 cases involving Rs. 265.31 crores at the level of High Courts.

3. The Legal Cell has also been monitoring the progress under the "Kar Vivad Samadhan Scheme" since its inception in September, 1998, and also issuing, in consultation with Ministry of Law, clarifications, directions and instructions to field-formations under the scheme. The response has been quite appreciable in as much as 13883 declarations have been filed covering an amount of Rs. 1791.14 crores. A sum of Rs. 690.99 crores is likely to be recovered as determined by the declarants under the Scheme.

Future plans

1. Legal Cells in the CBEC, has initiated several steps to streamline the litigation process and for monitoring of progress. A Special (Litigation) Cell, has been constituted to pursue the matters pending and coming up before the Supreme Court on day to day basis. The Litigation Cell has been active in obtaining information from the CAS of the Supreme Court and passing it on to the Legal Cell in the Boards' Office for onward dissemination to the field-formations. Efforts are on to computerise the date base of the Cell so as to further enhance its functional efficiency.

2. A proposal has also been initiated, in consultation with Ministry of Law, for empanelment of competent and knowledgeable advocates for handling court cases in various High Courts and CEGAT to be operated at the level of Chief Commissioners.

Arrears of central excise

Arrears of Central Excise as on 30th November, 1998 were Rs. 6016.50 crores approx. as compared to Rs. 5283.75 as on 31.3.98. Measuring like administrative, legal and pursuasive as are considered necessary continue to be taken in order to liquidate the arrears.

Audit - central excise

CBEC receives 500 to 600 DAPs every year, comments on which are required to be furnished on time bound basis. Action Taken Note on all the Audit Paras included in the Audit Report of C&AG are prepared and furnished to the Office of the C&AG.

During the current financial year, a concerted drive was made to send ATN on pending APs pertaining to previous years. As against 635 DAPs included in Audit Reports of previous years (1990-91 onwards), 444 ATNs have been sent upto 31.12.1998 which is 70% of the total pending paras.

Apart from the above, 299 DAPs were received till 31.12.98, out of which action has been taken in respect of 174 DAPs.

Customs

Arrears of customs revenue: Arrears of Customs Revenue (Confirmed Demands) as on 30.11.98 is Rs.53031.08 lakhs, as compared to Rs.28844.38 lakhs as on 1.4.1998. Considering the total Customs Revenue, these arrears form a very small percentage of the total revenue. Arrears of revenue are kept under constant watch and their recovery is pursued.

Audit: During the year 1998-99, 197 Draft Audit Paras relating to Customs duty have been received from the C&AG of India for inclusion in the Audit Report for the year 1997-98 (Revenue Receipts - Indirect Taxes - Customs). As on 1.12.98 replies in respect of 70 paragraphs out of the said paras have been sent to C&AG for vetting.

During the year 1997-98 out of the 202 Draft Audit Paras advance remedial/corrective action taken notes on 70 paras have been furnished to C&AG for vetting.

Adhoc exemptions: Adhoc Exemption is given on non-commercial imports by Government institutions, charitable organisation engaged in relief and rehabilitation work, import of scientific and technical equipments by research and development institutions etc. These organisations are not engaged in any commercial activities. Government allows them relief by way of adhoc exemption from payment of Customs Duty on import of these goods which are otherwise not covered under general exemption notifications.

During the period 1.4. 98 to 31.12.98, 88 adhoc exemption orders were issued, out of which 10 were for commercial exemption, while the remaining 78 related to non-commercial exemption.

Liberalisation of baggage rules: On the recommendations of the Estimates Committee, Baggage Rules have been liberalised by allowing import of one duty free laptop/ notebook computer by the tourist as his personal effects under rule 11 of Baggage Rules, 1998.

Disposal of detained baggage: Government have accepted the recommendation of the Estimates Committee regarding disposal of detained passenger baggage at International Airports under which now the balance amount from the sale proceeds after deducting customs duty etc. is refunded to the owner/passenger.

Customs court cases: The following steps were taken to improve the functioning of the department-

i) Instructions were issued to all the field formations

that all references received from the trade may be attended promptly and replied within a maximum of four weeks. The information received from FAX of E-Mail should be replied by E-MAIL.

ii) A simplified procedure was evolved to allow filing of Bill of Entry in joint name of the lessor and lessee in case of project import.

iii) A simplified procedure was evolved for duty free clearance of goods imported for display or use at fairs exhibitions, etc.

iv) The scope of fast track clearance was extended to manufacturer, importer of electronic goods having investments of rupees three crores and above as against the earlier limit of Rs. Thirty Crores and above.

v) A procedure was evolved to allow movement of export cargo by container/trucks from the hinterland to ports/ air cargo complexes.

vi) State Government undertakings, acting as custodians of Customs areas like 'air cargo complexes' and 'inland container depots' were allowed to dispose of unclaimed/uncleared cargo under simplified procedure.

vii) A simplified procedure was evolved for movement of export goods from factories, 100% EOU, EPZ, etc. on the basis of self certification and the scale of physical examination of export cargo was also reduced substantially.

viii) REWARI, BHIWADI, and RUDRAPUR notified as new Inland Container Depots u/s 7(aa) of Customs Act, 1962.

ix) New Courier Imports and Exports (clearance) Regulation, 1998 were notified under which imports as well as exports through courier mode is allowed.

In addition to the existing facilities at Mumbai, Delhi, Chennai and Calcutta, the facility was extended to Bangalore, Hyderabad, Ahmedabad and Jaipur also. Under the new regulations the courier parcels may be brought by passenger flight as well as cargo flight.

x) Import of additional items was allowed at Jaipur and Pune Airports.

xi) Loading/unloading of additional items was allowed at Dahej Port, Kakinada Port and Dahanu Port.

xii) "Py-3 field" and "Dahej" have been declared as coastal ports for coastal trade.

xiii) A "sub-exchange office at Ludhiana" has been appointed as a Foreign Post Office.

xiv) Countervailing duty was exempted on imports of goods from Nepal to India, manufactured in small scale industries in Nepal on the pattern of exemption given to similar small scale industries in India.

xv) Detailed instructions were issued laying down guidelines to eliminate/minimise irregularities in clearance of goods from bonded were houses.

xvi) The Exim Policy, 1997-2002 was extensively amended to give boost to exports and to simplify the procedures for import, manufacture and export of goods. The existing Customs & Excise notifications have been amended so that these are aligned with the provision of the amended EXIM Policy.

Till recently the EOU units were subjected to "Manufacture and Other Operations in Warehouse, Regulations, 1966" which required physical control by the Central Excise Officers of such units. These regulations have been amended to remove the physical controls to a very great extent and to shift the stress on account based control. To create a level playing field for the EOUs manufacturing Marine Freight Containers, with imported containers, it has been permitted to allow them clearance into DTA without payment of duty provided the containers are exported within 6 months from its clearance, EOUs have been permitted to donate used computers duty free after two years of their use to the recognised non-commercial educational institutes and recognised charitable hospitals/library and public funded research and development institutions.

xvii) In order to give relief to hotel industry to render services, Zero duty EPCG scheme was extended to it. Exemption for 10% CVD was also extended.

xviii) 100% EOUs/EPZ Units were permitted to switch over to DTA under Zero duty EPCG scheme.

xix) Import of Capital Goods required for Bio-tech Products was permitted under Zero duty EPCG scheme.

xx) Import of Capital Goods required for manufacture/ exports of nine products of engineering sector was permitted at the reduced threshold limit of Rs. One Crore under Zero duty EPCG scheme.

xxi) Import of Jigs fixtures, dyes and moulds was allowed without any value restriction under EPCG scheme.

xxii) The operation of DEEC scheme was extended to the ports of Kakinada and ICDs at Agra, Faridabad, Guntur, Jaipur, Jalandhar, Nagpur, Tirupur and Varanasi.

xxiii) Exemption from Bank Guarantee was extended to manufacturer/exporters under DEEC and EPCG schemes.

xxiv) The Special Advance Licensing Scheme was operationalised to promote import of Electronic Hardware products.

xxv) To facilitate imports by holders of DEPB, it has been decided that the DEPB holders whose DEPB books are registered at seaports of Mumbai, Calcutta, Cochin, Kandla, Mangalore, Marmugao, Chennai, Nhavasheva, kakinada, Vishakhapatnam, Haldia and Tuticorin Airports at Ahmedabad, Bangalore, Mumbai, Calcutta, Delhi, Hyderabad and Chennai and ICDs at Bangalore, Delhi, Moradabad, Ludhiana, Hyderabad, Agra, Faridabad, Guntur, Surat, Ahmedabad, Kanpur, Pitampur, Malanpur and Nagpur can be allowed imports of goods at any of the above mentioned Sea Ports/Airports/ICDs.

It has also been decided that the DEPB holder whose DEPB scrips are registered at any of the Customs station namely Air Caargo Complex, Coimbatore, ICDs at Coimbatore, Tirupur, Salem and Singanalur can make import at any of these customs station.

The DEPB holders have been allowed exemptions from payment of Special Additional Duty @4% for goods imported under DEPB scheme.

DEPB Scheme has also been extended to ICDs at Jodhpur, Salem, Tirupur, Singanalur, Waluj and Malanpur.

xxvi) The power for conversion of Shipping Bills into drawback shipping bills has been delegated to the commissioner of Customs in relaxation of rule 12 (1) (a) of Customs & Central Excise Duty Drawback Rules, 1995.

xxvii) Exemption has been allowed from payment of Customs Duty for fastners and polywadding materials when imported for the purpose manufacture of export products.

xxviii) Section 75-A of Customs Act, 1962 has been amended to reduce the period of three months provided in section 75-A to two months, within which period the drawback shall be paid to the exporters.

Anti smuggling measures

The drive against smuggling and duty evasion continued unabated during the year 1998-99. All the Commissionerates along the coast, the land borders and inchare of the international airports remained fully alert to prevent smuggling of contraband both into and out of the country. A number of remarkable seizures of contraband were effected during the year by various Commissionerates and the DRI. The success of the anti-smuggling efforts is clearly reflected by the fact that contraband goods worth over Rs.362 crores were seized during the year 1998-99 (upto November, 1998). In addition, cases of duty evasion to the tune of Rs.400.35 crores were detected, (upto Nov., 98), out of which an amount of Rs.59.71 crores was recovered even before completion of investigations/issue of Show Cause Notices. The pressure on the organised syndicates engaged in the smuggling was kept up by promptly attending to post -seizure activities like investigation prosecution as well as detention under COFEPOSA ACT. Steps were also taken to update existing dossiers and opening new dossiers of fresh gangs which had come to notice of various field formations involved in the anti-smuggling activities. Timely action was also initiated for disposal of the contraband goods as well as forfeiture of properties acquired with the funds generated by smugglers.

In addition to interception of smuggled goods, all the customs houses and DGRI stepped up efforts to detect cases of attempted Commercial frauds and a large number of cases involving violation of Import-Export Control Laws, evasion of customs duty, by misdeclaration of content, value etc., fraudulent claims of export benefits like drawback and duty free imports under Advance Licence/DEEC and DEPB schemes were unearthed. Many of these cases involved both evasion of customs duty and illegal remittances amounting to crores of rupees.

Customs formations all over India also made extensive efforts in tracking down the narcotics smugglers especially those engaged in illicit trafficking of heroin/ganja/hashish and mandrax The efforts were very fruitful and it resulted in some excellent seizures apart from busting of several major gangs involved.

Special efforts were made to upgrade the collection of intelligence on Indo-Pak, Indo-Nepal, Indo-Bangladesh border and Indo-Sri lanka coast line.

The DRI, the apex intelligence agency in the field of anti-smuggling, continued to maintain close liaison with the Coast Guard, CRPF Income-tax, NCB and all other field formations of Customs and Central Excise in the country.

The year also witnessed continued efforts at better coordination with the intelligence/enforcement agencies of other countries. The Director General Level talks between India and Nepal as also between India and Sri Lanka to discuss measures to curb smuggling and on other related matters were held in Delhi.

The break-up of important contraband goods seized during years 1995-96, 1996-97, 1997-98 and 1998-99, is as follows:

Value (Rs. in lakhs)

Commodities	*1995-96*	*1996-97*	*1997-98*	*1998-99 upto Nov. 98 (Prov.)*
Gold	5676	5449	5845	1270
Syn. fabrics	2262	2231	3875	3814
Elec. goods	5107	2514	3174	2755
Indian currency	523	331	683	406
Foreign currency	5153	5312	4874	1452
Narcotics drugs	7331	4132	9442	3725

Sector wise break-up of value of contraband goods seized during the year 1998-99 (Prov.) as compared to four previous years.

Post-seizure work handled during year 1998-99, in comparison with the previous four years, is as follows:

Value (Rs. in lakhs)

Sector	*1994-95*	*1995-96*	*1996-97*	*1997-98*	*1998-99 upto Nov. 98 (Prov.)*
No. of seizure	55030	54307	49434	46838	21849
Value of goods seized (Rs. in lakhs)	58746	65937	57056	67725	36234
No. of persons arrested	1229	1332	1077	1190	517
No. of persons convicted	334	153	181	20781	81
No. of detention orders issued under COFEPOSA	385	281	288	235	108
No. of persons actually detained under COFEPOSA	335	290	258	214	97
No. of detention orders issued under PIT NDPS	169	97	83	90	39

No. of persons actually detained under PIT NDPS	132	90	76	68	28
Evasion of duty (in lakhs)	N.A	353	84	288	514

The year 1997-98 and trend continued in 1998-99 witnessed an increase in legal imports of gold as compared to previous years with the newly introduced scheme of import of gold through specified agencies under the OGL scheme. Details of import of gold during last 3 years are as follows :

Customs marine wing

Customs Marine Wing under the overall charge of Commissioner, Directorate of Preventive Operations (D.P.O.) is responsible for procurement and supply of various categories of support equipments to all the field formations under the CBEC, engaged in the anti-smuggling work. During the year 1998-99 the important work handled by the DPO in the above field is as follows:

Boats/vessels

(a) Out of the four wooden dhows of 80 ft. with designed speed of 13.6 knots being built by M/s N.M. Wadia Bilimoria, the first and 2nd CPD Panchvati and Suvarnarekha had been delivered and the work is in progress for the remaining dhows.

(b) A proposal for acquisition of Customs Patrol Vessels towards partial replacement/ modernisation of existing fleet with Customs field formations has been prepared for period of ten years and the same is under consideration of the Ministry.

(c) Proposal for setting up of in-house training

facilities has been submitted and is under consideration.

Vehicles

A total amount of Rs.44.57 lakhs (approx.) was released to various Commissionerates/Directorates from the Special Equipment Fund towards purchase of 13 vehicles including Cars, Jeeps, Gypsys and Mini Bus during the current financial year.

Baggage X-Ray machines

A total number of 58 Baggage x-ray machines have been procured and supplied to various Airports, Customs Caargo Compleses, Sea Customs Ports, Land Customs Stations, and other field formations. Further, on the request of Commissioners, a proposal for acquisition and installation of additional 45 XBIS are under active consideration.

Night vision binoculars

259 Night Vision Binoculars have been precured and 254 binoculars of these have already been supplied to the concerned Commissionerates.

Narcotic drugs & explosives detectors

A proposal for acquisition of 10 Nos. of Narcotic Drugs & Explosive Detectors to be installed at sensitive entry & exit points is under active consideration of the Ministry. Requisite information after serious follow up, regarding their usefulness by Customs Administrations abroad has been collected from Interpol. London and Customs sources abroad.

Door frame metal detectors

22 Door Frame Metal Detectors were procured and installed at various sites in the field formations of the Department.

Hand held metal detectors

413 Nos. of Hand Held Metal Detectors have been

received and 332 out of these supplied to various Commissionerates.

Hand held search lights

A total quantity of 377 Hand Held Search Lights have been received from the suppliers and 289 Nos. have already been supplied to the user Commissionerates.

Simple binoculars

A supply order for acquisition of 406 Nos. of Simple Binoculars has been issued.

Sniffer dogs

A proposal for acquisition of additional Sniffer Dogs for detection of Narcotic Drugs and Explosives and setting up Dog Squad Units at different sensitive entry & exit points is under serious consideration of the Ministry.

Fire arms

Army Headquarters consented during the year to release the requisite Fire Weapons viz., 1043 S.L. Rs.75 L.M.Gs. and 87 Nos. of Projector Mini Flares immediately on payment basis.

Printing, publications and publicity

The Directorate of Publicity and Public Relations looks after the requirements of Printing, Publicity and Public Relations of the Customs, Central Excise and Narcotics Department.

Printing and publications

During the year 1998 as many as 38 publications were brought out. Out of these, on monthly basis were CBEC Digest, ICE Trade Digest, ICE Law Reporter and ICE Legal Aid and those on quarterly basis were audit Bulletin. Monthly issue of the House Journal ICE was also brought out. In addition to the above, exceptional and adhoc printing jobs as and when received from the Central Board of Excise and Customs were also undertaken. The list of publications is given below:-

1. ICE Trade Digest
2. ICE Magazine
3. CBEC Digest
4. ICE Law Reporter
5. ICE Legal Aid
6. All India Central Excise Audit Bulletin-Quarterly
7. Customs Notifications (Printed and despatched to field formations all over the country and to subscribers. The Notifications are also offered for sale to Trade and Public at ours sales counter as per the new provision in force.
8. Central Excise Notifications (Printed and despatched to field formations all over the country and to subscribers. The Notifications are also offered for sale to Trade and Public at ours sales counter as per the new provision in force.
9. Service Tax Notifications (Printed and despatched to field formations All over the country and to the subscribers. The Notifications are also offered for sale to Trade and Public at ours sales counter as per the new provision in force.
10. Handbook-1998
11. Civil List-1998
12. Guide for Travellers
13. Indirect Taxation in India
14. Pocket Telephone Directory
15. Indian Customs EDI system-Import Module-for System Mangers
16. Indian Customs EDI system-Export Module-for System Mangers
17. Indian Customs EDI system-Export Module-for
18. Indian Customs EDI system-Export Module-for

19. Various Parliamentary Accounts Committee's Reports
20. Customs Appraising Manual (in 5 volumes)-Under Print
21. Guide for Travellers; (Leaflets)
22. Agenda Paper for the Conference of Chief Commissioners
23. Budget Bulletin-Customs
24. Budget Bulletin-Central Excise
25. ACR Forms for CBEC and its field formations
26. Citizen's Charter-adopted by the Customs and Central Excise Deptt.
27. Central Excise Tarrif-1998. Updated, published, despatched to field formations all over the country and offered for sale to Trade & Public.
28. Customs Tarrif-1998. Updated, published, despatched to field formations all over the country and offered for sale to Trade & Public.
29. Booklet on Service Tax.
30. Duty Drawback Schedule-1998.
31. Questions and Answers on Service Tax.

Publicity section: 2 short films on Kar Vivad Samadhan Scheme were made and were telecast through Doordarshan.

The Directorate made 2 jingles on Kar Vivad Samadhan Scheme for broadcast through AIR.

Classified Advertisements were released in important dailies.

Vision brochure and other publicity material like posters and pamphlets were distributed.

Activities of the directorate general of inspection

The Directorate conducted 45 inspections of various offices during the year. The Directorate also conducted studies on the following issues/subject:

1. 14th Report of the PAC (11 th Lok Sabha 1996-97 Union Excise Duties- Provisional Assessments arising out of Audit Paragraph 1.03 sub-para 8 (i to v) of the Report of the C&AG of India for the year ended 31 March, 1995 (No.4 of 1996) Union Government Revenue receipts- Indirect Taxes).
2. Procedural Safeguards to be observed for units availing modvat facilities.
3. Examining areas of major simplification in the procedure on excise side.
4. Evolving an alternate scheme for collection of excise duties.
5. Short levy due to incorrect valuation adopted by M/s. Indian Oil Corporation for sale of LPG.
6. Operation of Procedure under Customs Notification No. of 36/96(NT) dt. 23.7.96.
7. Service Tax- Decentralisation of administrative control from Headquarters to Divisional level.
8. Departmental Books/Manuals required by the field formations.
9. Review of existing procedure for custody and sale of Match Excise Banderols.
10. Review and simplification of forms prescribed by the Ministry/Department.
11. Memorandum on dealers invoice and Modvat credit scheme.
12. Study and recommendation of Committee on excise structure rationalisation.

13. Simplification of Central Excise Procedures vis-a-vis the impact on revenue.
14. Study on movement of petroleum through Kandla Bhatinda Pipeline (KBPL) for formulating duty payment procedure.
15. Study relating to the Review of Policy/Procedure pertaining to the 100% EOU/EPZ etc.
16. Study regarding formulatings of procedure for duty free exports to Govt. of India aided projects in Bhutan.
17. Study on payment of rebate to HMG Nepal in terms of notification 50/94 Central Excise (NT).
18. Study regarding variation in the prices of Copper and Brass Scraps noticed at Nhava Sheva Customs House by WRU, Mumbai.

Nepal refund: A delegation of officials from this Directorate General as well as from the Ministry under the leadership of Shri S.K. Malhi, DGI visited Nepal in October, 1998 to study and review the procedure of refund of Central Excise duty to Nepal and suggested measures for speedy sanction of rebate. As a part of the visit, the delegation also visited Raxaul LCs and Birganj LCs and studied the actual documentation followed by both the Land Customs Station.

Computerisation of nepal refund wing: With a view to make speedy payment of rebate to His Majesty, Government of Nepal, the work of Nepal Refund Wing is being computerised. During the period from 1.4.98 to 15.12.98, about 28000 invoices were processed and refund of Rs. 55 crores was sanctioned and paid as rebate to HMGN.

Functions of the Directorate General/Directorates under the CBEC and of the CRCL.

No.	*Name of the office*	*Functions in Brief*
(i)	Directorate General of inpsection and audit. Customs and central excise.	(a) To Study the workineg of the Customs, Central Excise and narcotics departmental machinery throughout he country. (b) To suggest measures for improvement of its efficiency and rectification of important defection it through inspection and audit, and by laying down procedures for smooth functioning. (c) To play the role of a primary Central Agency for advising the Ministry of Finance and the CBEC in technical as well as administrative matters, pertaining to Central Excise, Customs and Narcotics Departments.
(ii)	Directorate General of Revenue Intelligence	As the apex intelligence organisation, it is responsible for study and dissemination of intelligence against smuggling, identifying the organised gangs of smugglers and areas vulnerable to smuggling, targeting of intelligence against them and their immobilisation liaison with the intelligence and enforcement agencies in India and abroad for collection of intelligence and in-depth investigation of important cases having inter-collectorate and international ramifications, alerting field formations for interception of suspects and contraband goods, assessment of current and likely trends in smuggling and advising the Ministry in all matters pertaining to plug any loopholes and attending to such other matters as may be entrusted by the Ministry/Board for investigation.

(iii)	Directorate General of Anti-Evasion	Collection, collation and dissemination of intelligence relating to evasion of Central Excise duties, studying of price structure, marketing patterns and classification of commodities vulnerable to evasion of Central Excise duties, coordinating action with agencies like Income-tax, etc. in cases involving evasion of Central Excise duties, investigation of cases of evasion of Central Excise duties having inter-collectorate ramifications and advising the Board and the collectorates on the modus operandi of evasion of Central Excise duties and the appropriate remedial measures thereof.
(iv)	National Academy of Customs, Excise and Narcotics	(a) To impart training to direct recruits and to arrange refresher course for departmental officers.
		(b) To assist in formulating training policies and to implement the policies and to implement the policies approved by the CBEC by formulating schemes and syllabi of studies for the training of direct recruits and departmental officers.
		(c) To arrange study tours of Customs and Excise Officers from neighbouring countries under
(v)	Directorate of Organisation and Management Services Customs and Central Excise	To look after the functions relating to method studies, work measurement and staffing, besides management services, including man-power planning for the customs and Central Excise and Narcotics Department.

(vi)	Directorate of Statistics & Intelligence	(a)	To collect and consolidate data and statistics pertaining to realisation of revenue I rom indirect taxes and advise the Ministry and CBEC in forecasting Budget estimates.
		(b)	To collect statistics for compilation of statistical bulletin and statistical year book in respect of revenue, arrears, seizures, court pertaining to indirect taxes.
(vii)	Directorate of Preventive operations	(a)	To inspects, assess and evaluate the effectiveness of staff deployed on anti- smuggling duties in the Collectorates and in vulnerable areas. (b) To monitor, coordinate and evaluate the progress in cases of adjudications, prosecutions and reward to informers/officers in different Collectorates and to watch the progress in disposal of confiscated goods involved in prosecution cases. (c) To plan and assess the need for staff training, equipment, vehicles vessels, communications or other rescurces required for anti-smuggling work in different Collectorates and evaluate their with the matters concerning acquisition, procurement, purchases, repairs and reallocation of such equipment.
(viii)	Directorate of Publicity and Public Relations	(a)	Preparation, revision and publication of statutory and departmental manuals. (b) Consolidation of instructions issued by the CBEC in technical and administrative matters of Customs and Central Excise.
		(c)	Compilation of important judgements delivered by High

	Courts and Supreme Court on matters relating to indirect taxes.
	(d) Updating of all departmental manuals through corrections lists etc.
	(e) Undertaking publicity with a view to educating the public about the indirect taxes through brochures, posters, hoardings, radio, T.V. and press media.
(ix) Central Revenue Control Laboratory	To analyse sample of goods and render technical advice to the CBEC and its field formations in regards to dutiability or otherwise of various goods.
(x) Directorate of systems	All aspects of the implementation Customs and Central Excise Computerisation Projects including acquisitions of hardware, development and maintenance of the software, training of personnel and monitoring of expenditure budget on computerisation at the central and field.
(xi) Directorate of valuation	The main function assigned to this Directorate are:-
	(a) To assist and advise the Board in the implementation and monitoring of the working of the W.T.O Agreement on Customs valuation
	(b) To build a comprehensive valuation data base for internationally traded goods using past precedents, published price information or price obtained from other authentic source and to disseminate the price information on a continuing basis to all Customs formation, for on-line

viewing and as a means of assistance to day-to-day assessment with a view to detecting and preventing undervaluation as also for enabling assessment to be finalised speedily.

(c) To monitor valuation practices at various Customs formations and bring to the notice of the Board significant and emerging pricing patterns and also suggest corrective policy or other measure were needed.

(d) To maintain liaison with the valuation Directorate of other Customs Administrations and Customs Officers posted abroad.

(e) To study international price trends of sensitive commodities and pricing patterns of transnational corporations (e.g. transfer pricing) and Indian ventures with foreign collaboration and help evolve a system to combat planned undervaluation as well as valuation frauds.

(xii) Directorate General of Vigilance

It maintains the vigilance cases against officers of Customs & Central Excise. It also maintains proper surveillance on officials of doubtful integrity.

To maintain close liaison with the Central Bureau of Investigation, local Directorate of Revenue Intelligence and Commissionerate Vigilance Branches to ensure that the programmes of vigilance and anti-corruption are implemented in all Commissionerates of Customs and Central Excise and Narcotics Department.

(xiii) Directorate of Service Tax

Service Tax was introduced for the first time in 1994 only on three services and the scopes of the levy has been considerably enlarged by now bringing in a total of 27 services in the Service Tax net. Considering the increasing workload due to expanding coverage, a Directorate General of Service Tax has been created to be stationed at Mumbai. The main functions assigned to this Directorate are to:

(i) monitor the collection and assessment of service tax;
(ii) Study the implementation of Service Tax in the field and to suggest measures to increase revenue collection;
(iii) to undertake study of law and procedures;
(iv) to form a data base; and
(v) To inspect the Service Tax Cells in the Commissionerates.

The central board of direct taxes

Personnel

The Central Board of Direct Taxes is the apex body in the direct tax set up. It performs various statutory functions under the various acts and is responsible for formulation and implementation of policies relating to direct tax administration. The Board consists of a Chairman and five Members.

The Chairman is ex-officio Special Secretary and the Members are ex-officio Additional Secretaries in the Ministry of Finance. It has three attached offices under three Directors General of Income-tax viz. D.G. (Admn.), New Delhi, D.G. (Training), Nagpur and D.G. (Exemption), Calcutta. There are 23 Chief Commissioners of Income Tax who are in charge of assessment and collection of direct taxes at the regional levels. Besides, there are 7 Directors Generals of Income-tax (Investigation) who are in overall charge of investigation machinery on regional basis to curb tax evasion and unearth unaccounted money. The CCIT/DGIT are assisted by CIT/DIT in their jurisdictions. There is also appellate machinery comprising Commissioner of Income Tax (Appeals) to perform the work of disposal of appeals against the orders of Assessing Officers. The Income Tax Department employs a work force of about 60,000 officers and staff, of approximately 10% are gazetted officers in Group 'A' and 'B' and the remaining 90% are non-gazetted employees in Group 'C' and 'D'. The details of the sanctioned strength in different grades in the Income Tax Department as on 1.1.1999 is in Annexure-I.

The Income Tax Act has been amended through Finance (No. 2) Act, 1998 w.e.f. 1.10.1998 so as to redesignate the income tax authorities as under:

(a) Central Board of Direct Taxes.

(b) Directors General of Income Tax: or Chief Commissioners of Income Tax,

(c) Directors of Income-tax or Commissioners of Income-tax or Commissioners of Income-tax (Appeals),

(cc) Additional Directors of Income-Tax or Additional Commissioners of Income or Additional Commissioners of Income Tax (Appeals),

(cca) Joint Directors of Income-Tax or Joint Commissioners of Income-Tax,

(d) Deputy Directors of Income-Tax or Deputy Commissioners Income-Tax or Deputy Commissioners of Income-tax (Appeals),

(e) Assistant Directors of Income Tax or Assistant Commissioners of Income Tax,

(f) Income Tax Officers.

(g) Tax Recovery Officers,

(h) Inspectors of Income Tax.

During the year under review, 58 posts of DCIT and 63 posts of ACIT have been created and 220 posts in Leave/ Training/ Deputation Reserve have been converted into duty posts. Another Regional Training Institute, in addition to the four already functioning has also started functioning at Hazaribagh.

Direct taxes advisory committee

With a view to encouraging mutual understanding between the tax-payers and the Income Tax Department and to advise the Government on measures for removing difficulties of a general nature, there is a Central Direct Taxes Advisory Committee (CDTAC) at Delhi and 36 Regional Direct Taxes Advisory Committees (RDTAC) at important stations of all ' Chief Commissioners/ Commissioners of Income-tax. Representatives of trade and professional associations are nominated to these committees. The term of these committees is two years.

Revenue collections

(Rupees in crores)

	Budget Estimates 1998-99	*Collections upto Dec.'97*	*Collections upto Dec.'98*
Corporation Tax	26550.00	13823.36	16748.00
Income Tax	20930.00	11714.03	12727.00
Interest Tax	920.00	583.52	572.00
Total	48400.00	26120.91	30047.00

Budget collection of CT, IT and Interest tax upto December, 1998 (for the financial year 1998-99) shows an increase of 15.032% over the collection upto December, 1997 (Financial year 1997-98). Budget for Financial year 1998-99 has been estimated at an increase of about 26.30% over the collection during 1997-98. The increase in Corporation Tax, Income-tax and Interest-tax upto December, 1998 is 21.16%, 8.64% and (-) 2.04% as compared to the collection during the corresponding period of last year.

Arrear position

(Rupees in crores)

		(Corporation tax /Income tax) 1996-97	1997-98
	Total outstanding demand	33585	41230
	Reason-wise Analysis		
(i)	Amount not fallen due	9366	9973
(ii)	Amount claimed as paid but pending for verification	2055	2346
(iii)	Amount for which instalments have been granted.	310	574
(iv)	Amount stayed/kept in abeyance which includes amount stayed by Courts, Settlement Commission, ITAT, and I.T. Authorities.	15798	22516
(v)	Balance tax in arrears	6056	5821

Cost of collection

(Rupees in crores)

Year	*Revenue Collection(all Direct Taxes)*	*Cost of Collection*	*Cost Factor*
1994-95	25,689.30	382.75	1.49%
1995-96	33,383.71	430.30	1.29%
1996-97	38,895.08	486.48	1.25%
1997-98	48,280.40	715.37	1.48%

Measures to combat tax evasion

The Government is continuously striving to check tax evasion and accumulation of unaccounted wealth. In pursuance of this objective, systematic survey operations, search and seizure operations in appropriate cases, verification of information by Central Information Branches in a planned manner and scrutiny of a selected number of cases continue to be undertaken. This year, the emphasis continued to be on selection of bigger cases in respect of all areas of work. Special attention was given to investigation of some scam related cases.

For carrying out the aforesaid work: The field units of the Investigation Wing are headed by 7 Directors General of Income-tax, stationed at Delhi, Calcutta, Chennai, Mumbai, Ahmedabad, Lucknow and Bangalore. Their functions include investigating cases relating to tax evasion, carrying opt searches, surveys and verification of information pertaining to financial transactions. There are 17 Directors of Income-tax (Inv.), who work under them and are stationed in different parts of the country. Besides, there is also a Director of Income-tax (Spl. Inv.) at Delhi.

These Officers are assisted by a number of Additional Directors/Joint Directors/Deputy Directors and Assistant Directors of Income-tax.

The Directorate of Income-tax (Special Investigation) is a specialised agency to assist the Department who has been assigned the following broad functions :

a. Research into the latest techniques of tax evasion and investigation of the same.

b. Selection of cases of tax evasion having all India

c. ramifications for monitoring and co-ordinating the investigation and assessment work.

c. Co-ordinating with other Central Investigation Agencies on economic offences.

The results achieved in searches and surveys are as under-

Results of surveys

Year	*No. of Premises surveyed*	*No. of new assessees added*
1993-94	4,98,517	12,00,446
1994-95	7,92,006	15,16,721
1995-96	7,83,295	13,16,763
1996-97	8,18,982	16,58,302
1997-98	4,51,871	*23,78,194
1998-99 (upto October'98)	*60,089	*16,50,409

Result of searches

Year	*No. of searches*	*Value of assets seized (Rs.in crores)*
1993-94	5026	396.45
1994-95	4830	381.43
1995-96	4612	458.14
1996-97	4299	405.63
1997-98	3653	306.85
1998-99 (upto Nov.'98)	*3110	*140.33

Prosecution: Prosecution under the Income Tax Act is provided for offences against direct tax laws.

Pre-Emptive purchase of properties: The scheme of pre-emptive purchase of immovable properties by the Central Government as per the provisions of Chapter XXC of the Income-tax Act, 1961 has served as an effective deterrent against tax evasion through under-statement of the value of immovable properties in real estate transactions and has encouraged the tax payers in disclosing the true consideration involved in such transactions.

The Scheme is implemented by a high level body of the Appropriate Authorities, comprising of two commissioners of Income Tax and one Chief Engineer on deputation to the Income Tax Department. The power of Pre-emptive purchase is exercised in cases ol transactions where the Appropriate Authority the view that the consideration for transfer of the properties has been understated in the agreement to transfer. At the inception (1.10.1986) the Scheme was operative in only 4 metropolitan cities and has since been extended to 28 cities through-out the country Prior to 31.7.1995, a uniform limit of Rs.10 lakhs was prescribed for particular cities, notified under the Scheme. At present, the transactions exceeding Rs.75 lakhs in Mumbai, Rs.50 lakhs in Delhi, Rs.25 lakhs in Pune, Banglore, Calcutta, Chennai, Ahmedabad and Rs.20 lakhs in other specified cities fall within the purview of the Scheme. In the short period of about a decade, since its implementation, these provisions have resulted in a considerable increase in the declared component of the consideration in real estate transactions and have also substantially increased State revenues through stamp duty realisation.

From the date of commencement of the scheme on 1.10.1986, pre-emptive purchase orders in respect of 1144 properties have been passed till 30.11.1998 and although profit out of sale of these properties was not one of the objectives of the scheme, there has been a substantial realisation on this account also. A total number of 723 properties have already been sold till December, 1998 generating a surplus of Rs.230.13 crores. The statistical particulars furnished would indicate that the power of Pre-emptive purchase has been exercised with great circumspection, in only a handful of cases.

Statistical particulars pertaining to Pre-emptive purchases under Chapter XXC upto the month of November, 1998 are furnished below :-

	No. of forms 37-I received	*No. of NOCs issued.*	*Order passed*	*Write pending*	*Properties sold in public auction*
Mumbai	27211	18901	476	127	359
Calcutta	2228	1364	60	25	19
Delhi	16475	9880	149	124	90*
Chennai	9382	5204	81	22	55
Bangalore	8171	5711	125	49	77
Ahmedabad	8988	5347	217	44	124*
Lucknow	1792	1032	36	12	8
Total	74247	47439	1144	403	732*

Properties purchased 1140	Apparent consideration Rs. 849.36 crores
Properties sold* 732	Apparent consideration* Rs. 404.19 crores
Sales Price* Rs. 624.32 crores	Profit* Rs. 230.13 crores

Income-tax assessment

The number of effective assessees under the Income Tax Act increased from 131.68 lakhs during financial year 1997-98

The following figures will indicate the growth in number of income tax payers in the country:-

Year	*Number (in lakhs)*
1993-94	102.06
1994-95	102.85
1995-96	106.65
1996-97	116.43
1997-98	131.68
1998-99 (upto 30th June, 98)	135.08

The work-load and disposal of assessments during the last few years is as follows:-

Assessment year	*Assessments for disposal (in lakhs)*	*Disposal (in lakhs)*
1993-94	94.99	80.11
1994-95	100.05	75.93
1995-96	106.22	83.00
1996-97	121.11	104.49
1997-98	138.60	112.76
1998-98 (upto 30th June, 98)	54.60	3.60

The claims of refunds are disposed of expeditiously. The Figures of last few years will testify this:-

Year	*No. of claims*	*Disposal*
1992-93	77337	69052
1993-94	90363	72841
1994-95	98452	81730
1995-96	139314	104362
1996-97	157712	107782
1997-98	215546	141877
1998-99 (upto 30th June, 98)	152818	33295

Details of refunds arising out of appellate and revisionary orders in the last few years are as under:-

Year	*No. of claims*	*Disposal*
1992-93	68655	64005
1993-94	77236	74295
1994-95	65220	62123
1995-96	61794	58168
1996-97	54004	49283
1997-98	43554	40607
1998-99 (upto June, 98)	8879	5356

The Board has continued its efforts for early completion of assessments and for prompt disposal of refund claims and has been consistently impressing upon the Chief Commissioners of Income Tax/Commissioners of Income Tax the need for taking effective steps for the elimination of delays in these matters. The Board has further directed that all refunds should be despatched by Registered post acknowledgment due within 15 days of its determining, irrespective of the value of such refunds.

Condonation of delay in filing refund claims

Refund claims are required to be filed within one year from the end of the assessment year to which the claim pertains. The Board has been given power under section 119 (2) (b) of the Income tax Act to condone the delay if it considers desirable or expedient to do so for avoiding genuine hardship in any case. The number of applications received and disposed of by the Central Board of Direct Taxes during the last few years are given as under:-

Financial year	Number of applications received	Disposal (including cases brought forward)
1993-94	323	357
1994-95	234	152
1995-96	87	64
1996-97	138	81
1997-98	94	105
1998-99 (upto 30.11.98)	69	56

During the period 1.1.1998 to 31.12.1998, one hundred notifications and orders relating to grant of exemptions to charitable institutions, religious institution , sports bodies and professional organisations etc. were issued.

Appeals

Under the direct-tax laws, the first appeal is tiled before the Departmental Appellate Authorities i.e. Deputy Commissioner (Appeals) and Commissioner (Appeals). However, w.e.f. 1.10.1998 the first appeal is to be filed before Commissioner (Appeals) only. The following statement shows comparative figures relating to institution/disposal and pendency of appeals during the period 1.4.1998 to 31.8.1998 and the corresponding period in the preceding year.

Period	Opening pendency	Institution	Total	Disposal	pendency
		Appeals before DCs IT(Appeals)			
1.4.97 to 31.8.97	...	...	63,217	5,949	57,268
1.4.97 to 31.8.98*	...	...	44,759	3,520	41,239
		Appeals before CsIT(Appeals)			
1.4.97 to 31.8.97	1,35,174	36,898	1,72,072	21,574	1,50,498
1.4.97 to 31.8.98	1,31,264	32,370	1,63,634	22,793	1,40,841

**Those ale provisional figures Final figures are being collected*

Thus the pendency of appeals before these authorities was 1,82,080 as on 31.8.1998 as against 2,07,766 on the corresponding date in the preceding year. Targets for disposals of high demand appeals have been included separately in the Action plan target.

With effect from 1.10.1998, a new Section 260A has been introduced into the Income-tax Act which seeks to introduce direct appeals to the High Court doing away with the earlier system of filing reference applications.

This would considerably reduce unnecessary litigation and also facilitate expeditious disposal of cases. Towards strengthening the judicial machinery in each Chief Commissionerate, it is proposed to set up High Court Cell in each charge to monitor/co-ordinate matters with the High Court. Similarly a Supreme Court Cell is functioning at New Delhi to facilitate proper coordination between the judicial wing of the Income Tax Department and the Apex Court. Further, with a view to expedite disposal of cases in High Courts and Supreme Court, bunching of cases on similar issues is being done.

Legislation

New Legislation relating to direct taxes for the financial year 1998-99 is contained in the Finance (No.2) Act, 1998, Income-tax (Amendment) Act, 1998 and Income Tax (Second Amendment) Act 1998.

The important provisions of these statutes in the sphere of direct taxes are summarised below:-

I. *Rate of Income-Tax:*

(a) The exemption limit for individuals, HUF's etc. which was at Rs.40,000 has been raised to Rs.50,000. However, the tax rates continue to be the same as in the earlier years. The table below gives the income slabs and the rates of income-tax applicable to individuals and HUFs.

	Old Slabs Rates income (Rs.)		New Slabs	Rates
Lower Slab	40,001- 60,000	10%	50,001 - 60,000	10%
Middle, Slab	60,000 - 1,50,000	20%	60,001 - 1,50,000	20%
Higher Slab	Above 1,50,000	30%	Above 1,50,000	30%

(b) The tax rates of domestic companies has been continued at 35% and that of foreign companies at 48%.

II. Welfare Measure and Tax Relief

(a) As a part of the rationalisation of the Standard Deduction under section 16 of the Income-tax Act, it has been decided to raise the standard deduction for those persons with salaried income upto to Rs.1,00,000 f rom the present limit of Rs.20,000 to Rs.25,000. The standard deduction has been discontinued for employees having salary of over Rs.5,00,000 per year. The standard deduction for others will remain the same.

(b) Deduction equal to 100% of donations made to National Sports Fund and National Cultural Fund to be set up by the Government from the taxable Income of the donors has been allowed.

(c) A new section 80JJAA has been introduced providing for and additional deduction of 30% of additional wages to the new workmen for a period of three years beginning with which the new workman is employed. The workman, however, should be employed on regular basis and such a workman should be in employment for at least 300 days during the year. Separate conditions have been provided for the new and existing companies.

(d) A new section 80JJA has been introduced providing for deduction of an amount not exceeding Rs.5,00,000 for the assessee whose gross total income includes any profits and gains derived from the business of collecting and processing or treating of bio-gas, making pellets or briquettes for fuel of organic manure.

(e) Under the existing provisions of clause (26) of

section 10, any income which accrues or arises to a member of a Scheduled Tribe residing in any area specified in the clause either from any source in the areas or States specified or by way of dividend or interest on securities, is exempt from income-tax. This exemption has been extended to the members of Scheduled Tribes residing in the Ladakh region of the State of Jammu & Kashmir.

(f) Under the Income-Tax Act, cooperative societies enjoy certain tax concessions in respect of their income. The whole of the amounts of profits and gains of cooperative societies engaged in the business of banking or providing credit facilities its members, marketing of agriculture produce of its members, supply of agricultural implements, seeds etc. to the members, processing without the aid of power of the agricultural produce grown by its members, cottage industries, fishing and allied activities and the primary cooperative societies engaged in the supply of milk, oilseeds, fruits or vegetables etc. are exempt to f rom the income tax. Cooperative societies engaged in the activities other than those specified above are liable to tax on their business income in excess of Rs.40,000/-, in the case of consumers' cooperative societies and Rs.20,000/- in the case of other co-operative societies. With a view to encouraging and promoting growth of the co-operative societies. With a view to encouraging and promoting growth of the cooperative sector, the exemption limit of cooperative societies has been raised from Rs.20,000 to Rs.50,000 and in the case of consumers' cooperative societies from Rs.40,000 to Rs.1,00,000 by amending section 80 P of the Income-Tax Act.

(g) Section 80DD allows for a resident being an

individual or Hindu undivided family a deduction of Rs.15,000 for expenditure incurred in respect of handicapped dependence subject to certain condition. Section 80DDA allows a separate deduction, from the gross total 'income of an amount not exceeding Rs.20,000 deposited in a year in any scheme of LIC, UTI etc. specifically framed for providing recurring or lump sum payment for the maintenance and upkeep of a handicapped dependent. In order to allow a choice to the parent or the guardian to spent either on medical treatment of or for the future needs of the handicapped dependents, as the case may be, a new section 80DD has been provided by which the parent or guardian could claim a deduction upto Rs.40,000 for the medical treatment suited to his needs.

(h) In order to meet the rising cost of medical treatment and to mitigate the hardship faced by salaried tax-payers in such cases, the limit of 10000 rupees provided under section 17 (2)(v) of the Income-tax Act has been increased to Rs. 15,000/-.

(iii) Incentives for Infrastructure Development and Industrialisation

(a) A Five Year Tax Holiday and a deduction of 25% (30% in the case of Companies) of profit in the subsequent five years was allowed to an undertaking engaged in the business of generation and distribution of power or to an industrial undertaking set up in backward district provided the undertaking starts generating power on or before 31.3.2000. As the gestation period is too long for power projects, the above benefit has been extended to undertakings which commence generation, or generation and distribution of power on or before 31.3.2003.

(b) A Five year Tax Holiday and a deduction of 25% (30% in the case of Companies) of profit in the subsequent five years was allowed to an undertaking set up in industrially backward States specified in the Eights Schedule, which starts manufacture or production during the period beginning on the 1st day of April, 1993 and ending on the 31 st day of March, 1998. The above benefit has been extended to undertaking set up in industrially backward States as specified in the Eighth Schedule which starts manufacture or production upto 31.3.2000.

(c) A Five Year Tax Holiday was provided under section 80-IA with effect from the Assessment Year 1997-98 to approved companies engaged in Scientific and Industrial Research and Development activities. The incentive was made available to any company that had as its main objective, activities in the areas of scientific and industrial research and development and which had been accorded approval by the prescribed authority. The tax holiday has been extended by one year i.e. upto 31 st March, 1999.

(d) Under the existing provisions of 80-IA, a five year tax holiday in respect of profits and gains of an assessee engaged in telecommunication services is allowed with a further deduction of 25% (30% in the case of companies) of profits from such business in the next 5 years. The country needs to augment its telecommunication services. The benefit has been extended to radio-paging and domestic satellite services and also to network of trunking and electronic data inter-change services. In the case of domestic satellite service, this deduction will be allowable only to those Indian companies which own and operate the satellite for providing telecommunication services,

(e) Under the existing provisions of section 801A, undertakings engaged in the commercial production of mineral oil are entitled to a seven year tax holiday. With a view to encouraging oil refining within the country in view of the increased demand, the benefit of such tax holiday has been extended to undertakings engaged in refining of mineral oil, which commence production on or after 1.10.1998.

(f) With a view to promoting investments in housing, a new sub-section (4F) has been inserted in section 80-IA of the Income-Tax Act. An undertaking engaged in developing and building housing projects is eligible to claim deduction under section 80-IA, subject to conditions specified. Subject to the conditions being satisfied, 100% of profits from such business shall be deductible.

(h) The Government has identified national waterways, the fourth mode of transport, for improving the transport infrastructure in the country, Inland Waterways and inland ports play a vital role in improving a country's infrastructure. With the objective of improving the transport infrastructure, the inland waterways and inland ports have been included in the definition of "infrastructure facility" as given in section 801 A. They entitled to tax holidays.

(i) A new section 33ABA has been inserted to provide for tax incentives to the Petroleum and Natural Gas sector. A deduction is allowed in computing the taxable profits in case of an assessee carrying on business of prospecting for, or extraction or production of, petroleum and natural gas or both in

India and in relation to which the Central Government has entered into an agreement with such assessee for such business. The maximum amount of deduction shall be allowed as per the provisions of the section. The maximum amount of deduction will be restricted to 20% of the profits of such business, computed under the head 'profits and gains of business of profession' before making any deduction under this Section.

(j) A situation unique to the Petroleum and natural Gas Industry is the assignment or farm-out of participating interest held by an assessee in a production sharing contract to the third party. Section 42 of the Income-Tax has been amended so as to provide for the treatment of the unallowed expenditure in a case where the business of the assessee consisting of the prospecting for or extraction of production of petroleum and natural Gas is transferred wholly or partly or any interest in such business is transferred in accordance with the agreement.

(k) A new section 80HHBA has been inserted in the Income-Tax Act providing that an Indian company or a non-corporate assessee resident in India shall be entitled to a deduction of 50% of the profits and gains derived from the business of execution of housing projects aided by the World Bank and undertaken by the assessee in pursuance of a contract floated on the basis of a global tender. The deduction is available only if the assessee transfers 50% of profits and gains from the business of housing project, to a Housing Project Reserve Account.

(l) Under the existing provisions of Section 80HHE, 100% deduction is allowed on profits derived from export of computer software provided the sale consideration is received or brought into India in convertible foreign exchange. Software exports have grown exponentially in recent years. With a view to increasing India's market share in the international arena, the Explanation has been extended to include 'any customised electronic data' within the meaning of "computer software". The benefits of deduction have also been extended to supporting software developers. The benefit of export can also be passed on to software developers by software exporting companies subject to conditions.

(m) Under the existing provisions a five year tax-holiday is available to newly established industrial undertakings set up in free-trade zones and to units set up in software technology parks and also to export oriented units. The holiday has been extended to ten years.

(n) To boost the demand of commercial vehicles, full depreciation is available for commercial vehicles purchased in the Financial Year 1998-99. An enhanced depreciation is also available for commercial vehicles purchased in replacement of condemned vehicles of over fifteen years of age.

(IV) Widening of Tax Base

(a) Two more economic indicators, namely, holding of a credit card and membership of a club where the entrance fee is charged Rs.25,000 or more have been added to the already existing four criteria in proviso to sub-section 1 of section 139 of the Income-tax Act. It has also been made obligatory for any person fulfilling any one of the six economic criteria to file a return of income. However, certain exemptions have been made for senior citizens, non-residents, travel to neighbouring countries and travel to some countries on pilgrimage.

(b) It has been provided that a person shall quote his Permanent Account Number or his General Index Register Number till such time PAN is allotted for certain transactions. In the absence of PAN or GIR number, it will be necessary to file a declaration. The transactions for which quoting of PAN has been made compulsory have been notified separately.

(c) In the light of the fact that a large number of person having salaried income which are subject to deduction of tax at source do not file returns, it has been felt necessary that penal provisions are necessary to ensure that all such persons having taxable income file their return of income. Therefore, section 271 F has been amended to provide for a penalty of Rs.1000/- for not filing of return under sub-section (1) of section 139 before the end of the relevant assessment year.

(V) Measures for Development of Capital Market

(a) Corporatisation of Membership Card of recognised stock exchanges is exempt from capital gains if effected on or before 31.12.1997. To encourage more stock brokers to corporatise, increase their liquidity and consequently their volume of trading, section 47 has been amended to exempt such corporatisation of membership card of recognised stock exchanges from levy of capital gains tax if the same is made upto 31.12.1998.

(b) When share certificates are returned bearing distinctive numbers different from those appearing on shares which were earlier lent, the legal position of such exchange in terms of being a transfer under section 2(47) of the Income-tax Act attracting capital gains was not clear. Section 47 of the Income-tax Act has been amended to provide that any transfer in a scheme for lending of any securities under an agreement or arrangement, subject to the guidelines issued by the Securities and Exchange Board of India in this regard, which the assessee has entered into with the borrower of such securities, shall not be regarded as transfer.

(c) The deduction in respect of amortisation of certain preliminary expenses under section 35D of the Income-tax Act has been enhanced to one-fifths of the expenditure for each of the five successive previous years. The aggregate limit of expenditure is also enhanced to five per cent of the cost of the project or where the assessee is an Indian company at the option of the company of the capital employed in the business of the company.

(VI) Rationalisation and Simplification

(a) A simplified one page return for non corporate assesses called "SARAL" has been introduced to facilitate easy filing of returns.

(b) The definition of the term "actual cost" in section 43 is amended by insertion of Explanations 9 ' and 10 to sub section (1) in this section. Provisions have been made for reducing from the actual cost any claim of credit made and allowed under the Central Excise Rules, 1944, and any subsidy or grant or reimbursement which reduces the cost directly or indirectly.

(c) The issue relating to whether the value of the closing stock of the inputs, work in progress and finished goods must necessarily include the element for which MODVAT credit is available, has been the matter of considerable litigation over the years. To ensure that the value of opening and closing stock reflect the correct value, a new section 145A is inserted. This section provides that the valuation of purchase, sale and inventory shall be made in accordance with the method of accounting regularly employed by the assessee and such valuation shall be further adjusted to include the amount of any tax, duty, cess or fee (by whatever name called), actually paid or incurred by the assessee to bring the goods to the place of its location and condition as on the date of valuation.

(d) Sub-section (2AB) to section 35 was introduced by the Finance Act, 1997. This sub-section allowed weighted deduction of one and one-fourth of the expenditure incurred on scientific research and development by a company carrying on specified research on fulfilment of certain conditions. Due to difficulties experienced by a prescribed authority in monitoring these expenses, it has been decided to limit the weighted deduction to those expenses on scientific research made upto 31 st March, 2000.

(e) The profits and gains of any insurance business other than life insurance are computed in accordance with the provisions of section 44 of the Income-tax Act and the rules contained in the First Schedule. As per rule 5 of the First Schedule, the profits and gains of such insurance business are taken to be the balance of profits disclosed by the annual accounts under the Insurance Act, 1938 and are subject to the adjustments of expenditure or allowance which are not admissible under sections 30 to 43B. The Act amends rule 5 of the First Schedule so as to explicitly provide for the disallowance of provision for any tax, dividend, reserve of any other provisions, as may be prescribed, debited to such profit and loss account, putting an end to the litigation in this regard.

(f) Under the existing provisions, the Assessing Officer determines the sum payable by the assessee on the basis of assessment in accordance with the provisions of subsection (3) of section 143 of the Income-tax Act. There is no provision to issue refund under this sub-section. Provision has been made for determination of sum payable by the assessee as well as the refund of any amount due to him by the Assessing Officer while making an order of assessment under section 143(3).

(g) Under section 10(23G) of the Income-tax Act, any income by way of dividends, interest or long term capital gains of an infrastructure capital company or an infrastructure capital end on investment made by way of share or long term finance in an enterprise carrying on the business of developing, maintaining and operating any infrastructure facility which fulfils the conditions specified in sub section (4A) of section 80A is exempt from income-tax. In the absence of any control mechanism, it has not been possible to monitor if the funds are invested in infrastructure projects. For investments made from 1.6.1998, it has been provided that only those investments made in approved infrastructure capital companies shall be eligible for exemption. Any infrastructure enterprise has to approach the Central Government and seek necessary approvals before it can receive funds under section 10(23G). However, for investment made prior to 1.0.1998, the earlier provisions shall apply.

(h) Section 54H of the Income-tax Act caters to the situation where the transfer of the long term asset is by way of compulsory acquisition under any law and the amount of compensation awarded for such acquisition is not received by the assessee on the date of transfer. In such cases the period available to the assessee for investing the long term capital gains for the purpose of exemption is reckoned from the date of receipt of compensation and not from the date of transfer. Sections 54EA and 54EB of Income-tax Act have been brought under provisions of 54H.

(i) Section 37 of the Income-tax Act is amended to provide that any expenditure incurred by an assessee for any purpose which is an offence or which is prohibited by law shall not be allowed. This will result in disallowance of the claims made by certain assesses in respect of payments on account of protection money, extortion, hafta, bribes etc. as business expenditure.

(j) Producers of cinematographic films are obliged to furnish within 30 days from the date of completion of the film or within 30 days from the end of the financial year, whichever is earlier, statement containing particulars of all payments of over Rs.5000 in aggregate made by him or due from him to each person engaged by him. The limit has been enhanced from Rs.5000 to Rs.25000.

(k) To set at rest the controversy in this regard, an Explanation has been inserted after sub-section (2) of section 158BA of the Income-tax Act to clarify that assessments completed under Chapter XIV-B shall be in addition to regular assessments in respect of each previous year included in the block period. The dispute regarding meaning of the word 'execution' while calculating the period of limitation in section 158BE of the Income-tax Act, has been settled by inserting a clarificatory Explanation. An Authorisation is deemed to have been executed in the case of search on the conclusion of search as recorded in the last panchanama drawn in relation to any person in whose case the warrant of authorisation has been issued. In regard to requisition under section 132A of the Income-tax Act, the authorisation would be deemed to have been executed on actual receipt of books of account or other documents or assets by the authorised officer.

(l) Under the existing provisions, the sums referred to in clause (a) of section 43B is allowable as deduction in the previous year in which the sum is actually paid. The first proviso to section 43B has been amended so as to provide that any sum payable by the assesses as interest on any term loan from a scheduled bank referred to in clause (e) shall be allowed as deduction during the previous year if such sum is actually paid by the assessee on or before the due date applicable in his case for furnishing the return of income under sub-section (1) of section 139.

(m) The Fifth Central Pay Commission had recommended a change in the designation of Assistant Commissioner of Income-tax (Senior Scale). Income-tax (Senior Scale) and Assistant Director of Income-tax (Senior Scale) as Deputy Commissioner of Income-tax and Deputy Director of Income-tax respectively. This necessitated redesignating the existing Deputy Commissioner of Income-tax and Deputy Director of Income-tax as Joint Commissioner of Income-tax and Joint Director of Income-tax, respectively. The above changes in designation made if necessary to amend the various sections of the relevant Direct tax enactments, so that the statutory powers continue to be exercised by the substituted authorities as a result of redesignation.

(n) Section 10(23F) exempted income by way of dividends or long term capital gains of a venture capital fund or venture capital company from investments made by way of equity shares in a venture capital undertaking. The condition for minimum lock-in period of three years before such equity shares could be transferred has been withdrawn by the Act. The ambit of venture capital undertaking has also been extended to include domestic companies whose shares are not listed in a recognised stock exchange in India and which are engaged in the business of developing, maintaining and operating any infrastructure facility.

(o) Under the existing provisions of section 32 of the Income-tax Act, depreciation is allowable only on tangible assets, being buildings, machinery, plant or furniture. The scope has been widened to include depreciation on intangible assets, being know-how, patents, copyright, trademarks, licences or franchises.

(p) Under the existing provisions, every person carrying business or profession as per section 44AA of the Income-tax Act is required to maintain books of accounts and other document to enable the assessing officer to compute his total income. This is required if the income exceeds Rs.4000 or the total receipts or turn over exceeds Rs.5,00,000 in any of the three immediately preceding previous year. In case where the business or profession is newly set up, the limitations apply for such previous year. The above limits have been enhanced from Rs.40,000 to Rs.1,20,000 and from Rs.5,00.000 to Rs.10,00,000.

(q) Under the existing provision, where an expenditure incurred by the tax-payer in respect of which he either offers no explanation regarding the source of such expenditure or where explanation offered is found unsatisfactory, the expenditure is treated as 'income' under section 69C. There is no corresponding provision for disallowance of such expenditure. This used to enable the tax payer charged to tax under section 69C to claim the expenditure as deduction under section 37 defeating the very objective of the section. Section 69C has been amended by which unexplained expenditure deemed as income cannot be allowed as deduction under any head of income.

(r) Loss from house property is not allowed to be carried forward and set off against income arising in subsequent years. A new section 71 B has been inserted to provide that where the net result of computation under the head "Income from house property" is a loss to the assessee and such loss cannot be or is not wholly set off against income from any other head of income in accordance with the provisions of section 71, so much of the loss as has not been so set off or where he has no income under any other head, the whole losses shall be allowed to be carried forwarded set off in the subsequent assessment years against the income from house property upto a maximum of 8 assessment years.

(s) Under the existing provisions of sub-section (213) of section 192, the person responsible for making payment of salary can take into account income from other heads (not being a loss) and taxes deducted thereon for the purpose of calculating and deducting tax at source from salary cases mostly because the drawing and disbursing officer cannot allow adjustment of loss from house property against salary income. Section 192(2B) has been amended so as to allow adjustments of loss from house property against the income from salary for the purpose of determining the tax deductible from salary. The person responsible for deducting tax at source can now make necessary adjustment and deduct appropriate amount of tax.

(t) Under the existing provision, penalty under sub-section (2) of section 272A of the Income-tax Act is imposable for failure to deliver in due time a copy of the declaration under section 197A or for failure by the person deducting tax to furnish a certificate of deduction, to the person to whom such payment is made or credit is given within the prescribed period. These defaults are continuous is nature and attract penalty at the rate of Rs.100-200 per day without any maximum limit. The maximum limit of penalty imposable in such cases shall not exceed the amount of tax deductible or collectible, as the case may be.

(u) Under section 264 of the Income-tax Act, 1961 the existing provision, the Commissioner of Income-tax is empowered to revise an order passed by the subordinate authority where no appeal has been filed. There is limitation of one year for filing the application but there is no time limit for the Commissioner of Income-tax to dispose off the application. A limit of one year has been prescribed for disposal of such application with a view to reduce the delay in disposal.

(VII) Special Provisions for Business Reorganisation

(a) Section 47 of the Income-tax Act has been amended providing that transfer of any capital asset or intangible asset from a proprietary concernor a firm to a company on succession shall not be regarded as transfer attracting levy of capital gains subject to fulfillment of prescribed conditions. However, if the conditions are not complied with, the benefits availed of by the firm or the proprietor shall be deemed to be the income of the succeeding company.

(b) Section 72A has been amended to provide for carry forward of accumulated loss and unabsorbed depreciation in the hands of the successor companies for the unexpired period available to the predecessor firm or the proprietary concern. However, in case of non compliance of any of the conditions laid down, the loss and depreciation shall be deemed to be the income in the hands of the successor company.

(VIII) Rationalisation of Appellate Provisions

(a) Under the existing provisions, the appeal fee payable to Tribunal was Rs.250/- for appeals involving assessed total income upto Rs.1,00,000 and Rs.1,500 when the assessed total income exceeded Rs.1,00,000. Such a small scale of fee is not sufficient deterrent filing of a large number of unnecessary appeals on decided issues and on issues having petty tax effect, thus slowing down the disposal of appeals. The scale of fee payable to Appellate Tribunal has been enhanced as under by amending sections 253 and 254 of the Income-tax Act:-

Particulars	Fee for filing the appeal before ITAT
Assessed total income Rs. 1 lakh or less	Rs.500/-
Assessed total income is more than Rs.1 lakh but not more than Rs.2 lakhs	Rs.1500/-
Assessed total income is more than Rs.2 lakhs	1 % of the assessed income subject
Miscellaneous applications under section 254(2)	Rs.50/-
Stay petitions	Rs.500/-

(b) The fee for filing an appeal before the Appellate Tribunal under other direct tax enactments, namely, Wealth-tax Act, Gift-tax Act, Interest-tax Act and Expenditure-tax Act, has been enhanced from Rs.200/- to Rs. 1000/-.

(c) With a view to helping quicker disposal of appeals before the Appellate Tribunal, the Act has enhanced the limit of total income in a case for disposal by a single member bench from Rs. 1 Lakh to Rs.5 Lakhs by amending section 255 of the Income-tax Act.

(d) According to the existing provisions, no direct appeal arising out of the order of the Appellate Tribunal lie to the High Court. The assessee or the Commissioner has to request the Appellate Tribunal for reference of question of law to the High Court. If the Appellate Tribunal decides against such reference, High Court can be moved to direct the Appellate Tribunal to make such reference and state the case. This process consumes a lot of time before the decision on merits of the case if finalised. The Act has inserted a new sub-heading, "CC-Appeals to High Court" and sections 260A, 260B in Chapter XX and has also amended sections 256,257,260 and 261 to provide that an appeal shall lie against the orders of the Tribunal directly to the High Court.

(ix) Measures to Check Tax avoidance

Under Clauses (22) and (22A) of section 10 Educational and Medical Institutions were allowed blanket exemption on their Income if they did not exist for purposes of profit. This provision was misused to a large extent by the tax payers by floating educational and medical institutions for the purposes claiming tax exemption. The blanket exemption has been replaced by a control mechanism by which the educational and medical institutions not financed by the Government and having gross receipts of over rupees one crore per annum are required to apply to the Central Government and seek approval under section 10(23C) of the income-tax Act.

(x) Miscellaneous

(a) The Export Import bank of India was formed by the Export-Import Bank of India Act, 1981. Section 37 of the said Act provides that the Export Import Bank of India shall not be liable to pay income-tax, surtax or any other tax, in respect of any income, profits and gains specified therein. The Act has omitted section 37 of the aforesaid Act to make the Bank liable for payment of income-tax or any other tax, in respect of profits and gains accruing to the bank.

(b) The method of computation of the income of Foreign Institutional Investors from securities or capital gains arising from the transfer of such securities is given in section 115AD. The Act amends clause (a) of sub-section(l) so as to extend the tax concessions available on income of Foreign Institutional Investors on their investment in listed securities to unlisted securities also.

(c) Under the existing provisions, the scope of Authority for Advance Ruling is restricted to a determination of a question of law or fact in relation to a transaction which has been undertaken or is proposed to be undertaken by a non-resident applicant. The Act has amended Clause (a) in section 245N whereby advance ruling will also mean a decision by the Authority in relation to an assessment pending before the Income-tax Authority or the Tribunal in respect of a resident applicant and such decision will include the decision on question of law or fact arising out of the assessment order for which application has been made. However, the resident applicant has to fall within the class or category of persons as notified by Central Government in this regard. A new section 245RR has been inserted in the income-tax Act which bars the Income-tax Authority or the Appellate Tribunal from deciding any issue in respect of which an application has been made by the resident applicant to the authority.

(xi) Wealth Tax

The existing provisions of section 2(ea) of the Wealth-tax Act, exempt from wealth-tax a house meant exclusively for residential purposes and which is allotted by a company to an employee or an officer or Director who is in whole time employment, having a gross annual salary of less than Rs.2 lakhs. In view of inflation and general rises in the salaries, section 2(ea) is amended so as to enhance the limit of gross annual salary to Rs.5 lakhs. The Act has also amended the said section so as to provide for exemptions from wealth-tax in respect of any residential property that has been let out for a minimum period of 300 days in the previous year and also any property in the nature of commercial establishment or complexes. Explanation (b) of section 2(ea) excludes from the meaning of urban land, any land held by the assessee as stock in trade for a period of five years from the date of its acquisition by him. The Act amends the Explanation so as to make land held by the assessee as a stock in trade for a period of ten years from the date of its acquisition by him, not includible in the definition of urban land, and hence not chargeable to wealth-tax. Under the existing clause (vi) of section 5, one house or part of a house belonging to an individual or a Hindu Undivided family is exempt from wealth-tax. The Act amends this clause so as to extend this exemption also in respect of a plot of land comprising an area of 500 sq. meters or less.

(xii) Abolition of Gift Tax Act

Under the Gift-tax Act, which was enacted in the year 1958, gift tax was chargeable at the prescribed rate on the value of taxable gifts made by a person during the relevant previous year. Over the years, the implementation of the provisions of Gift-tax Act has neither yielded any substantial revenue nor resulted in fulfilling the objectives of effectively combating the tax evasion. The provisions in the Income-tax Act are considered sufficient to take care of the attempts for tax evasion. Hence with a view to simplify and rationalise the direct tax provisions, section 3 of the Gift-tax Act is amended so as to provide that the provisions of this Act shall cease to apply and shall have no effect whatsoever in respect of any gift made on or after the 1st day of October, 1998.

(xiii) Expenditure Tax

Under the existing provisions of the expenditure tax Act, taxis charged on expenditure incurred in a hotel where the room charges for a unit of residential accommodation are one thousand two hundred rupees or more per day per individual. The Act has amended the section 3 of the Expenditure-tax Act to enhance this limit to two thousand rupees or more per day per individual.

(xiv) Kar Vivad Samadhan Scheme, 1998 (KVSS, 98)

(a) The Provision of Kar Vivad Samadhan Scheme, 1998 introduced by Finance (No.2) Act, 1998 are contained in sections 86 to 98 of the Act. The twin objectives of the Scheme are to reduce tax areas as well as litigation relating to such arrears both in various direct and indirect tax enactments.

(b) The Scheme seeks to provide a quick and voluntary settlement of tax dues outstanding as on 31.3.98 by offering complete waiver of interest and penalty and waiver of a part of the tax arrears. It also provides immunity against institution of prosecution proceedings and imposition of penalty. The assessee on his part shall seek to withdraw appeals pending before the various appellate authorities and Courts.

(c) The amount to be paid for full and final settlement of tax arrears determined on or before 31.3.98 but remaining unpaid on the date of declaration has been specified in the Scheme for various direct and indirect tax enactments.

(d) A person desiring to avail of the Scheme is required to file a declaration in the prescribed form before the designated authority notified for this purpose. The designated authority, thereafter, shall pass an order determining the amount payable for settling the tax arrears. The settlement becomes effective on payment of the stipulated amount and the appeal or reference filed before any authority, tribunal, are deemed to have been withdrawn. Where writ petitions or appeals have been filed before the High Court or Supreme Court, the declarant is required to move an application for withdrawing such petitions. Any amount paid in pursuance of declaration made under the Scheme is not refundable under any circumstances.

(e) The Scheme is not open to following cases/persons:

   (i) Cases where prosecution for concealment of income or for offences under indirect tax enactments has been launched or where a person has been convicted for such offence.

   (ii) Cases where no show-cause notice or notice of demand has been issued under any indirect tax enactment.

   (iii) Cases where an order has been passed by the

Settlement Commission under section 245D(4) of the Income-tax Act or under section 22D(4) of Wealth-tax Act.

(iv) Persons against whom prosecution proceedings have been initiated under Chapter IX or XVII of the Indian Penal Code, Foreign Exchange Regulations Act, Narcotics Drugs and Psychotropic Substances Act, Terrorist and Disruptive Activities (Prevention) Act, Prevention of Corruption Act and Trial of Offences Relating to Transaction in Securities Act and

(v) Persons against whom order of detention has been issued under the COFEPOSA Act.

(f) The Scheme came into force on the 1st day of day of September, 1998 and ended on 31 st day of January, 1999.

Foreign tax division (F.T.D.)

Double Taxation Avoidance Agreements (D.T.A.As.)

The attempt of various countries to assert their jurisdiction to tax world-wide incomes of their residents and also exercise jurisdiction with regard to incomes accruing or arising within those countries gives rise to the problems of double taxation. The Double Taxation Avoidance Agreements (DTAAs.) endeavour to provide tax-payer protection against taxation of the same income in two countries. These Agreements, besides providing a reasonable element of legal and fiscal certainty for carrying on international operations, also stimulate the flow of trade, capital, technology and personnel. The co-operation between the tax authorities is also established.

During the period from January to December, 1998, negotiations were held with the Delegations from Bahrain, Crotia, Egypt, Japan, Kyrgystan, Nepal,

Netherlands, Nigeria and Qatar. During this period, DTAAs. between India and the following countries were signed at Government level on the dates indicated below:

1.	Czech Republic	1.10.1998
2.	Morocco	30.10.1998
3.	Portugal	11.9.1998

D.A.T.As. with Belarus, Canada, Russian Federation and South Africa and Amending Protocol to the existing DTAC with Finland were notified in the Gazette of India. As on date, India has notified comprehensive Double Taxation Avoidance Agreements, covering all sources of income, with 57 countries. Similarly, agreements limited to income from the operation of aircrafts exist with 13 countries and those limited to shipping profits with 6 countries. India has also an agreement limited to estate duty with the United Kingdom.

International Cooperation

The Central Board of Direct Taxes is a Member of the International Fiscal Association, Netherlands.

- A High Level Indian Tax Delegation visited. New Delhi on 30.3.1998 for holding talks with the Indian tax authorities under the "Mutual Agreement Procedure" of the Double Taxation Avoidance Agreement. Some of the disputed issues were resolved.
- A High Level Nepalese tax delegation also came to New Delhi from 28th to 30th June, 1998 for attending the second meeting of the Indo-Nepalese Joint Committee constituted under the DTAA between the two countries. The discussions were held in a cordial atmosphere and further talks on some of the disputed issues will be taken up in the next meeting.

- A delegation from Central Board of Direct Taxes represented India at the London Conference on Electronic Commerce organised under the aegis of the International Fiscal Association on 9th May, 1998.

- Chairman, Central Board of Direct Taxes represented India and chaired a session at the OECD Emerging Market Economy Forum Workshop held in Paris on 17-18th September, 1998. The workshop discussed the problems of elimination of double taxation faced by the participating countries.

Grievance calls

The Income-tax Department has a three tier Grievance Redressal Machinery as below:

1. Central Grievance Cell directly under the Chairman, CBDT

2. Regional Grievance Cells under Chief Commissioners/ Directors General of Income-tax.

3. Outstation Grievance Cell under each outstation Commissioner/Director of Income-tax.

There is a Director of Grievance in the Central Board of Direct Taxes, directly reporting to the Chairman, CBDT

The Central Grievance Cell acts on complaints directly received by it and supervises the Regional and Outstation Grievance Cells.

During the period 1.4.1998 to 30.11.1998, the Grievance Cell has redressed 62 grievances. All efforts are being made to redress the grievance as quickly as possible.

The Central Board of Direct Taxes released its citizens' Charter on 27.11.1998 declaring the commitment of the Income Tax Department to provide excellent and fair services to the taxpayers.

The objectives of the Charter are to be fair, helpful and Assessing Officers and the disposal during the same period was efficient. Efficiency is sought to be enforced through setting a time limit for certain activities including redressing all complaints and grievances within 30 days.

This charter is in accordance with the decision taken in the Conference of Chief Ministers in May, 1997.

The Charter also expects citizens to be prompt, honest and accurate in payment of taxes.

Inspection division

The Inspection Division of the Central board of Direct Taxes functions directly under the Chairman, CBDT with a countrywide jurisdiction. It has been carrying out inspections and ensuring proper and effective implementation of the policies, directions and instructions of the CBDT. It has also been evaluating systemic and other shortcomings and achievements of various policies with a view to improving the functioning of the Income-tax Department. It has three units, two in Delhi and one at Calcutta. The Units in Delhi are headed by two Additional Commissioners of Income-tax and the Unit in Calcutta is headed by the Joint Commissioner of Income-tax.

During the period from 1.4.1998 to 31.12.1998 the Inspection Division had conducted inspection of 25 Charges of Commissioners of Income-tax functioning under various Chief Commissioners of Income-tax in respect of the following:

1. Issue of certificates under section 230A of the Income-tax Act.
2. Utilisation of information collected in surveys under section 133A in the course of assessments.

3. Comparison of appraisal reports with assessments in search cases.

4. Disposal of statutory and grievance petitions by the Commissioners of Income-tax.

5. Availability of office space as well as staff quarters under various Commissioners charges and utilisation of already sanctioned funds for purchase/ construction of flats/bldg./ plots for Office and residential accommodation.

The Inspection Division prepared detailed reports about the working of Officers in the aforesaid charges in respect of assigned areas of work, highlighting areas of concern and giving suggestions for improvement in the functioning of the department. The shortcomings noticed in the course of inspection were brought to the notice of Central Board of Direct Taxes and the concerned Chief Commissioner of Income-tax for taking appropriate remedial action.

Valuation cell

The Valuation Cells have statutory powers in respect of the following:-

(i) Determination the cost of construction for assessment purposes under the Income-tax Act;

(ii) Determining the value of properties for purposes of Wealth-tax, Capital Gains and Gift-tax Act;

(iii) Estimation of fair market value of immovable properties in cases of transfer of real estate falling within the jurisdiction of Appropriate Authorities under Chapter XXC of the Income-tax Act, 1961; and

(iv) Determining the fair market value of attached properties which are auctioned for recovery of tax arrears.

As on 1st April, 1998, the Valuation Cell had a pendency of 1261 cases. During the period from 1st April to 30th November, 1998, 2418 cases were received on reference from Assessing Officers and the disposal during the same period was 2183 cases.

Audit and public accounts committee division

Duly recognizing the role played by the C&AG and the Public Accounts Committee of Parliament in a democratic system, the draft paragraphs and System appraisals proposed for inclusion in the C&AG Report and received from them are promptly examined in the Central Board of Direct Taxes in it's A&PAC Division and Ministry's comments are furnished to the C&AG. This division also furnishes information to the Public Accounts Committee by replying to their Advance Questionnaire and Questions raised after the oral evidence is taken by the Committee.

During 1998-99, the C&AG called for comments of the Ministry on 918 draft paragraphs proposed for inclusion in their Annual Report for the year ended 31.3.1998. These were attended to, and replies in 300 draft paragraphs have been furnished ask on 23.12.1998. Action Taken Notes on 259 paragraphs out of 300 included in C&AG Report for 1996-97 were processed and sent to the C&AG for vetting, out of which 116 vetted ATNs have been furnished to the Monitoring Cell. The reviews on topics "Functioning of Internal Audit in the Income-tax Department", "Method of accounting of revenue collections and refunds - functioning of Central Treasury Units, Zonal Accounts Offices and Computer Cell" and "Deductions in respect of profits and gains from newly established industrial undertakings after a certain date (Section 80-1)" were also received and processed. Parawise comments on the Reviews, "Method of accounting of Revenue Collection and Refunds" and

"Functioning of Internal Audit" have been furnished to audit. Specific comments on 21 illustrative cases mentioned in the Review on "Duductions under section 80-1" have also been furnished. Public Accounts Committee have selected two of the above Reviews in addition to the four review/Audit Notes included in Audit Report for 199596 for oral evidence of the Ministry during 1998-99. The Department gave oral evidence on the 'Taxability of PILCOM' taken up by the PAC on 1.12.1998 and on Audit of Accounts under section 44AB of the Income-tax Act on 9.12.1998.

Member (Revenue and Audit) is one of the member of the "Specified Authority" constituted under Section 72A of the Income Tax Act with the Secretary, Ministry of Industry, Department of Industrial Development, as its Chairman. The provisions of Section 72A facilitate the rehabilitation of the Sick Industrial Establishments by merging them with healthy units by allowing set off of losses and depreciation of the sick unit against the income of the healthy unit, provided adequate steps are taken by the latter to turn around the sick unit by infusing funds, managerial skill etc. These cases are examined and processed by A&PAC division. 20 such cases were examined and considered in a meeting of the Specified Authority held during the year. Two cases were recommended by the "Specified Authority" to the Central Government for issue of declaration under section 72A(l) of the Income-tax Act. Another case was recommended for issue of final certificate under section 72A(2)(ii) granting tax benefits subject to certain clarification.

Office/residential accommodation and infrastructure

There are at present 453 Income-tax offices in the foreign country. These offices are located in Government buildings constructed by CPWD/purchased ready built or in hired buildings (where the Government building has not been constructed so far). With a view to enable the CBDT to purchase ready built office accommodation/ residential accommodation for the Income-tax Department in order to meet the shortage, especially when the CPWD is unable to undertake the construction work due to their pre-occupation with on-going projects, funds have been allotted under the budget.

In the previous year funds to the tune of Rs.35.25 crores were utilised for purchase of residential accommodation at Coimbatore, Pune, Chennai and Mumbai and a total area of 28527 sq. ft. was added to the existing space.

The Central Government has provided a sum of Rs.55.30 crores for this purpose. Several proposals for acquiring ready built office and residential accommodation at Bombay, Pune, Ahmedabad, Bhopal, Moradabad and other places are under CBDT's active consideration.

The Board have continued to take steps to improve other infrastructure facilities by augmenting the no.8 staff cars and taxis/computers for the Income Tax Department.

Attached offices of CBDT

The following three Directorates-General are attached to CBDT:

1. Directorate General of Income-tax (Admn.), Delhi
2. Directorate General of Income-tax (Training), Nagpur
3. Directorate General of Income-tax (Tax-Exemptions), Calcutta.

The Directorate General of Income-tax (Admn.) supervises the work of Director of Income-tax (RSP&PR), Director of Income-tax (O&MS), Director of Income-tax

(System), DIT (IT), DIT (Audit), DIT (Recovery). DIT (IT) works directly under the Board in so far as secret matters relating to departmental examinations are concerned. DIT (Vigilance) who is the Chief Vigilance Officer of the Department reports directly to the Board.

The DGIT (Trg.) is head of National Academy of Direct Taxes, Nagpur, five Regional Training Institutes and 26 Ministerial Staff Training Units at various places in the country.

The DGIT (Tax-Exemptions) was created in October, 1987. There are 4 Directors of Income-tax (Exemptions) at Delhi, Calcutta, Mumbai and Chennai functioning under the administrative control of DGIT (Tax Exemptions).

Directorate of income tax (IT)

The Directorate has two wings viz. Inspection and Examination. The functions of the Inspection Wing of the Directorate of Income-tax are as under:-

(a) to lay down general guidelines for inspection by Addl./ Joint Commissioners of Income-tax and by the Commissioners of Income-tax;

(b) to obtain inspection programme from the Addl./ Joint Commissioners of Income-tax, Commissioners of Income tax and to monitor the progress of inspection;

(c) to examine and review the inspection reports received in the Directorate and to provide feed back to the Commissioners of Income tax and Chief Commissioners of Income-tax on the quality of assessments and inspections as adjudged from the inspection reports;

(d) to issue general instructions to the field officers and to remedy the defects noticed, on review of inspection reports;

(e) to report, periodically, to the Board on the Review of inspections;

(f) to bring out an annual review of inspections containing the following:-

   (i) Review of inspections planned and carried out;

   (ii) performance of the Joint Commissioners (Special Range), as reflected from the inspections made by .the Commissioners of Income-tax;

   (iii) the quality of inspection reports of the Addl. Commissioners of Income-tax/Joint Commissioners of Income-tax,

   (iv) instances of good work done 'by the Joint Commissioners, Deputy Commissioners/ Assistant Commissioners and Income Tax Officers;

   (v) shortcomings and defects noticed in the work of Addl./Ioint Commissioners, Deputy Commissioners/ Assistant Commissioners and Income-tax Officers

   (vi) highlighting the qualitative performance of the Departmental Representatives and the difficulties and the problems experienced by them in their day-to-day functioning.

There are five categories of inspections being monitored by the Directorate, namely:

(1) Inspection by the Range Addl. Commissioners of Income-Tax/Joint Commissioners of Income-Tax of the work of the Deputy/Assistant Commissioners and Income-tax Officers.

(2) Inspection by the Commissioners of Income-tax of the work of Addl./Joint Commissioners, Deputy/

Assistant Commissioners working in Central Charges.

(3) Inspection by the Commissioners of Income-tax of the work of Joint Commissioners (Special Ranges).

(4) Inspection by the Commissioners of Income-tax of the work of Officers, in the headquarters.

(5) Inspection by Commissioners of Income-tax of the work of Departmental Representatives.

The following table indicates the number of inspection reports and the number of reports scrutinised during the last five years:

Financial year	*No. of reports received*	*No. of reports scrutinised*
1994-95	525	210
1995-96	847	316
1996-97	779	323
1997-98	600	355
1998-99 (upto 24.12.1998)	62	117

From 1991-92, review of inspection reports involved examination of the inspection notes in 6 Scrutiny cases, one recovery case and 3 cases completed under section 143(l)(a). As a result of scrutiny, cases reflecting appreciable work done by the Assessing Officers, sub-standard work done by the Assessing Officers, high quality inspections, inadequate inspections, useful advice/suggestions given by the Inspecting Officers and mistakes of recurring nature committed by the Assessing Officers are extracted for highlighting the same in the Annual Review.

As per Action plan laid down by the Board for 1998- 99 reviews of the 40% of the Inspection Reports received upto 31.12.98 are to be completed in the following quarter, i.e., upto 31.3.1999.

Examination Wing

The main function of the Examination Wing of the Directorate of Income-tax (income-tax) is to conduct Departmental Examinations.

(1) A high degree of secrecy and efficiency has been ensured by complete computerisation in the Examination Wing. Substantial changes have been introduced in the Examination System. Some of these are summarised as under :-

(i) Application forms for appearing in the Examination have been modified in the light of Revised Rules for Income-tax Officers and Income-tax Inspectors' Examination, 1994

(ii) Entrance cards with photographs of the candidates affixed there on have been introduced for both the Examination.

(iii) Standardised formats have been introduced (DE-I to VIII) for getting the requisite information from various Examination Centres.

(iv) Permanent Roll Numbers have been issued to all the candidates prefixed with the Centre Codes of the Examination Centres.

(v) A secret code has also been allotted to each Chief Commissioner of Income Tax charge to be printed on each of the Answer Books.

(vi) Uniform answer books have been introduced in format DE-IX and IXA.

2. As per Action Plan for the year 1998-99, four Departmental Examinations, i.e. Income-tax Officers, Income-tax Inspectors, Ministerial staff and Group 'D' Employees for promotion to LDCs cadres were held during the year 1998. The Result of the Examination for Income-tax Inspectors has been

declared on 20.11.1998 whereas the result for Income-tax Officers Examinations was declared on 7.1.1999. So far the results of Examinations for Ministerial Staff and Group 'D' Employees are concerned, the same are declared at the level of Chief Commissioners/Commissioners of Income tax concerned.

The Departmental Examination for Assistant Commissioners of Income Tax (Probationers.) of 51st Batch was held in the month of September, 1998 and result thereof has been declared on 1.12.1998. 94% candidates were declared successful in the said Examination.

3. Besides conducting Departmental Examinations for various cadres as detailed above, the following miscellaneous functions are also carried out by this Directorate:

(a) Review, amendment and interpretation of the Rules, and setting the Syllabus for various Departmental Examinations,

(b) Implementation and review of the policy regarding Departmental Examinations and issue of instructions to the Commissioners all over India,

(c) Disposal of the various queries and references from the Chief Commissioners of Income-tax/ Commissioners of Income-tax and from various Staff Associations,

(d) Disposal of various complaints, Grievance and Representations made by the candidates.

(e) Preparation of the detailed briefs for the counter affidavit to be submitted to Central Administrative Tribunal/Court in reply to the petitions filed by the candidates against refusal to grant special permission to appear for the Examination, rejection of representation etc.

(f) Para-wise comments on Applications filed before CAT/Court by various candidates against revised Rules for Income-Tax Inspectors and Income-Tax Officers Examination, 1994 were prepared during the year and sent to the Chief Commissioners/ Commissioners concerned.

(g) Payment of Honorarium to were made to various officers for setting of question papers and evaluation of answer books in respect of the Departmental Examinations conducted by this Directorate.

Directorate of income-tax (audit)

During the Financial Year 1998-99, nine Inspections of Audit Wings have been completed upto November, 1998 as against the target of 10 Inspections for the financial year.

- During the year 1998-99 (upto September, 1998) 12 quarterly reviews were prepared, 6 pertaining to Internal Audit and 6 to Receipt Audit, showing position of settlement of Major and Minor Objections.
- 300 Draft Paras which were included in the Comptroller & Auditor General's Report for 1996-97 were processed and analysed. Action Taken Notes have been sent to the Board in 269 cases.
- Till September 1998 Internal Audit and Special Audit Parties detected 3425 cases of major irregularities with tax effect of Rs.21,03,407(000). A Comparative Statement on the performance of Audit

Parties for the period 1.4.1998 to 30.09.1998 with that for two earlier Financial Years is given below:-

		1996-97	1997-98	1998-99 (Upto 30.9.98)
1.	No. of IAPs as on 31 March 101	103		103
	No. of SAPs	40	40	40
2.	No. of cases checked by:			
	(i) Internal Audit Parties	1,35,592	1,51,038	60,280
	(ii) Immediate (SA)	42,432	47,420	15,408
3.	Total No. of cases in which mistakes (Major) were detected	7,177	7,296	3,425
4.	Revenue effect of (3) above (in thousand)	33,54,120	41,20,980	21,03,407
5.	No. of Internal Audit Objections settled			
	(a) Major	8,080	6,235	1,008
	(b) Minor	5,546	4,661	142
6.	Revenue effect of (5) above (in thousand)			
	(a) Major	36,33,295	25,16,933	3,89,719
	(b) Minor	21,254	17,614	598

Directorate of income (recovery)

The Directorate of Income-Tax (Recovery) was created in December. 1978, with the purpose of collating, compiling and reviewing, on behalf of the Central Board of Direct Taxes, quarterly dossiers of cases involving outstanding demand of above Rs.1 lakhs in respect of cases of film circles and Rs. 10 lakhs and above in other cases.

The Slab-wise details of outstanding demand in the dossier cases with demand above Rs. 1 Crore, as on 30.09.98 is as under:-

Slab	*No of cases*	*Amount involved (Rs. in Crores)*
Rs.1 crore to Rs. 5 crores	1732	373581
Rs.5 crore to Rs. 10 crores	270	184766
Rs. 10 crores and above	311	2314281
TOTAL	2313	2872628

- The Directorate conducts review of dossier cases involving demand of Rs. 1 crore and above. The cases involving demand above Rs. 5 crores are examined by DG (Admn.). The dossiers involving demand above Rs. 10 crores are overseen by Member (R&A) and those between Rs. 1 to 5 crores are monitored in the Directorate. Special attention is paid to the collection of arrears in high demand cases.
- A comparative analysis of dossiers as on 31 st March, 1998 and 30th September, 1998 shows that reduction/collection in respect of dossiers above Rs. 1 crore due to the efforts of this Directorate and the field formations was to the extent of Rs. 1583 crores.
- The Directorate conducts recovery inspections of the field offices. 21 Recovery Inspections were conducted during F.Y. 97-98. Consequent upon inspection suggestions were made to the Board for strengthening the recovery machinery particularly the institution of Tax Recovery Officers. 25 Recovery inspections proposed in the current year are at hand.
- The Directorate processes write off/partial write of proposals received from Chief Commissioners of Income-tax.
- A new write-off manual, updated with the latest instructions/ circulars of Board has been finalized. This would be useful to the officers in the field in their write off work.

Directorate of income-tax (RSP&PR)

This Directorate is responsible for research on Tax matters, printing, compilation of Economic and Administrative statistics, publications, publicity and Taxpayers' Education programme.

(a) During the period 1.4.1998 to 31.12.1998 the important features of publicity and public relations work done this Directorate are as follows:-.

(i) Kar Vivad Samadhan Scheme-1998 was launched by the Finance Ministry the year. It was in operation from 1st September, 1998 to 31st January, 1999. All aspects of multi media publicity and advertisements relating to this scheme were managed & co-ordinated by the Directorate of Income-tax (RSP&PR).

(ii) In the area of press publicity, 21 titles covering subjects such as Salary, Tax Return, Advance Tax, Permanent Account Number, Widening of Tax Base, TDS etc. were publicised. A special ad. was brought out on 15th August, 1998 under the title "Right to Contribution".

(iii) The Income-tax Telephone Directory-1998 was printed and distributed.

(iv) Administrative Handbook, 1999 was printed and distributed to all the Officers of the Department.

(v) Focusing on the importance of mandatory requirement, a full page advertisement of PAN with forms 60 and 61 was widely published. Another full page advertisement specifying the urban agglomeration of various specified cities was also published on Widening of Tax Base, which was widely appreciated

(vi) For creating better awareness amongst the tax payers, 12 titles under tax payers information series were updated out of which two have been printed. The rest are under the process of printing.

(vii) Citizens' Charter-November, 1998 was published in the form of bilingual posters and brochures. These were supplied directly to 452 stations in the country which have Income-tax establishment. In order to have continuous liaison with various Newspapers, Ad. Agencies, publishers and also those regions and charges within the department which are available on Internet, e-mail address was obtained for the department. Mayur Bhawan and Hans Bhawan offices of the Directorate were provided with e-mail facility.

(ix) From all the Wings of the Directorate, Fax messages are required to be sent very often to a large number of Chief Commissioners, Directors General, Commissioners and Directors etc. It used to be a herculean task to repeatedly dial each fax no. and send the message. The process used to consume several days for each message. In order to handle this problem better, Enhanced Fax Facility was installed in Mayur Bhawan and in Hans Bhawan. Now, if one message is to be faxed to a large number of addressees stationed in various cities of India, it has to be faxed by the Directorate only once dialing a specific code no. The message gets flashed to all the addressees within a short duration. Delivery reports are received on the fax and the procedure costs less as compared to the MTNL rates.

(x) CDs of Direct Taxes Ready Reckoner and a book titled Filing of Income-tax Returns, 1998 by Persons in Occupation of House Property having Car/Telephone/ Credit Cards, Club Membership etc. were got sent to the CCsIT and DGsIT. CBDT News Letter and Circulars/ Instructions/Notifications were sent to the CCS/DGs/CsiT Important Circulars and forms pertaining to Samadhan/ Saral/1/6 criteria were faxed throughout the country through enhanced tax facility.